Thick Description and Fine Texture

Also of Interest

John A. Popplestone and Marion White McPherson,
An Illustrated History of American Psychology

J. R. Kantor
Psychology and Logic
The Logic of Modern Science
The Scientific Evolution of Psychology
The Aim and Progress by Psychology and Other Sciences
The Science of Psychology: An Interbehavioral Survey
Cultural Psychology
Tragedy and the Event Continuum
Psychological Comments and Queries
Principles of Psychology

The University of Akron Press
Akron, Ohio

Thick Description and Fine Texture:

Studies in the History of Psychology

Edited by David B. Baker

Copyright © 2003 David Baker

All rights reserved

All inquiries and permissions requests should be addressed to the publisher,

The University of Akron Press, Akron, OH 44325–1703.

Manufactured in the United States of America

First edition 2003

07 06 05 04 03 5 4 3 2 1

Library of Congress Cataloging-in-Publication Data

Thick description and fine texture : studies in the history of
psychology / edited by David B. Baker. — 1st ed.

    p. cm.

Includes bibliographical references and index.

  ISBN 1–931968–02–0 (alk. paper)

  1. Psychology—Historiography.   I. Baker, David B.   II. Title.

  BF81.T47 2003

  150'.7'22—dc22

2003021622

The paper used in this publication meets the minimum requirements of American
National Standard for Information Sciences—Permanence of Paper for Printed
Library Materials, ANSI z39.48—1984.∞

Contents

Thirty-five Years of Archival Achievement:

Essays in Honor of John A. Popplestone and
Marion White McPherson

David B. Baker

TO HONOR THE CONTRIBUTIONS of significant persons, the academic world has at its disposal any number of award mechanisms. Most ubiquitous are items that become the private property of the recipient, including honorary degrees, all manner of chronometers, and countless variations of engraved decorative icons. Once bestowed, the gift and recipient are often relinquished to a restive setting, removed from the currents they once occupied.

In the hierarchy of academic acknowledgment, being honored with a collection of essays generally indicates that a person's legacy is lasting and relevant. Unlike acknowledgments that inhabit personal spaces, these works reside in the public domain and serve as a perpetual reminder of past accomplishment and contribution. And so it is with this volume that pays tribute to two pioneers in the history of psychology, John A. Popplestone and Marion White McPherson.

Their founding of the Archives of the History of American Psychology at the University of Akron in 1965 was a watershed event in the history of psychology in the twentieth century. In bringing together the primary sources in the history of psychology, they brought a new legitimacy to the study of the subject. Historians of psychology had a place to hang their hat, historiography gained muscle, and scholarship broadened.

To honor their legacy a festschrift conference was convened at the University of Akron on April 7, 2000.[1] A vestige of nineteenth-century German academic life, the festschrift was conceived as an expression of esteem from students who had profited from the mentorship of a beloved and accomplished professor. For Popplestone and McPherson, the archives were their university office and historians of psychology their students. Indeed their reach was far and wide, touching not only the lives of individual scholars but also shaping the corpus of the new history of psychology that was emerging in the 1960s. Shepherding this new movement from its infancy through the century's end, they created, challenged, provoked, and persevered to leave a record that has no equal.

Who better then to begin this volume than the founders themselves, answering several questions demanded by the historical record. Following the introduction, nine distinguished scholars in the history of psychology share in the reflected glory of the good works of Popplestone and McPherson. The composition of the authors reflects much of the contemporary scene in the history of psychology. Some are historians and some psychologists, all keenly aware of the primacy of original source material in historical scholarship. Each was invited to reflect upon the process of archival research.

As with any selected work the reader is free to read at will, the essays offering insights into a myriad of issues familiar to anyone who has reached for an archival folder or considered the provenance of an artifact. As one considers these diverse and informing essays, what emerges is a sense of the journey available through archival research. The panoply of available methods reminds us that historiography is dynamic and continually open to new interpretation and knowledge. The ways in which individual writers collate archival elements to produce a coherent narrative also reminds us that such undertakings are a human endeavor, capable of inducing a range of affect and experience. It seems fair to say that the journey is a satisfying one.

The opening essays, offered by two established editors in the history of psychology, Professor Michael Sokal and Professor John Burnham, provide a focused and personal examination of some of the tools and techniques of historical analysis. Sokal's discussion of microhistory offers a range of possibilities for considering the data of individual lives, whereas Burnham brings the reader along in his search for meaning in the use of oral history.

The genre of historical biography is well represented in the papers of Professors Ludy T. Benjamin Jr., C. James Goodwin, and Leila Zenderland. Interestingly, each of the biographical subjects is part of a cohort whose careers reached full stride in the second and third decades of the twentieth century. Benjamin shows in detail how a seeming paradox of identity can be unfolded through an examination of personal and professional personas. Goodwin offers a perspective on the use of personal diaries, illustrating that the vagaries of autobiographical note taking can offer valuable insights into the interaction of person and place. Expanding the scope, Zenderland carefully walks the reader through the steps involved in deconstructing social policy to reveal the influence of the personal, professional, and political.

Just as biography provides rich historical narrative, so too do the tensions in the culture at large. The essay offered by Professor Hendrika Vande Kemp illustrates how one can take on a topic of massive proportions and in the process distill some essential facts and provide credence to areas of neglected historical analysis.

Professor Ryan D. Tweney treats object as subject in a fascinating piece in which the instruments and apparatus of psychology provide the raw data for considering transformations in the ways in which knowledge is generated, analyzed, and interpreted.

Completing the volume are two essays that reflect the essential nature of the archival adventure. Above all else, the Archives of the History of American Psychology serve an educational function. The holdings are there not only to preserve the historical record but also to see that it is always available to those who come in search of answers to questions about the often ethereal past. Archival work connects the past with the present and offers possibilities for the future. In it are contained patterns and interconnections. Archives can mentor and can reveal the influence of mentors on succeeding generations. Such is the case for Professor Donald A. Dewsbury, whose archival adventures reveal much about the nature of finding an intellectual family and home. Bringing us into the present, Professor Raymond Fancher offers the perspective of a teacher of the history of psychology whose graduate students participate in an archival rite of passage that affirms the importance of the archival record.

Taken together, these collected works honor two important people and the institution they created. In doing so, they celebrate the expression of creative and careful scholarship made possible by the efforts of John Popplestone and Marion White McPherson, who in founding the Archives of the History of American Psychology not only gave us an institution for today and tomorrow, but also gave us permission to see the possibilities of the past.

Looking Backward

John A. Popplestone and Marion White McPherson

IN 1965, THREE BEGINNINGS took place that mark the end of one developmental phase of the field of the history of psychology and the beginning of the next: Division 26, the Division of the History of Psychology, of the American Psychological Association (APA), the *Journal of the History of the Behavioral Sciences*, and the Archives of the History of American Psychology (AHAP) all came into existence in the same short time period, all nurtured by Robert I. Watson, and all three have flourished in the years since.

Here, we would like to boast a little about what has happened in the archives. Quantifying growth is easily done: from nothing to more than twenty-seven hundred linear feet of documents ready for use, more than fifteen thousand photographic records, over six thousand test records, and so forth. But these statistics, like so many numbers, tell a story only in one language without a contextual, interpretative setting.

In these years since the beginning we have become a different institution, existing in different times, serving a different population and reflecting a different psychology. For openers, the collection policy announced in 1965 was embedded in the social and intellectual unrest of those times. For example, the 1970 Kent State shootings were only twelve miles away from the Akron campus and closed it down while the second annual meeting of Cheiron was being held with the AHAP as host.

We specified at the beginning that we would be interested only in North American psychologists, not European or other nationalities and not in psychiatry, psychoanalysis, or anything else, and that this restriction was not a narrow nationalism but only a means of limiting our focus. We also said that our interest was in the whole field of psychology and in all psychologists. That is, we are not going to be elitist in terms of people and not hierarchical in terms of kinds of psychological activity.

One of the considerations here was that, traditionally, most archival programs were in academic settings, which meant that academic psychologists were more likely to have a place that would be interested in their papers (the program at Harvard was the exemplary example). But those psychologists who were employed in nonacademic settings, particularly those in the independent practice of psychology, were quite unlikely to have someplace where their papers would be welcomed and protected.

We assume that Columbia University and Barnard College did not have an archive program in 1956, and for this reason Harry Hollingworth *did* deposit copies of his unpublished autobiography with the Nebraska Historical Society. But other copies of the autobiography, along with the rest of his papers and those of his wife, Leta Hollingworth, were still in his possession at death. We obtained them from his daughter, by his second marriage, and they are now in Akron, safe.

This policy of inclusion by AHAP was in contrast to many older historical and archival interests that tended to be restricted to "important" people, places, and events. In the spirit of the 1960s we were to be egalitarian, reflecting a psychology that was pluralistic in content and diverse in membership. By and large we have stayed with this definition, but we are now a little less interested in typical people—although they are still represented—and we are a little more sophisticated, we hope, in predicting what historians in the future are going to find of interest. What is called "important" today will be of interest tomorrow. And the obscure tends to remain so.

One special collecting project that reflects this attitude began in the earliest days and was only terminated in 1997. We had selected six people, neither stellar nor obscure, as typical faculty members, and asked them to save whatever came across their desks; everything that a typical faculty member had to deal with in our times. Gradually, most lost interest and dropped out, but one conscientious person lasted from the start of the project until his retirement. This is a unique record, which we hope some historians in the future will find immensely interesting.

At Mystic Seaport in Connecticut is a pavilion devoted to an exhibit called "Neptune's Attic." The seaport administration explains that although its collecting policy is now very specific and focused, it was not always thus, and all sorts of interesting, but irrelevant, things have washed ashore—as it were—and ended up there. This exotica is "Neptune's Attic." We could almost do the same thing, "Psychology's Attic," from some of the surplus things we have found embedded in the papers of psychologists. For example, we could include a large collection of items related to Edward Muybridge, the early photographer of movement, a collection of California wine bottle labels, a lock of Rosalie Rayner's hair, the altimeter of Wolfgang Köhler, and an eight-ball which a speaker liked to place on the podium before beginning his remarks. We were almost offered Einstein's brain, but wiser counsel prevailed. (Actually we would have declined since he was not an American psychologist.) We do have the complete records of obtaining a degree from a Florida diploma mill, from application through dissertation to the final conferring of the Ph.D. in counseling psychology with subsequent membership in APA.

We are still trying to represent the whole of psychology and the diversity of the people who do psychology, but we also recognize that the task is different today from what it was when we began. For openers, there are simply many more psychologists in whom we have to be interested than there were extant then. To underline this, and using APA as the example, in 1965 there were twenty-three interest divisions, and by 1999 there were fifty-two. The field has grown and diversified. The 23,500 APA members of 1965 are overwhelmed by the more than 155,000 who belong today. In a relatively short time, the American Psychological Society (APS) has formed and grown to include some 15,000 members.

Many more archival programs exist today than in 1965. Then it was a rare university, hospital, or clinic that had an archival program. Now many institutions do, and they stand ready to help preserve records that would have perished, except for our efforts. Today many records can receive excellent care at home. We still feel that we can give a psychologist special treatment and understanding, but we also are happy to learn that a collection is well housed elsewhere when we do not receive it.

J. E. Wallace Wallin, who was ninety-three years old at the time of his death in 1969, left his papers to the University of Delaware, his alma mater—an appropriate bequest. However, we had a call from the archivist at Delaware one day asking us if we might be interested in accessioning the Wallin papers. His reason was that they simply could not make any sense out of them; they seemed to be in no order with which they could deal. What he was really saying was that the papers of this psychologist did not fit the usual archival expectation, partly because they were psychological and partly because of Wallin's career and personality. My answer was that we would take on Wallin if the family agreed with the transfer. Wallin's daughter did agree, and the transfer was made. Later when she came to visit Akron, and saw the inventory and the gray boxes that held her father's papers, she was pleased.

Another anecdote indicates the special quality of care that we can give. One of our student workers came to one of us one day with a typescript and the question of just what it was and how should the inventory describe it? She said, "It seems to be the start of a novel or perhaps a short story." And then I read, "This little boy seems to be sitting at a table. There is a violin on it and the little boy is thinking about. . . ." Only a rare psychologist would not recognize a story stimulated by Card 1 of the Thematic Apperception Test.

From the beginning, the mission of the archives was providing protection and service where it would otherwise be missing. There was never an intention to dominate the field, to corner the market of manuscript materials in psychology. But in those early days fewer resources were available to psychologists, and we had to do more for the field simply because no one else was helping us. In the first years in particular, we heard repeated horror stories when one of us arrived too late. "Dad burned everything," or, "I just could not keep all that stuff so it was thrown out," and, "when Mother went into the nursing home we closed the house down and those things must have gone then." We hope that today we have forestalled some of that sort of destruction.

In 1965 we were novices and Akron was an obscure midwestern university that housed an archive that was an unknown. Most psychologists did not understand that the writing of history requires the preservation and use of primary sources, the unpublished documents that are produced by a career in psychology.

A common misunderstanding in those early days was to hear us talk about "papers" and have the listener respond with the collected reprints of published research articles. That sort of thing does not happen anymore, although psychologists are still amazed and somewhat apprehensive when they consider that the historian is dependent upon what has survived, by chance, as data. All that has changed. The Archives of the History of American Psychology at the University of Akron are well known, internationally, which is, of course, why the university has supported this very special, rather elitist enterprise all these years.

Very early, one of our archival consultants explained, "In the 1920s a university that wanted prestige built a bell-tower; in the '60s they founded an archive." And he added, somewhat sinisterly, "The cost is about the same." At one point Akron's then vice president for academic affairs told me, "It used to be that when I went to meetings of academic vice presidents people would look at my badge and say, 'Oh, Akron, where the rubber comes from.' But now they look at my badge and they say, 'Oh, Akron, where the psychology archives are.' " I knew then that my budget was safe.

Of course not all academic administrators have been supportive. The dean of the College of Liberal Arts, Robert Oetjen, once said to me, "You know John, when I encounter a scientist who is knowledgeable about the history of his discipline I know that I am dealing with an incompetent." He later presided over my demotion as department head.

More than a thousand people have actually donated things to us. But many more have received brochures and other mailings as we have tried to be visible. Activities such as chairing the Task Force on Centennial Celebrations help to keep the archives at Akron conspicuous.

The changes in the field of psychology and the changes in the salience of the archives have been accompanied by a third set of changes in the field of the history of psychology. In 1965 Division 26 had 234 charter members; today that number exceeds eight hundred, nearly a fourfold increase, just about proportional to the growth of the membership of APA.

In 1969 a second forum for history research (and fellowship) came when the Cheiron Society was organized, originally around the core of the alumni of a workshop in the history of psychology. Cheiron was created as an interdisciplinary society with the original name International Society for the History of the Behavioral and Social Sciences, which forms the acronym ISHOBSS and required the shift to Cheiron. There is now also the European Society for the History of the Human Sciences, and members of both societies attend both meetings. Cheiron is dominated by psychologists with an interest in the history of the field, both in North America and Europe. The Forum for the History of Human Science (FHHS) was founded in December 1988 as an interdisciplinary group with a stated purpose "to promote scholarship in the history of the social and behavioral sciences." The organizational meeting took place at the 1988 History of Science Society (HSS) annual meeting, and the group sought affiliation status with HSS as an interest group. We expect that FHHS will prove to have a membership with a dominant component of trained professional historians with an interest in the history of psychology, while Division 26 will be professional psychologists with an interest in the history of the field. Cheiron seems to be mostly psychologists acting like historians.

The arrival of the historians is changing the field. Psychologists writing about psychology are generally friendly and tolerant of their field and its problems, but the outsider looking in is sometimes hostile, negative, and even seems to see psychology as an enemy. These people take Foucault seriously. However, they are a highly sophisticated group and bring new points of view to the field. One of these people describes himself as a member of the loyal opposition. Perhaps that says it as well as anything else.

Thirty-five years ago the members of Division 26 and most of the members of Cheiron, but not all, were self-taught historians coming to the field with only a rough and ready knowledge of historiographic techniques and skills. Many of them wrote very good history, did use primary sources, and managed to create a discipline that was very different from the history of psychology that had been too frequent prior to 1965.

Over the years, some of the questions we are asked have been repeated, but sometimes the answers change.

What kind of permanence do the archives have? Will they outlast your enthusiasm and interest? Will the archives go on? How can we be sure that the administration at Akron will continue to support the archives? The answer to this good, reasonable question has remained the same over the years. How can anyone guarantee that anything will be permanent? Who would have thought that the Merrill-Palmer institution would close its doors? Who could have predicted that the Vineland Training School could end so ignominiously? And, on a larger field, who would ever have predicted the collapse of Marxist-Leninism on such a vast scale? When the University of Akron administration and Board of Directors established the psychology archives it was, of course, with the intention that it was permanent. Archivists like the term "perpetuity." A project of this sort, with its national and international attention needs to be done well. If it were to be abandoned national and international opprobrium would replace praise and regard. They know this. Currently, the University of Akron continues to be generous. We have been supported for thirty-five years. In 1994 we moved into new quarters, and the succession has been assured with the appointment of David Baker as the new director in 1999.

"Is the collection on microfilm?" and *"Are you on the web?"* are two similar questions still being asked. Microfilm is not really seen as a solution to any of our problems. It fades, gets a disease, and generally does not have the kind of permanence that paper and ink possess. Also, a confidential item in a file can be pulled from a box before the box is given to a patron and returned when it goes back on the shelf, regaining its position in the collection.

We are especially careful about confidential material. The donor may stipulate that certain items are to be closed under various conditions and may also specify the level, or time, when they may be inspected, copied, or quoted. Or we may decide that some material is simply too sensitive, for the present, to be made public. We maintain that one does not lose one's privacy simply by being dead. And one's associates and family have the same rights. Because we are not a governmental agency, like the Library of Congress, we may restrict access, and our legal department is even touchier about these things than we are.

Lastly there is an aesthetic side to all this. People like to hold in their hand the real document, the thing itself, and staring at a ground glass screen is not the same thing. So we have no expectation, at the present, to go to microfilm. The saving in space would be the compelling reason to use it, and we do not feel that this has come yet.

We are in the process of computerizing the inventory and other finding aids. It is a significant undertaking and one that will meet the needs of our donors and patrons.

Popplestone's favorite question still being asked is *"How did you ever get an idea like this?"* said with an inflection that says "how come a dork like you is able to come up with something so splendid?" He has answered this question so frequently that it seems redundant to answer it again but perhaps we should.

In 1965, we were both identifiable as clinical psychologists; our teaching and research were concerned with personality, mental retardation, and psychometrics. Teaching was in the clinical area. But the head of the department asked one of us to teach the history of psychology course, which was far from our main interests and not an area of special expertise. But, on the other hand, we are not afraid of history, or of the past either. In 1965, after about four years of teaching a course in history, one of us complained that there was a very low standard of what passed for research in the field and predicted that unless the historians began to use primary sources and had archival material available, a field of respectable historical writing would never exist.

A mutual friend had been involved in the recent establishment of the Archives of American Art, and that interesting project probably helped to suggest a psychology archives. Also we were reminded many years later of an article in the *American Psychologist* signed "Historiophile" (actually Saul Rosenzweig) which urged a psychological museum. But that was not in consciousness at the time, and neither the earlier Rafi Khan nor the David Boder "museum" attempts were known to us.

In any case, the dean, who was an historian, authorized pursuit of the possibility. Visits to the Archives of Labor History at Wayne State University and the Archives of American Art at the Institute of Arts in Detroit were helpful, and the influential support of Robert I. Watson sped things along. In October 1965, the University of Akron Board of Trustees author-ized the Archives of the History of American Psychology and at the same time created the University of Akron Archives.

AHAP at that time was without released time, without a budget, and with space limited to a desk in a library office, with a part-time student assistant and some handsome letterhead. We had the good wishes of many, but not all, of the university administrators.

"Why in Akron?" This suggests that the American midwest is as remote from civilization as is Baffin Land or the upcountry of Belize. West Coast people feel it should be on the West Coast, and East Coast residents think it should be in either Washington or New York. In fact, with modern meth-ods of travel and communication, it can be anyplace. In this case our will-ingness to do the work and the university's willingness to provide housing and money settled the issue.

Journalists—and some others—ask, *"What is the most interesting request you have had?"* We have several favorites. One is our participation in the Ellis Island restoration project. The concept was to allow the modern vis-itor to experience vicariously what the arriving immigrant experienced, to evoke the physical and psychological examinations. But the staff were not able to find the tests that had been given. Manuals and descriptions abound, but the actual objects did not. Then a friend of the Ellis Island exhibit staff suggested they try Akron. We had the tests—in fact we had enough extras that we could lend Ellis Island what was needed. We have not been out to see the restored station but an article in *LIFE* magazine did illustrate the "Ship Test" we loaned them, although it did not give us credit. So we are awaiting the chance to see it. Neither of us has an Ellis Island experience in our families—we came in by another route—but this *does* mean that we now can share some of this part of the history of Amer-ica with so many others.

In another, not particularly psychological experience, we were asked to make available some of the genealogical charts that had been prepared by the staff of the Vineland Training School and known as "The Jackson-Whites." The genealogies of the Jukes family and the Kallikak family were once "evidence" of the familial occurrence of social inadequacy. The Jackson-Whites are another such family, although not as well-known as the Kallikaks and the Jukes. We received an inquiry from a professional genealogist hired by the Ramapough Mountain Indians who were trying to achieve acknowledgment by the federal government as an Indian tribe. The genealogist asked to be allowed to examine the charts since they were believed to provide important information on the ancestry of their tribal members. A letter urging us to allow the genealogist to have access came from Ronald Redbone Van Dunk, chief, Ramapough Mountain Indian Tribe. We were happy to give access, once our legal department gave us clearance, and we wrote to Chief Van Dunk to assure him of our cooperation. We had never before written to an Indian chief and none of the manuals we consulted told us what the correct salutation was. They do prescribe the appropriate form for the Queen of England and the Pope, but not for an American Indian tribal chief. We have no idea how valid the claims of the Ramapough Indians are, but it was nice to do something for the Indians more concrete than just have the usual white, European-origin, liberal, guilt feelings.

A similar inquiry is, *"What is your favorite or most valuable or most important collection?"* Well, the Papers of Henry Herbert Goddard are very large—he was an important figure—and we have a lot of traffic in them. The Donald K. Adams Papers reflect the Gestalt movement and did receive a lot of use. The Papers of Barbara Strudler Walston will reflect many of the current, cutting-edge things happening in psychology now. She was involved in many activities. In fact the extent of her involvement and the recency of events has decided us on the indefinite postponement of preparing her papers for use. They are just too new and involve too many people on the contemporary scene.

As we have examined this question of what collection seems most important, the real answer is, "Whatever one is most recent." We acquired the papers and films of Rene Spitz on July 24–27, 1990. This is a very large collection—1,320 pounds of paper and 2,080 pounds of film. (We have these figures since the collection was released by The University of Colorado in Denver and came to Akron via air freight, in two shipments for security. And, since we shared the cost of shipment with the people in Colorado, we know the exact poundage.) Spitz is probably most easily identified as a psychoanalyst and psychiatrist of European background, and the work usually identified with his name is the anaclitic depression and hospitalism. But he was a member of APA from 1956 to his death in 1974, and was, at one time, frequently cited by psychologists. The collection begins in Europe before 1938 and includes psychoanalytic materials from the pre-Hitler era, a period in which historians of psychoanalysis say the records are very sparse. He seems to have had a wide correspondence with many workers in personality, child development, and early studies of psychopathology in children. The films, particularly *Grief,* are still in demand, mostly by people in television production.

We are frequently approached by the producers of television programs, particularly educational television, for help with visuals, photographs, and film clips. They are delightful people to work with, and it is something of a thrill to give things to them because of the potentially huge impact. If a scholar uses our materials and they are seen by a few hundred other scholars that is just fine—that is our main reason for existence, after all. But when a single film clip is going to be seen by millions and have the potential for influencing them for the better, it is really having impact.

What financial support do the archives receive?

Strangely, the question about "the bottom line" which dominates the thinking of the staff of the archives is rarely of concern to the inquiring consumer-donor. Perhaps the worth of the project seems so self-evident that the question does not seem salient. However, to those of us who are intimately concerned with operation and execution, money is important and rare.

Through the years the University of Akron has generously provided our salaries, supplies and services, travel, and space, heat, maintenance, and auxiliary services (like audio visual support), just as for an academic department. We have never been overwhelmed by surplus abundances but, on the other hand, the university has allowed us the basic subsistence budget without which nothing would have taken place. However, the amount of work does increase every year, intake is sometimes a little overwhelming, and there is a gap between what the university can provide and what AHAP needs to carry out its goals.

Except for a very few grants, we have not been able to generate any significant extramural support. For example, in 1966 a National Science

Foundation official, Murray Aborn, a psychologist, in the course of saying no told us, "There is no need for a psychology archive since there are no competent historians of psychology." He *was* invited to the festschrift conference of 2000 but did not attend.

We generate funds by selling photographs to book publishers and others. Some publication royalties are assigned to us. One of these is an AHAP-based publication, *An Illustrated History of American Psychology*. It has gone through two English language printings, as well as an abridgement in Japanese. And over the years we have had spontaneous gifts from organizations and individuals who have felt that we deserve help. Some psychologists have included the archives in their wills, and one has even made the archives his heir.

In order to structure these spontaneous gifts, an organization, "The Friends of the Psychology Archives," was initiated in 1995. The friends have sent a mail solicitation every year since, and the annual gifts are now a major support of the work, particularly in providing the salaries of our student workers who prepare the finding aids.

In 1965 when the field of the history of psychology took a great leap forward with the creation of the journal, the division, and the opening of a special subject matter archive, we all felt that maturity, if not here *now*, was soon to be obtained. At the archives we were sure that the directed preservation of primary materials was a necessary and perhaps even sufficient condition for the writing of good history. The field is certainly much better now than it was in 1965, and we think that most of us would allow a prediction that it will be even better in the future. But we must also entertain the proposition that an ideal history may never exist. Perhaps our goals and aspirations can never be fully experienced. This is not a statement of pessimism but simply one of looking at our record with some pride—the idealism of 1965 may have been less mature than a present-day realization that perfection may be pursued but may not be apprehended.

CHAPTER 1

"Microhistory" and the History of Psychology:

"Thick Description" and "The Fine Texture of the Past"

Michael M. Sokal

IT IS AN HONOR TO PARTICIPATE in a celebration of all that John Popplestone and Marion White McPherson have done for all of us. At times like this I'm especially pleased to take advantage of the phenomenon of "reflected glory." And of course, the other contributors to this volume shine almost as brightly as the honorees. All are highly distinguished individuals who have written (among their many other works) some of the best scholarship available in the history of psychology. Most important, in terms of this presentation, their scholarship most effectively illustrates the value of "microhistory" and the "thick description" of "the fine texture of the past."

I believe that I can offer other interesting illustrations of the value of such approaches to psychology's past and can even suggest two or three alternative means of implementing concerns for individual scientific lives and careers. Indeed, I want to sketch something of the range of approaches and interpretations—that is, to present what might be thought of as "type specimens" of several of one thousand flowers—that such attention to the "fine texture of the past" can support. I'll do so through a review of some of my own ongoing, recent, and (unfortunately) not so recent research, most of which focuses on the life and career of James McKeen Cattell (1860–1944).[1] Best known as a distinguished experimental psychologist, Cattell was also—even more

1

significantly—the owner and editor of *Science* magazine for fifty years, from 1894 through 1944.[2]

James McKeen Cattell was born in Easton, Pennsylvania, in 1860, the son of the president of Lafayette College and grandson (and namesake) of its wealthiest benefactor. After he graduated from Lafayette, his grandfather's wealth allowed him to study at Johns Hopkins and in Germany. He earned a Ph.D. in 1886 at the University of Leipzig under Wilhelm Wundt, prophet of the new experimental psychology.[3] Cattell's experiments measured a wide variety of reaction times under a wide variety of conditions. However, instead of employing Wundt's preferred method of "Selbst-Beobachtung"—a term that means, literally, "self observation," and is often (and incorrectly) translated as "introspection"—Cattell refocused his experiments away from the reactor's report of his own mental activity to the experimenter's "objective" measurements of the behavior of his "subject." Though Cattell was, apparently, the first to use this term, the full implication of this shift of scientific attention emerged only many years later. Instead, in the 1880s and 1890s, Cattell himself stressed that he consistently measured reaction times in milliseconds, and continually emphasized the extreme precision of these measurements.

As the English speaker who knew more about Wundt's work than anyone else, Cattell then spent two and one-half years at St. John's College, Cambridge, where he introduced his English hosts to this "new psychology."[4] More significantly, while in England Cattell fell under the influence of Francis Galton—a cousin of Charles Darwin—and especially Galton's interest in the differences between individuals, the variation that makes natural selection possible. Cattell was especially taken with Galton's anthropometric laboratory, which gathered data on such differences and even attempted to measure variations in such physiological traits as strength of squeeze and lung capacity. In 1889 Cattell returned to America to assume at the University of Pennsylvania (what he later claimed to be) the world's first professorship in psychology. In 1891 he moved to Columbia University, and his work was associated with that institution for the rest of his career, for better or for worse.

At Columbia Cattell extended Galton's interests by introducing a series of anthropometric "mental tests," a term he later claimed to have coined.[5]

These employed the procedures he had used in Wundt's Leipzig psychological laboratory to measure how individuals differ with respect to such traits as sensory acuity, reaction time, and short-term memory. Throughout this work, Cattell continued to emphasize the precision of his measurements and began to employ descriptive-statistical techniques to report his data. Around 1895 Cattell brought Franz Boas to Columbia, not because of his well-recognized anthropological expertise, but largely because Boas (with his Ph.D. in physics) understood as Cattell never did the mathematics underlying the concept of correlation that Galton had recently developed. Cattell also implemented Galton's ideas—in particular, Galton's vision of a positive eugenics—outside the laboratory, as he and his wife, Josephine Owen Cattell, had seven children. But in emphasizing the quantitative precision of his results Cattell lacked any functional notion of what they meant; that is, of how the traits he measured actually helped those he tested to live and act in the world. Through the 1890s, as American psychologists resonated more strongly than ever with the functional concerns perhaps best expressed by William James, the limitations of Cattell's approach grew ever more apparent.

Finally, in 1901, under the influence of Boas, one of Cattell's students dealt the clichéd deathblow to Cattell's testing program. This student—Clark Wissler, later a distinguished anthropologist—showed that none of results of any one of Cattell's tests correlated with those of any other test, and that none of these results correlated at all with any accepted measure or estimate of student performance, ability, or aptitude. Indeed, he even showed that student attendance correlated better with any of these estimates than did the results of any of Cattell's tests. Cattell had already begun to shift the focus of his attention away from his laboratory. But though others continued to try to use his anthropometric tests in (what were known as) "schools for the feebleminded"—at least until 1908, when Henry H. Goddard brought to America the work of Alfred Binet[6]—Cattell abandoned this effort. But he never abandoned his belief in the value of highly precise quantitative methods.

Cattell's shift from the laboratory began as early as 1893, when he began laying plans for what emerged the following year as *The Psychological Review*.[7] Like most scientific journals of the period, the *Review* was privately

owned, and Cattell's editorial interests always reflected—at least in part—
the fact that with his university salary alone he could not live in the style
to which he had become accustomed. Cattell jointly owned and edited the
Review with James Mark Baldwin (of Princeton and Johns Hopkins) until
late 1903, when he sold his share of the journal to Baldwin after a bitter
controversy. Even earlier, late in 1894, Cattell took over the ownership and
editorship of *Science*, the weekly journal founded by Thomas Edison and
supported for years by Alexander Graham Bell, which had just ceased publication after many years of significant financial losses. Cattell soon suc-
ceeded where Edison and Bell had failed, and in 1900 Cattell arranged for
Science to become—even while still privately owned—the official journal
of the American Association for the Advancement of Science (AAAS). This
arrangement served both well, and the AAAS's membership soon boomed.
As *Science's* circulation grew equally fast, so did Cattell's advertising revenue. Within a decade, he earned more from advertising in *Science* than he
did as a Columbia professor.

The Psychological Review and Science were only the start of Cattell's jour-
nalistic empire. It gradually grew to include *Popular Science Monthly* and
The American Naturalist (failing journals that Cattell took over in 1900 and
1907, respectively); *School and Society* (an analog to *Science* that Cattell edited weekly for educators from 1915); and *The Scientific Monthly* (which
continued as the *Popular Science Monthly* after 1915, when Cattell sold the
original name). In 1906 Cattell began gathering data for and periodically
producing volumes of *American Men of Science* and also established The
Science Press to publish all he edited.[8] From 1915, James McKeen Cattell
and Josephine Owen Cattell (who served as unacknowledged managing
editor for all these publications) regularly produced two weekly and two
monthly journals from "Fort Defiance," their isolated family home about
fifty miles north of New York City. Cattell formally continued as professor
at Columbia, but graduate students in psychology soon realized that they
had to look elsewhere for active mentoring.

Cattell nonetheless remained involved in Columbia affairs, most actively protesting what he perceived as violations of academic freedom and
frequently condemning the policies of university President Nicholas Murray Butler. As early as 1907 his colleagues noted that Cattell was often "in

a contentious rather than a helpful frame of mind" and that he was "chronically opposed . . . to anything anybody does," and regretted that "Cattell is opposed to so many things." In 1913 Columbia tried to force Cattell into retirement. His colleagues defended him, arguing that his significance for American science vastly outweighed any difficulty his behavior might cause—and the university ceased its efforts. But four years later, after Columbia fired Cattell for his opposition to American conscription policy once the nation entered World War I, few defended him.[9] By that time his criticism of Butler grew more personal; for example, he compared the president with his daughter's doll, as both would "lie in any position in which they were placed." Many at Columbia—including Franz Boas and John Dewey, both of whom he had brought to the university—concluded that "Cattell has outlived his usefulness to the university."[10] But though some argued analogously with respect to Cattell's usefulness to the AAAS, the association did nothing to challenge Cattell's editorship of *Science*. After all, the journal was Cattell's private property, and its assets far outweighed the AAAS's.

After the war, Cattell continued editing his journals, founded The Psychological Corporation in an attempt to organize the rapidly expanding field of applied psychology, and devoted himself to AAAS affairs.[11] He served, for example, as chair of the AAAS executive committee for almost twenty years, and though many found his leadership stifling, few actively opposed it, especially during the 1920s when the association was richer than it ever had been. After all, they noted, Cattell had turned sixty-five in 1925, and among themselves they figured they wouldn't have to tolerate him for many more years. But after 1929—when *Science*'s advertising revenue dropped and Cattell sought a scapegoat—he fired and hired a succession of four permanent secretaries, alienated other potential AAAS supporters, and used his position to smother any opposition to his policies. Finally, in 1941, those who opposed his leadership banded together to force his resignation as the chair, at age eighty-one. He died three years later, and *Science* became the property of the association under the terms of an agreement that provided an exceptionally large annuity for Cattell's heirs for many years.

Historians and psychologists knew the basic outline of this life and career when I began my work in 1968, though many details (such as, particularly, Cattell's significant financial interest in many of his ventures) emerged only after I began immersing myself in "the fine texture of the past." Doing so became possible when one of Cattell's four sons deposited a large collection of his father's papers at the Manuscript Division of the Library of Congress. Even more significantly, during a 1971 visit with another of Cattell's sons at the family home of Fort Defiance, my wife, Charlene Key Sokal, literally fell through the floor of an outbuilding and discovered a cache of papers that more than doubled the size of the Library of Congress collection. I can't claim that this collection rivals in significance the great resources that Popplestone and McPherson have brought together here in Akron since the mid-1960s, which now comprise the Archives of the History of American Psychology, but it has supported my scholarly career for many years. As pre-teens my now-adult children used to speak of Cattell as their imaginary brother Jimmy. I also owe much to the Library of Congress, and am especially indebted to Mary M. Wolfskill, director of the staff of the Manuscript Division's Reading Room.

One example relates to my attempt to understand just what led Cattell to his interest in measurement—an interest that led to his psychological tests—and why he emphasized as strongly as he did the precision of his quantitative results. I still remember how excited I was to discover that, when he graduated from Lafayette in 1880, Cattell had been scheduled to give his class's valedictory address on "The Ethics of Positivism." To be sure, I have yet to find the text of this address, either at Lafayette or in the Library of Congress collection. That didn't stop me from arguing that anyone who spoke on Comtean positivism in 1880 must have immersed himself in a philosophy that emphasized—with its law of three stages and the hierarchy of knowledge—the authority of quantitative approaches to the world. Indeed, I still think this argument makes much sense, and I spent much time and effort explicating Gilded Age America's interest in Comtean ideas and tracing the paths through which these ideas might have reached rural Pennsylvania by the late 1870s.[12] But even as I continue to argue that Cattell derived (what I came to call) his "scientific ideology" largely from a study of Comtean positions, it was not until many years later that I looked further and asked, why did Cattell focus on positivistic ethics?

What indeed were "the ethics of positivism"? Since Comte denied the teachings of Christianity he had to look elsewhere for the basis of ethical behavior, and he found it in the concept of altruism, which emphasized the good that individuals do for others. Comte soon identified as his model of altruistic (and hence ethical) behavior the sacrifice of the mother in childbirth, and practitioners of his "Religion of Humanity" found themselves revering images of mothers and infants that uncannily resembled the Madonna and Child archetypically portrayed by Renaissance artists. Although critics came to characterize this concept as "Catholicism without Christianity," it did serve to emphasize the importance of family and, for many, the centrality of the mother in many family settings.

As I delved into the details of Cattell's early life I came to realize that in many ways the family of his childhood exemplified Comte's ideal. His father, William C. Cattell, was a highly effective college president and, like most of his generation, was also an ordained minister—in his case, a Presbyterian—to whom students and colleagues looked for emotional sustenance. In all others aspects of his life William Cattell exhibited an extreme genteel neurasthenia that most evenings left him nervous and edgy and at times forced him to withdraw entirely from the practicalities of life. Such complaints remain common today, of course, and early twenty–first century psychologists use other terms to explain them. However, 130 years ago neurasthenia was the diagnosis of choice for those upper middle-class Americans who exhibited these symptoms, and the condition seemed to be prevalent (or at least common) among those who, like William Cattell, saw themselves as learned.[13] One incident illustrates just how the elder Cattell suffered. It occurred during a European visit, when his wife walked away for a few minutes, and President Cattell could not find her. As Israel Platt Pardee—a young friend who accompanied the family—recorded:

[Dr. Cattell] at once became terribly excited, called to me to come with him, and he started away from the docks almost at a run, his high hat on the back of his head, his umbrella under his arm and talking to himself at a great rate; said he would call the town crier out but that he would find Lizzie. He seemed to be getting more and more excited all the time. I could hardly keep up to him and could hardly keep from shrieking with laughter, for it did not seem to me so serious a thing. . . . We tore up the middle of the street, and the Doctor passed a lot of little boys playing in the street. He threw one boy one way and another boy another way. This showed how terribly upset he was for there is no kinder man to children than he is. We passed a carriage going in the opposite direction; I happened to look in and saw Mrs. Cattell. . . . I stopped them and then tore off after the Doctor, but he was so excited I could hardly make him stop or make him appreciate the fact that the lost were found.[14]

As this episode suggests, in his suffering William Cattell found himself emotionally dependent upon his wife and children, and only the devoted care and attention of his wife, Elizabeth McKeen Cattell, could calm his nervousness. The details of his desk diaries reveal all sorts of further examples of this dependency and of the ways in which his family, especially his wife, became the center of his emotional world. After his death, Elizabeth Cattell's own letters to her sons highlighted just how much she missed the chance to dote on her husband, and she regularly recalled how he had always looked to his family in time of need.

As a twenty-year-old student in Germany, Cattell spent an inordinate amount of money—even for somebody who could look to his grandfather's wealth—on a copy of Raphael's *Sistine Madonna*, which remains in family hands. For the rest of his life Cattell carried with him the ideal of the close-knit family with the mother at its center, but deferring always to the father's interests. This idea did much to shape the details of Cattell's personal life and helps explain why, for example, he and his wife had seven children. It also suggests why he chose to have them live in relative isolation at Fort Defiance and to have Josephine Owen Cattell "home school" their children (to use today's term), to protect them from influences outside the family. Indeed, as they aged, the Cattell children found themselves called upon to help produce their father's journals, and even in their forties their father interfered in the careers of several of them. Cattell's emphasis on the centrality of family life also found its way into his dealing with his Columbia colleagues. For example, as a well-known proponent of academic freedom in the early 1910s, Cattell found himself called to defend his colleague Harry Thurston Peck, the eminent Latinist, whom Columbia had discharged for moral turpitude. Cattell briefly supported Peck, but when he found that Peck had indeed seduced his wife's maid he joined others in condemning his behavior. Such actions, he claimed, struck at the very heart of family life and, for Cattell, that was simply unacceptable. He even argued editorially in *Popular Science Monthly* against the common early twentieth-century policy of prohibiting married women from teaching in public schools.[15] He did so for two reasons: such a practice prevented the best-educated women who wanted to keep their jobs from marrying and thus from contributing to the mental quality of the next generation; and it also set before girls just the model he believed they ought to avoid, the unmarried and hence childless educated woman.

To return to Cattell's science, I believe strongly that the ways in which his parents related to each other—the "dynamics" of his family, to use early twenty-first century terms—led Cattell to the ethics of positivism, and thus to other aspects of Comtean positivism, and eventually to the "scientific ideology" that determined the course of his scientific career. To be sure, I cannot trace his precise thought processes as a late adolescent. (Can anyone trace the thought processes of adolescent males?!) Moreover, in response to my earlier exposition of this point, a commentator once complained that I had diverted attention from the "meat" of history of science and that my analysis had little to do with the ways in which science actually developed and emerged. Such critics at times argue that historians of science should concern themselves solely with the ideas of their subjects, that such personal matters are nothing more than the "accidentals" of the past, and that focusing on them only serves to perpetuate Alfred North Whitehead's Fallacy of Misplaced Concreteness. I hope, however, that readers of this volume find these arguments as specious as I do, and my auditors will agree that an interest in the emergence of scientific ideas can often lead to a concern for the personal. Indeed, this train of thought brings to mind a comment I first heard almost thirty years ago. Newton famously is supposed to have answered the question, "How did you solve your problems?" with the aphorism, "by always thinking on them," but as Charles Rosenberg once remarked in my hearing, most of us wouldn't want to spend much time with anyone who put that method into practice! The point is that few if any of those doing science ever "always think" on the scientific problems that consume their professional lives, and that—

like all of us—their minds are involved with many ideas and feelings. And a concern for the full range of these mental activities and emotions, that is, for the "fine texture" of an individual's life, can often allow historians to understand their subjects more fully than otherwise.

My opening paragraphs promised that in sketching the value of "microhistory" I would offer alternative approaches to making sense of this "fine texture." As some of you might know, I strongly argued several years ago for the value of adult life-span developmental psychology in understanding the lives, careers, and scientific work of men like Cattell. After all, I argued, both psychologists and historians seek to understand how individuals live and work and think. If some of what earlier scholars had called "psychohistory" has proved more fanciful than many of us prefer, psychologists have developed many other approaches to their subject to rival psychoanalysis. In the 1980s I thus emphasized the work of Daniel J. Levinson, presented most fully in *The Seasons of a Man's Life* (1978), which—though admittedly informed by Freudian and Jungian ideas—derived primarily from an empirical study of dozens of mid-twentieth-century, middle-aged, middle-class, career-oriented white male Americans. In doing so, I argued against the possibility of using Levinson's ideas in trying to understand the lives of other kinds of individuals and noted that they wouldn't work for William C. Cattell; after all, he had a calling to the Presbyterian ministry, rather than a career. And I certainly wouldn't recommend their use in any analysis of the lives of most nineteenth century individuals. Since then, however, a biographer of Henry David Thoreau has issued a book titled *Thoreau's Seasons*, which (though I haven't read it) supposedly applies ideas about modern American men to a life that ended about a century before Levinson wrote.[16] Cattell, at least, lived in the twentieth century, and though he never worked effectively within any large-scale organizations (like Columbia University), he was as career-oriented as any of the "organization men" about whom social critics of the 1950s complained.

My work implementing these ideas thus made extensive use of Levinson's terms. I identified as Cattell's "hero" Francis A. March (the Lafayette professor who exemplified the possibility of a scholarly life) and explicated the notion of "mentor" by reference to Francis Galton. In his study Levinson had found that many of the men he studied had "dreams" that helped direct, or at least chart, their lives and careers. For Cattell I identified both a personal dream (centered around his family) and a professional dream (centered around, first, his scientific work and later, around his journals). Indeed, this transition allowed me to pick up adult life-span developmental psychology's most notorious notion, that of the "mid-life transition." The "mid-life crisis" popularized by Gail Sheehy—whose most recent book focuses on Hillary Clinton—is a concept that has been used to excuse all sorts of actions. But for the men whom Levinson studied, their early forties proved to be years when they begin to realize more fully than ever before that they would never achieve all that they had dreamed, and many thus begin to reevaluate their goals and some made changes in their lives. As I worked with these ideas it shocked me to realize that the paper proving that Cattell's tests correlated with nothing of meaning appeared when he was forty-one years old! In any event, I have explicated these ideas most fully in a paper that appeared as a chapter in the festschrift for Robert E. Schofield.[17]

I found the response to this paper most interesting, as many men about my age—and I was in my early forties when I wrote it—found themselves resonating with what I had to say, while most women did not. One close woman friend even argued that anything I had interesting to say about Cattell derived solely from my immersion in the details of his life, the fine texture of the past to which I keep returning. Any attempt (she continued) to embed my understanding of Cattell in any sort of analytic framework (such as Levinson's) merely served to distract from my insight. I won't now debate this point further, but will note that any attempt to apply any sort of analytic framework—Levinson's or anybody else's—will not work without the kind of "thick description" that I am advocating.

Perhaps more than with most scientists, Cattell's achievement—largely through the journals he edited—depended heavily on his relations with those around him, and his contemporaries often commented to each other on Cattell's forceful character. At times this trait emerged as an admirable self-confidence. In the mid-1880s, for example, even as he challenged Wundt's view of reaction-time experiments, Cattell did so by offering an alternative experimental approach that, as noted earlier, focused more on a laboratory subject's behavior than on his self-observation of his mental activity. In the same way, his opposition to American conscription policy in 1917 embodied at least in part an anti-militaristic spirit that had earlier led him to criticize similar attitudes in Germany and England.

But just as regularly—and indeed, perhaps more often—his dealings with others exhibited an egotism and arrogance that alienated those around him and eventually had a negative impact on *Science* and on the AAAS. Certainly his denunciations of those who disagreed with him—like his criticism of Butler cited above—often embodied personal ad hominem criticisms that questioned the moral standing of those he attacked. Even as a graduate student at Johns Hopkins in the early 1880s, he charged that university President Daniel Coit Gilman "had not taken as much interest in me, as he might have done."[18] A few months later, when the faculty chose to award its fellowship in philosophy to John Dewey rather than to Cattell, he lashed out at them and challenged their authority. Cattell thus became the first student ever to be expelled from Johns Hopkins.

As he expanded his testing program through the mid-1890s and first *The Psychological Review* and then *Science* began to thrive later in that decade, Cattell did seem briefly to mellow through his late thirties. But the failure of his anthropometric testing program and the mendacity of several of his colleagues in connection with his sale of his share of *The Psychological Review* again brought out by 1902 the most combative aspects of his character. In that year, for example, he threatened officials of the Smithsonian and Carnegie institutions that he would use his journals to undermine their authority if they did not accept his views on scientific organization, and his personal attacks soon filled columns of the *Popular Science Monthly*. Although early twenty-first-century American academics often look to Cattell as a martyr in the cause of academic freedom, all who followed the events of 1917 realized at the time that his opposition to the draft represented only the proverbial last straw. Even those who supported Cattell's goals for the AAAS noted that, in firing and hiring four successive permanent secretaries through the 1930s, he "went out of his way to be troublesome,"[19] and by planting spies in the AAAS Executive Office, he undercut its leaders' authority. In 1929, even as psychology's grand old man and president of the first International Congress of Psychology to be held in the United States, Cattell personally attacked the experiments reported by William McDougall with an ad hominen attack that many remembered for years.

If I may be permitted an aside at this point, I'd like to use this incident to illustrate some of the riches that Popplestone and McPherson have gathered for our delectation at the Archives of the History of American Psychology. That is, documenting the details of this episode proved difficult for many years, as most of the documentary evidence I've found relating to Cattell's attack consists primarily of correspondence among his American colleagues sharing their embarrassment at his actions before an audience of the world's most eminent psychologists. And as those who wrote and were written to all heard Cattell's statements, none had to tell the others precisely what Cattell had actually said. This state of affairs led me in the 1970s to seek out as many psychologists who attended the congress as I could identify, and to ask them all what happened. I thus spoke with about a dozen different distinguished American psychologists, all of whom opened their accounts by highlighting the shock they felt at Cattell's remarks and emphasizing how they were burned on their memories. I hesitate to steal any of John Burnham's thunder, but I must report that though each of the dozen or so distinguished individuals told me that he or she would never forget what Cattell said to McDougall, my efforts led to a dozen or so different and mutually contradictory accounts.

Fortunately, however, as C. James Goodwin illustrates in a later chapter, Walter R. Miles was an obsessive diary keeper who attended the Congress and—even more fortunately—his diary is one of the many riches that Popplestone and McPherson brought to Akron. Let me thus quote some excerpts from Miles's entry for Thursday, September 5, 1929. Cattell said: "These experiments are interesting but of course they are wrong. . . . I must be permitted to say that your methods are not [valid]. . . . There is not sufficient correlation . . . that can be demonstrated. . . . Dr. McDougall, do you know why they were a failure (No.) I do (and will tell you later)."

How does a historian account for such behavior, both in an adolescent and in an older adult? My first attempts appealed to the image of Cattell as a young man spoiled by his doting parents and indeed by the setting in which he grew. An older friend (Israel Platt Pardee, whose description of the elder Cattell's response to the apparent disappearance of his wife I've already quoted) once described Cattell as a "Mama's boy," and as a student at Lafayette he became used to the deference of its faculty. These professors did expect Cattell to do as much and work as hard as his classmates, and they upheld all of the college's standards. But Cattell was bright and hard working and fulfilled their expectations readily. And, after all, most taught in McKeen Hall, and he was their president's son and the grandson (and namesake) of their major benefactor. He was thus deferred to, and he grew to expect such deference from all those whom he met, including those in positions of authority. This attitude also owed much to the late nineteenth-century Easton society, which knew Cattell as the scion of the upper middle-class family that has assumed the leading social role in their community. But this explanation seemed less than satisfying, until I re-read (for perhaps the tenth time) F. Scott Fitzgerald's 1926 short story, "The Rich Boy." This story contains what may be Fitzgerald's best-known observation: "the very rich are different from you and me." And despite Ernest Hemingway's derision in his 1936 short story, "The Snows of Kilimanjaro"—he even had earlier responded that "yes, they have more money"—I came to believe that Fitzgerald's portrait of his story's protagonist, Anson Hunter, has much to say about those who share wealth. After all, the Cattell family had a twelve thousand dollar income in 1886, and though this wealth paled in comparison to Hunter's, it certainly supported a genteel lifestyle in Easton, Pennsylvania. In Fitzgerald's story, even as a boy Hunter noticed that his friends' parents "were vaguely excited whenever their own children were asked to [his] house," and he soon came to recognize their "half-grudging American deference." Most notably, Hunter soon "accepted this as the natural state of things" and developed "a sort of impatience with all groups of which he was not the center." As Fitzgerald continued, this impatience "remained with [Hunter] for the rest of his life."[20] Like anyone raised within a particular setting, Hunter found nothing unusual in his experience, and neither did Cattell, who throughout his life expected all to defer to him and his desires. As Nicholas Murray Butler discovered when he happened to disagree with Cattell, Cattell reacted nastily when others refused to defer to him.

Having cited one writer of fiction, I'd like to mention (however briefly) two others whose work I've also found most useful. The first, C. P. Snow, is perhaps best known for his analyses of "The Two Cultures" and his arguments that the gulf between science and technology, on the one hand, and the arts and humanities, on the other, must be bridged. Indeed, his own career—as a physicist, novelist, and (most notably) as a government administrator—embodied such a bridge. And his fictional portrayal of academic life in early twentieth-century Cambridge—which shared much in common with the late Victorian Cambridge where Cattell spent three years—shed much light on many aspects of Cattell's character. If nothing else, for example, the second of *The Masters* on whom Snow's 1951 novel focuses always spoke of his colleagues as "men of science"—rather than scientists—and Snow's explication of this term helps explain why Cattell chose that usage for his directories.[21]

Critics might harp that Snow's novels emphasize the particular at the expense of the general. But other novelists—even as they embody their analyses in accounts of individuals living in a particular time and place—try to address the general affairs of humankind. And I believe that Iris Murdoch's late twentieth-century novels have much to say to those of us who seek to understand the past. To be sure, reviews of some of her novels by those who claim a sharp aesthetic sense argue that "writing this bad cannot be faked." On the other hand, I believe that those of us interested in the evolution of ideas have all sorts of good reasons to look to the author of such philosophical treatises as *Metaphysics as a Guide to Morals* (1993).[22] After all, how many philosophers have been honored by being created a Dame of the British Empire?

In particular, I wish to cite two particular passages, the first from her 1989 novel, *The Message to the Planet*. On its very last page, she has her protagonist, Alfred Ludens, speculate that if a friend had not acted in a particular way, "none of this would have happened at all." In reply, Gildas Herne—perhaps the most generally insightful and moral character in the book—concludes, "Don't let's play that game. Innumerable things could have altered other things. Everything is accidental." That's the message of the novel's title. In the same way, the omniscient narrator of her 1993 novel, *The Green Knight*, claims that "if at that moment Clement had caught sight of the dog and had managed to capture him, the fates of a number of people in this story would have been entirely different. Such is the vast play of chance in human lives."[23] I think it behooves those of us who seek to reconstruct the past to keep in mind the significance of chance, fortune, and accident in the lives of careers and development of those about whom we write. After all, to cite an incident in my own life, the sheer accident of my wife falling through the floor at Fort Defiance so many years ago made possible much of what I've done professionally since then. And of course, to return to my thesis, a full realization of the significance of such accidents depends upon attention to "the fine texture of the past."

After emphasizing what historians can learn from novelists, I should return to what psychologists can tell us. To do so, I'd like to emphasize the efforts of one psychologist, Jill C. Gitten, a student (whom I have never met) who participated in Donald Dewsbury's 1997 University of Florida graduate seminar in the history of psychology. She has looked to a set of psychological ideas in conjunction with some of the microhistorical detail I presented in 1981 in *An Education in Psychology*, my edition of Cattell's student journal and correspondence, to offer a different, though complementary, understanding of his behavior. Gitten read through Cattell letters (as excerpted in Ludy Benjamin's *A History of Psychology in Letters*) with a copy of the DSM-IV, the fourth edition of the American Psychiatric Association's *Diagnostic and Statistical Manual* (1994), at hand; those working in (almost) all psychotherapeutic traditions regularly employ its concepts. Gitten focused on the DSM-IV's category 301.81, "Narcissistic Personality Disorder," and highlighted the traits correlated with this diagnosis. These include "a grandiose sense of self-importance," "fantasies of unlimited success, power [and] brilliance," "a sense of entitlement," "interpersonally exploitative" behavior, and "arrogant, haughty behaviors or attitudes." To illustrate these traits she quoted from the letters Cattell wrote in his early twenties. For example, he wrote, "A paper like this gives me a very secure place in the scientific world [and] makes me equal to any American living"; and "I imagine—though I have often been told to the contrary—that I am quite clever in getting along with all sorts and conditions of people"; and "I could write a paper . . . most damaging to Prof. Wundt. It is to be hoped for his sake as well as mine that he passes me on the examination"; and

"Prof. Wundt lectured yesterday and today on my subject . . . I know a good deal more about it than he does."[24]

Today's psychotherapists utilize such diagnoses as a tool to help their clients gain insight into (and perhaps begin to have some control over) their own relations with those around them,[25] and Cattell obviously cannot use these insights in these ways. I believe that historians can find them useful in seeking to understand their attitudes and actions and, especially, to convey their understanding of their impact on the institutions within which they work. They certainly have helped me understand Cattell and to share my understanding with others.

Let me close by sketching one other way in which historians can (I believe sincerely) gain further (and perhaps deeper) access to "the fine texture of the past." When I've mentioned my concern for "thick description" before academic audiences during the last decade, I'm often asked about the impact of anthropologist Clifford Geertz and his ideas on my approach to history. After all, in a recent autobiographical essay Geertz presents a "budget of terms" that begins with "thick description" and continues with twenty-three other items "around which a [fuller] conception of . . . 'culture' could be built." To be frank, however, I had not heard of Geertz when I began to explicate my approach to the past that has gradually emerged in my work since 1968. On the other hand, I found myself resonating with one statement in Geertz's recent autobiography. There he argues that, "To discover who people think they are, what they think they are doing, and to what end they think they are doing it, it is necessary to gain a working familiarity with the frames of meaning within which they enact their lives."[26]

I doubt that most historians would disagree with this claim, and separately and together we have developed all sorts of methods to help us gain the kind of "working familiarity" for which Geertz calls. Reading this statement led me to realize more explicitly than I had before that, in many ways, I've been living Cattell's life during at least the past two decades. I won't argue this point in detail here, and I don't want to claim too much except to say that I've spent at least the past decade and a half devoting most of my professional time and attention to organizations and institutions that seek to promote science and scholarship. Of these, the journal

I'm now editing is perhaps the most analogous to the institutions to which Cattell devoted his professional life. To be sure, I would not wish to compare *History of Psychology* with *Science*, even during Cattell's last years as editor, when that journal fell into disarray. But certainly my work as Executive Secretary of the History of Science Society, and with the federal funding agencies I've served, has involved me more fully than most historians with the kinds of decisions and responsibilities that dominated Cattell's own professional life. In all, I believe that I am—to some degree at least—following the advice often attributed to Native Americans by not criticizing a man until I have walked a mile in his moccasins. Again, I have no wish now to claim too much or to cite specifics. But I believe strongly that my professional experiences have greatly enriched my analysis of Cattell's actions in, most recently, both my account of his early editorship of *The Psychological Review* and in my chapter in the just-published 150th anniversary history of the American Association for the Advancement of Science.

Attention to the fine texture of my own past reveals a concern for such matters long before I began working on Cattell. I edited the undergraduate newspaper of the engineering school I attended. In other settings I have argued that my interest in editing (and indeed in organizational affairs) derived in large part from my study at Case Western Reserve University with Melvin Kranzberg, the founder of the Society for the History of Technology and the founding editor of *Technology and Culture*.[27] I have often claimed that my approach to the institutions with which I work follows directly from the insights I've gained in writing institutional history and, indeed, that my organizational work represents a kind of "applied history of science."[28] Reductionists could thus ask, "Which came first?" I believe that any reductionist approach to the past simply serves to oversimplify its "fine texture," and I think that many of us would agree that an interest in this fine texture—the ideas, the individuals, their institutions, and how they all interacted—led us to history in the first place. In our efforts to explain all, let's not move too far from this attraction.

CHAPTER 2

Interviewing as a Tool of the Trade:

A Not-Very-Satisfactory Bottom Line

John C. Burnham

IN THE ARCHIVES OF THE History of American Psychology are many treasures. They exist in a matrix of ordinary materials that enhance the value of the treasures. Or it may turn out that quite ordinary materials will in the future turn out to be the treasures. One never can know for sure.

These clichéd observations serve as a two-sided base for my attempt to discuss interview material in the history of psychology. I want to suggest, with examples, that interview material is often disappointing, if not in general overrated.[1] But I wish to make these cautionary remarks in the context that one never knows but that someone, at some future time, might find in interview material value that I, at least, do not now see.

Some years ago I sent the archives some notes from my own interviews, just in case I should never get around to using the material. It is from these interview notes (and they are personal notes, not recordings) that I wish to draw some examples—and in the process demystify my deposit so that no one will imagine that it contains any material of particular interest. I know that it is a deadly task to explicate the unimportant because it is unimportant, but I hope to attract at least a little of your attention by laying out exactly how the interviews were so unfruitful.

I should explain that in the 1950s, so-called oral history had just come in with much fanfare, and interviewing was, if not all the rage, certainly a fresh approach to recent history. As a self-consciously up-to-date historian, I tried to share this enthusiasm. And beginning in 1958, my postdoctoral teacher, David Rapaport, thought that it would be an excellent idea for me just to get to talk to major figures, even if nothing substantial came of it. I think he, too, had a high opinion of the potential of interviews, but perhaps from a perspective that was not altogether historical. Therefore I set about, when I could, talking to great people in psychology and psychiatry. And if the greats were not available, I at least could talk to long-lived participants. I therefore spent a substantial part of my life from 1958 to 1961 on interviews.

Looking back, I think much of my effort was not well directed—in part because I often did not have time to prepare adequately or did not have the wit to exploit the interview process as I might have. But I also think that interviewing was just not as productive as it might be. For example, I did a full oral history of E. G. Boring, taped and transcribed. The result produced virtually nothing that he did not in one form or another have in print. When I did go beyond the set narrative and asked him about the suicide of a colleague (which I had heard blamed on Boring), he seemed to me to be guileful and evasive, or at least he played dumb, so that nothing was added to otherwise available written material. Altogether my experience with Boring, whose historical sense should have been valuable, did not elevate my estimate of the worth of interviews. When I got William Healy, the founder of child guidance, on tape, I found that he was insecure in his memory and was cribbing from an autobiographical account published some years before, even at one point openly reading from it into the tape recorder. I do not wish to suggest that my interviews were, on the whole, negative experiences. I made the acquaintance of some very, very fine and often gracious people. And I did get some material of value. I think that the interview material that I obtained from Augusta Bronner, who worked with Healy in child guidance, for example, was valuable and unique. That transcription is available and has been used by a number of scholars. I particularly treasure the material I more or less accidentally received from someone in a different field, William F. Ogburn, the great sociologist, for it turned out that I had virtually the only biographical information about the man, because everything else got pretty well thrown out.[2]

But I think more typical is my experience interviewing John B. Watson in 1955. I have written this up as a comic episode, in which he tried to get a poor graduate student—who happened to be a functional teetotaler— drunk on whiskey during the interview.[3] But even though I stayed relatively sober, virtually everything Watson had to tell me came from his personal myth, which he had published some years before. He was not disingenuous but was simply trapped in the stories he had told himself and others over the years so that his memories were not very useful to a historian.

Let me, then, describe some of my other experiences, and readers can judge for themselves—and perhaps sample more generally the kinds of problems that John Popplestone and Marion White McPherson have had to deal with and have, I believe, dealt with in such an intelligent way.[4]

Let me start out by telling briefly about my visit to Karl and Charlotte Bühler in 1958, when I happened to be in their vicinity.[5] I found a miserable German-speaking couple of a substantial age (he was seventy-nine) exiled in California, which for them was a remarkably alien culture. Worse still, these academics were reduced to doing private practice clinical psychology for economic reasons. I had no idea except in most superficial terms why I was told to see these people, and I had not had time to study their material, much of which was in a German largely inaccessible to me anyway. They represented a soft, theoretical, if not philosophical, European tradition that had only indirect connections to the hard, behavioral American psychology with which I was familiar.

Karl Bühler (1879–1963) was a gentle and charming person who was willing to talk about the happy times when he started working with Oswald Külpe on the theory of thinking. He informed me that Külpe was a fine musician and a bachelor and very kind. Bühler told me (but not in any detail at all) how he developed his ideas and experiments and how his Gestalt psychology differed from that of Max Wertheimer, whom he considered one-sided because Wertheimer, like the structuralists, dealt with particular things. Bühler went on to recall many great days, such as a delightful evening with John B. Watson (which may have sensitized Bühler to conditioned reflexes) and his many associations in the German-speaking world. Bühler still had an excellent memory, at least for the career he had left behind, and while I was charmed, I was left sad by his sense of loss.

All this time, Charlotte Bühler kept coming in and interrupting. She was very assertive and insisted that I give her equal time for her career. At this point, in 1958, Charlotte Bühler (1893–1974), as far as I could figure out, was a second-rate child psychologist with ideas that, again, may have made sense in the philosophical and theoretically-oriented world of prewar Central Europe, but were not interesting in American psychology of the 1950s. She was easy to stereotype as a woman who had been studying a minor subject and was marginalized as women often were then. But she had to tell me—and now I shall start closely paraphrasing my notes—how when she was in Gymnasium at the age of sixteen, she invented some experiments on thought processes. Two years later, in the library she discovered that some Karl Bühler had similar ideas. She started her study with Carl Stumpf, however, where she was a contemporary with Kurt Lewin. (I believe the notes say that she did not get an assistantship with Stumpf, but Lewin did.) Stumpf sent her to Külpe with high recommendations. Karl Bühler was then away at war, and so her attention focused on Külpe, and she developed a crush on him. She met Karl at the funeral of Külpe (he died in 1915), and Karl and Charlotte were married within weeks. Kurt Koffka was the main witness at the ceremony. She became pregnant immediately after the marriage, and so it was suggested that she work on fairy tales and child psychology. She then rehearsed for me how she was led into studying adolescents, how she spent time in America with E. L. Thorndike and encountered behaviorism. Eventually she came to emphasize creativity and life as a whole. But what really stimulated her interest in talking to a historian was her claim to priority for an idea that Arnold Gesell and Lawrence Frank had taken from her in Vienna in 1924–25, the idea of sequence in development.

Little did I realize at that time that this unpleasant, unhappy woman was undergoing a transition and would very, very soon become a major agent and symbol of the new Zeitgeist that favored so-called humanistic psychology.[6] Neither the personal impression I received nor the content of the interview indicated anything either outstanding or extraordinary to me. So in this interview, I lost both the significance of the past and at the same time the significance of the future.

Most of my interviews were not like that one. Unlike my work with Boring, Healy, and the Bühlers, my 1950s interviews were usually focused on my own research project for the 1950s: the impact of Freud in the period before 1918. In some ways, this narrowness was an advantage, because I was not doing the kind of inclusive dredging that one might attempt for a biography or even a broad history of ideas. But my very restricted focus also meant that there were very many questions I did not ask or openings that I did not pursue—although sometimes the interviewees went off on their own, and I may or may not have taken notes on what they were saying. I am sorry to say that I was often just not interested in what happened after 1918, even if my interviewees were eager to talk about it. In those cases, I made notes on such material only occasionally.

Indeed, my most common experience, if I caught someone still doing research, was to have that person want to tell me about what he or she was at the moment most excited. Such people often did not want to go back and talk about research or professional activities long since superseded. Indeed, even many of those who were retired still wanted to talk about the most recent problems on which they had worked. Or, worse still, they showed the Zeigarnik effect and wanted to tell me about research that was never completed or published—often for good reason.

At one point, in March 1959, I made a quick visit to the campus of the University of Michigan. There I talked to a number of leading figures who had a variety of interests and came from different generations. The most interesting was Norman R. F. Maier (1900–1977), who was one of those shrewd participants who viewed the world of psychology from the vantage point of his own professional activities and, simultaneously, from a global and historical perspective. He also had a tendency to acerbity that made me like him at once. Maier had taken his doctorate at Michigan in 1928, although he had also studied at Berlin. His own research was in the field of neuropsychology, and he later took up work in applied psychology.[7]

The most valuable observation that I obtained from Maier does not appear in my notes, although the idea framed everything he had to say about the way in which psychology at Michigan developed. But I still to this day remember his description of how, in a relatively short period of time after World War II, a group of psychologists associated in one way or another with the Yale department (and their allies) reconstituted the whole profession of American psychology by directing funding and students to "chosen" departments and withholding resources and personnel from others.

My actual interview notes (and, again, I paraphrase closely, as I shall with other reports that follow) also reflect the fact that my interviewee took advantage of my permissiveness or open-endedness, even though I started out as usual with my single-minded inquiry about the impact of psychoanalysis.[8] Maier explained that after World War II, the biological emphasis in psychology at Michigan worked at a disadvantage. The students all went into clinical psychology because the Veterans Administration would pay for that. "People didn't get paid for running rats," Maier observed tartly (he was himself, of course, a rat runner). The Institute for Human Adjustment was set up separately from the department. The administration told Charles Griffitts, a long-standing professor, to find a director, and he finally put himself in temporarily. The new unit included many joint appointments. These people with joint appointments did not get any money from the psychology department, but they did sit in on department meetings, and it was clear that Maier did not appreciate their influence there. He believed that clinical psychology had degraded psychology because clinical psychologists were losing status to physicians.

But, Maier continued, Donald Marquis (who came to Michigan from Yale in 1945) had seen which way the wind was blowing, and so he hired clinical psychologists. Before Marquis, there had been no Freudians at Michigan. Freud, Maier believed, had been treated as a historical personality by psychologists at Michigan.

Maier's sense of institution and history was unusual among my interviewees. Mostly my informants talked about people and tended to see the discipline of psychology in terms of people, and of course my questions may have reinforced this tendency—or else I easily was led into this mindset. One of the others to whom I spoke at Michigan was John F. Shepard (1881–1965). Here was someone who had attended St. Lawrence University, from which he was graduated at the age of twenty in 1901. In 1902–3, he studied at the University of Chicago, but from 1903 on, he was at Michigan, first as a graduate student and then as a faculty member specializing in biological and comparative psychology.[9] My impression when I interviewed him was that his outlook had not developed much since the World War I era.

Shepard left Chicago, he said, because Walter B. Pillsbury had wired James Rowland Angell at Chicago for a teaching assistant.[10] Shepard's memories of Chicago were interesting because they all came from a particular year and therefore were relatively uncontaminated by later experience. He worked with Angell and George Herbert Mead in Chicago. He heard John Dewey lecture, but Shepard took no courses from him, and Dewey, Shepard reported, was not a good speaker. Angell, he said, was a good lecturer who spoke freely and was never at a loss for the best words. Even then, Angell was a little in administration, a tendency that, of course, was fulfilled when he later became president of Yale.

Mead, said Shepard, was not as approachable as Angell. He or his wife had much money. Mead generally sat down in a big armchair with his hand up on the desk as he lectured. He was not as facile a speaker as Angell, but Shepard found his presentations very suggestive.

Shepard also spoke about other students at Chicago. Warner Fite ran the laboratory, and Shepard remembered that he smoked a lot.[11] Frank Pierpont Graves, later president of the University of Washington, worked with Dewey, but he was more interested in education, although Shepard worked with him in the psychology laboratory. John B. Watson was two or three years ahead of Shepard, and so he did not see him much; Watson was occupied with his dissertation. Watson was thought to be bright—by Angell, at least, Shepard added with just a little edge. Years later, he noted, Watson had the reputation of going off and drinking when he attended professional meetings.

The only Michigan faculty member of whom Shepard spoke was Charles Horton Cooley, who was a poor lecturer. He wound his feet around the chair, and he had a speech defect. But he did have a good sense of humor. Shepard even remembered one story told by Mrs. Cooley. She one evening was looking at clothing in a catalogue, apparently thinking of underwear for Cooley. "Charles," she said, "here's a union suit with only one button." "Well," he said, "that's about all that mine have now!"

I did get Shepard to talk a little about behaviorism. Yes, he said, he took note of it. Indeed, Clark L. Hull in his autobiography claimed to have heard about Watson in Shepard's class.[12] Shepard thought Watson had a point, but he just did not understand E. B. Titchener. Shepard's own work with animals involved the higher cognitive processes, although structuralism, he said, had no place for animal work. He built his first big animal maze in 1910, and he spent years attempting to control the experiments. He found that the animals were getting cues from the flooring in the maze, and this made him think that much of the animal work in psychology was flawed.

One particularly venerable figure was also still around Michigan at the time that I visited, and that was Walter B. Pillsbury (1872–1960). He held the amazing record of having served on the editorial board of the *American Journal of Psychology* for sixty-three years! Pillsbury had taken his Ph.D. at Cornell in 1896 with E. B. Titchener and had come to Michigan in 1897, where he officially founded the psychological laboratory. The author of many books and articles, he was president of the American Psychological Association in 1910 and represented a functionalist and eclectic viewpoint. Pillsbury's activity and longevity had permitted him to see and hear most of the founders of twentieth-century psychology, and, again, I asked him about people, thinking to obtain material and insights that might not be written down. Pillsbury is relatively well written up, and so I did not obtain much about the man himself that was not in his 1932 autobiography or his obituary.[13]

Pillsbury repeated some of the material out of his autobiography and out of the history of the department of psychology at Michigan that he had written only a few years earlier, such as the story of his attempt to compliment Watson's lab at Johns Hopkins and having Watson misunderstand him to be making a sarcastic remark. It was under these circumstances that I did not, therefore, get much by way of biographical detail, except that the college where he was teaching mathematics before he started graduate work at Cornell closed, or at least the students left!

The group at Cornell in the mid-1890s was a small one; Titchener had been there only since 1892. Pillsbury did have some observations about

Titchener. He was, said Pillsbury, a man of positive views. Because he was clear and dogmatic and enthusiastic, he was a good lecturer. He also strove for simplicity. Everything was either right or wrong. Titchener, according to Pillsbury, was in the 1890s developing ceremony in his lecturing. But Pillsbury did not think Titchener overworked himself. Pillsbury particularly noted that Titchener lectured only once a day, which was a very light load for those times.

Pillsbury lived adjacent to Titchener, whom he came to know as a person "with a small salary and a huge family." Then Clark offered Titchener thirty-five hundred dollars a year, which was an enormous sum in those days. (Dewey came into Michigan at nine hundred dollars in 1894.) Cornell met the offer, and Titchener stayed, for he was not keen to give up his lecturing, as presumably he would have had to at Clark.

Titchener said that his academic robe gave him the right to be dogmatic, and he carried this identity consistently. One day in town he encountered Pillsbury, who was carrying a bookcase down the street. Titchener took the bookcase away from Pillsbury and carried it, explaining to him that as a young and unestablished person, Pillsbury would lose status carrying the bookcase, but that he, Titchener, because of his established position, could not lose status.

At Michigan, Pillsbury found that psychology had been started by the two assistants to John Dewey, James H. Tufts and George Herbert Mead. There was, therefore, already some good apparatus available. Both Tufts and Mead went with Dewey to Chicago in 1904, and Pillsbury thought that it was best that all three stayed away from experimental psychology. Mead had actually started a fire in the lab when he was trying to varnish a human brain.[14]

Pillsbury's immediate predecessor at Michigan was Edgar Pierce, a Hugo Münsterberg Ph.D. Pierce married the daughter of a man who owned a chain of hotels, and Pierce left after a year to work behind the counter, but he maintained his membership in the American Psychological Association. Münsterberg was scandalized, and he got Henry Rutgers Marshall to move to have Pierce expelled from the association. At the meeting, James Cattell got up and said that it did not make any difference—the man could be an architect if he wanted. Despite Münsterberg, Pierce later endowed the department of psychology at Harvard. Pillsbury considered Pierce a very good psychologist.[15]

Pillsbury spent several summers in Europe. In 1902, he was in Oswald Külpe's lab. He found Külpe informal and kindly, but the laboratory was very primitive by American standards. There was not even an ordinary telegraph key.

Pillsbury ran into Freud's name when he started giving the abnormal psychology course at Michigan. Then when Pillsbury wrote his book on attention and was in Paris, he heard Pierre Janet's lectures, and he learned more about Freud's early work.[16] But Pillsbury thought of Freud primarily in connection with the field of abnormal psychology. William Alanson White came and lectured on insanity while Pillsbury was at Cornell. Pillsbury knew Albert Barrett at Michigan, whom he considered a good psychiatrist. But Barrett worked in a teaching situation, and after he died, the people in psychiatry at Michigan tended toward neurology.

I did get to ask Pillsbury about Watson and behaviorism. His impressions were various. He was scandalized when both Watson and his wife were smoking at the speakers' table at some meetings (he must have meant the head table at a banquet or similar gathering). Only a few years later, they were divorced. He found Watson to be aggressive. But there was no behaviorist controversy at Michigan: "I didn't accept it."

Pillsbury also visited the pioneers of Gestalt psychology. He saw Wertheimer the first year that the Gestalt group got started—this was 1913—and he understood their general attitude and approach. He also got a great deal from a visit to Wolfgang Köhler in 1925 or 1926. Pillsbury believed that a major factor in the failure of Gestaltists to have more influence in psychology was their "early mortality."

A quite different sort of interview that I had in 1957 was with the pioneer clinical psychologist, Florence Mateer (1887–1961). Mateer had attended West Chester State Normal School and taught school before going on to the University of Pennsylvania.[17] She subsequently went to Clark and received a master's degree and then, in 1916, a Ph.D. She took her master's degree from G. Stanley Hall, but, according to Mateer, he did not know enough about clinical psychology, and so she worked with William Burnham for her doctorate, which was on conditioning children.

Mateer recalled working at Vineland with Henry H. Goddard from 1910 to 1912. She was a Goddard student at her normal school, and she later accompanied him to the Bureau of Juvenile Research in Columbus, Ohio.[18] Goddard had visited Alfred Binet and brought the famous tests back and translated them—with difficulty, Mateer noted. She was the only person there who read French and German, and she took over the library.[19] She also worked supervising during the summer sessions that were held there for teachers. In addition, she was doing statistical work. While Goddard and Edward Johnstone were out giving lectures, Mateer was finding errors in their work, which disgusted her very much. Mateer said that Goddard could not really handle German. Moreover, he did not have a productive relationship (and perhaps less than that) with the psychologists at Clark. At Vineland, Mateer had time for research, and she translated the 1911 edition of the Binet Scale. She also rewrote the Kallikak study.

At Clark, Mateer found Hall very available to students. When she came to do her dissertation, Dr. Osborn of Women's and Children's Hospital provided her the children for study. This contact led to collaboration, and the two of them, Mateer and Osborn, started experimental work on calcium deficiency as a factor in mental deficiency.

After her Ph.D., Mateer went to a state institution, Waverley in Massachusetts, where she had to report to physicians. There the question was primarily whether or not the patient could be classified as insane. But it was apparently during her two years of service in a clinic at Harvard Medical School that Mateer learned about mental diseases. Mateer found Aaron J. Rosanoff (who worked with Grace Helen Kent) and Stanley Cobb (then in upstate New York) to be friendly to psychology. At that time, it was clear, clinicians had little idea of the later distinction between the mentally abnormal as opposed to the mentally deficient.

Mateer knew most of the pioneers of clinical psychology, as became evident as she talked about how she had learned about Freud. The earliest exposure that she recalled was seeing an article in German while she was at Vineland. Also she remembered hearing about Jung and his techniques from her French teacher, whom she characterized as a sickly Belgian at the University of Pennsylvania who one night in class wandered off onto the subject of Jung. And Mateer very definitely recalled seeing the articles in the 1910 *American Journal of Psychology* following Freud's visit to Clark.

Mateer's recollection was that the first thing she read was Freud's case history of a five-year-old boy.[20] Before joining Goddard, she had worked with a four-year-old boy—her brother. She did a careful observational study of his acquisition of vocabulary, but in the course of her research, she accumulated material on his mother fixation, his speech inversions, and so on. But she was unable to put it in context. There was no precedent for it. This was in the spring of 1906, and the study was published in 1908.[21] Later, when she came to know Freud's teachings, she regretted her lost opportunity.

Lightner Witmer was first rate, Mateer reported, at remedial reading. His assistant, Reuel Hull Sylvester, came down to Vineland when she was there to get a copy of the Goddard Form Board. Sylvester by accident turned it upside down, and so he created the Sylvester Board.[22] Those who were interested in testing the mental abilities of immigrants brought out some tests for that purpose that grew out of Mateer's Binet blocks (she dated this as about 1911). In her Vineland period, she recalled, two or three people from Vineland went down a line of immigrants being processed for admission and picked out a couple of likely defective people.

Let me conclude with two examples of interviews of another kind.

One was Robert Sessions Woodworth (1869–1962), known in his lifetime as the dean of American psychologists.[23] I talked to him in the summer of 1955 and exclusively about knowledge about Freud. I was deeply impressed by the clarity of his thinking. His memories were quality productions, because he had been so aware all of his career, and he remembered his awarenesses as well as the usual concrete impressions.

Woodworth was sure that he mentioned Freud in his course on abnormal psychology by 1905–6. He had undated notes in the file that show that he at least took up the dream interpretation material. He gave that class for many years. In his own memory, Woodworth believed that he had become acquainted with Freud's ideas very early. While he was with William James at Harvard in about 1897, Woodworth had written a paper on dreams, and he was much taken with Yves Delage's theory that dreams did not follow events of the preceding day because of satiation for the

events of the day. Dreams, therefore, were about that which was unfinished, unsatisfied. When Freud's book came out in 1900, Woodworth got
hold of it very soon. (But, again, he could find in his notes no datable
material.)

Stepping back, Woodworth commented that psychologists actually had
gotten to know about Freud rather quickly. Both the *Interpretation of
Dreams* and *The Psychopathology of Everyday Life* contained psychological
material. So, too, did Richard von Krafft-Ebing's book on psychopathic sexuality, Woodworth noted at that point. Woodworth credited Hall's interest
and the Clark lectures of 1909 also for psychologists' learning about Freud's
ideas. Then Woodworth referred me to Boring's historical work, in which
Boring contended that Hall was interested in any novelty.

Woodworth could not recall that any of his students, however, became
very interested in Freud. In 1911, in the Ladd and Woodworth book on
physiological psychology, one will, he pointed out to me, find a mention
of Freud on page 586—in a section Woodworth wrote.[24] Woodworth's *Dynamic Psychology* of 1918, however, came before the Freudians started using
that word "dynamic." But Woodworth did mean to write in that book
about the ways in which members of all schools of psychology discussed
cause-effect relationships. In later years, Woodworth had great reservations
about the scientific status of Freud's ideas. Woodworth considered them
hypotheses. And he thought they should be tested, but he believed that
the psychoanalysts were not cooperative.

Woodworth did personally know many of the analysts. He was invited
to a psychoanalytic meeting at least once. When he voiced his skepticism,
the analysts, he recalled, were up in arms; they wanted to psychoanalyze
Woodworth on the spot. Once, perhaps in 1920, Alfred Adler was in New
York at the behest of his stalwart followers. One ex-patient wanted to provide funds for Adler to propound his views at the medical school, but it
was not allowed. Therefore the psychology department arranged a course
of lectures. At least one student became a strong proponent of Adler.
Woodworth, as host for the occasions, found Adler a not disagreeable personality.

Woodworth then observed what the literature might have revealed, that
Edwin B. Holt and Watson were favorably impressed by Freud—especially

Watson. Watson later on made critical remarks about Freud, but early on he was impressed. Woodworth thought that Freud's freedom in treating sex was what interested Watson.

In 1912, when Woodworth was in Germany, Külpe asked him why American psychologists had fallen for Freud. Woodworth denied that they had. Külpe then wanted to know, if that were the case, why don't they speak up?

Woodworth provided me with two fundamental insights that have guided my writings on the impact of Freud. It was he, in more informal conversation that is not recorded in my notes, who directed my attention to the fact that psychologists as intellectuals got to know Freud but as professionals did not, for the most part, integrate psychoanalytic ideas into psychology for some time. The second insight he provided was the fact that interest, even improper interest, in the sexual content of Freud's writings led many psychologists to read Freud.

The last example I propose to bring to your attention is Frederic Lyman Wells (1884–1964).[25] I interviewed Wells on two occasions, once in 1955 and once in 1959. In both cases, I pursued the impact of Freud, but in 1959 I had a great deal more time and was able to ask much more systematic questions.

I had looked forward with particular anticipation to talking with Wells, because in print his contemporary observations, written before 1930, had been consistently shrewd and informative. I knew of no participant observer who had better insight and perspective on the profession of psychology in the early decades of the twentieth century. In my own writing, I drew for generalization on his eyewitness observation more than on that of any other contemporary. While in my interviews I found a lively, impressive senior citizen, his interest, in the 1950s—five years into retirement—did not seem to extend much beyond rather provincial, local interests of the Boston area community, of which, of course, he had an excellent command. I am left with the question as to why he did not grow with the profession after he was involved in the 1920s in the first attempts to organize clinical psychologists.

I was initially interested in Wells in 1955 because he was at that time one of four survivors from the famous 1909 group photo of Freud at Clark

University (Goddard, Jung, and Ernest Jones were the others). In 1955, Wells recalled for me that he had already become quite familiar with Freud's work before 1909. In the summer of 1907, when, after taking his Ph.D. at Columbia, he first went to McLean Hospital as a clinical psychologist, the psychiatrists there were very interested in psychoanalysis. G. V. Hamilton, who was on the staff, was the first to mention Freud to Wells. Wells was already interested in linguistic lapses and associations, and so Jung's work with association was particularly of interest to him. By 1911, Wells published a criticism of psychoanalytic ideas, which he believed were not based on rigorous enough methods such as he had learned working as a Ph.D. student under Cattell.[26] Even at the Clark conference, as Wells recalled, he had made himself unpopular by speaking his mind. The host, G. Stanley Hall, had no use for Wells after that. But Wells found both Freud and Jung to have delightful personalities, and he had a long talk with Jung (Wells was proficient in German; as a child, he had attended school in Germany). Freud, Wells recalled, had an upset stomach.

In Boston, the community in which Wells was at home, psychoanalysis came rather more slowly than in other centers, but when it came, he said, the Bostonians went for it hard. Wells believed that the emphasis on sex was what really put psychoanalysis across. Walter Dill Scott, Wells remembered, was bitterly opposed to psychoanalysis on account of the sexual emphasis.

Wells commented on the physicians who were interested in Freud's teachings, noting that they were in general very fine men, and he knew many of them from his experience in Boston and from a year he spent at Ward's Island in New York in 1911–12. I asked him especially about psychologists who early were conspicuous Freudians. One was L. E. Emerson of Boston and sometimes of Ann Arbor, whom Wells characterized as being in both psychoanalysis and psychology. Emerson was of course a psychologist, but he was definitely psychoanalytically oriented and did not have much status among his fellow psychologists. But Emerson, Wells emphasized, was a very learned psychologist, indeed, more of a scholar (more than what, my notes do not reveal). Emerson was sponsored by his intimate associate, Morton Prince, but his was a voice in the wilderness in Boston for years. Edwin B. Holt of Harvard (despite his book on the Freudian wish) was not a remarkable proponent of psychoanalysis while he was in Boston. Wells did not think that he was dynamic enough in his outlook.

It was in 1959 that I had a chance for a more leisurely interview. At that time, there was little biographical material on Wells, and so I obtained quite a bit. But that material has been rendered mostly obsolete by a very full obituary that appeared after he died.[27] Still, I was able to record a number of interesting details. For example, Wells started out in philology. He did have an undergraduate course in psychology at one point at Columbia when he was an immature eighteen, but it was a snap course by a popular professor who used William James's *Psychology: Briefer Course*. Wells become interested in the psychology of language and in questions that could be answered only by psychology. He therefore majored in psychology, with minors in anthropology and German philology. He was close to another student, a man who was central to the formation of modern anthropology, Edward Sapir. Franz Boas, the Columbia anthropologist, helped Wells decide about a career. Sapir panned professors who were not as clever as he, and most were not. Boas, however, apparently was. Wells recalled how he—together with Sapir—attacked the scholarship of the day independently, and the two needed no teachers. Wells started with the intention of teaching, but he never had a passion for teaching and was not good at it, although he did like to teach seminars. At one point, he was one of two assistants at Columbia to Cattell and Woodworth.[28] So when S. I. Franz left McLean, a position opened up for Wells (and, after that, with a few sideline exceptions, he did not follow the teaching route).

Much of my time with Wells was taken up with getting general impressions of people. He particularly was helpful in suggesting some of the personal dynamics in the Columbia department at the opening of the twentieth century. Woodworth, he noted, was both nice and friendly. Indeed, he was so amiable that one could not help liking him. Wells remembered particularly that he gave a good course on the psychology of movement. And Woodworth, Wells commented, was not a prude. Cattell, Woodworth, and Thorndike were the trio at Columbia. Cattell might inspire awe, Thorndike admiration, and Woodworth affection. Affection toward Cattell and Thorndike was not possible.

Wells noted that one had to get on with Cattell. Only one person was

thrown out of the department while he was there—a graduate student—
and Wells did not know why Cattell did not like his work. Wells did notice
that many students went from psychology into education, especially
when Thorndike might be pulling them in that direction. Other assistants
in those years, Wells observed, were educationists at the start or went
into it. There was complaint made at the time, he recalled, that psychology
did not hold people, that they went either into philosophy or into education.

Wells had sized most people up, and so I pursued his memories of his
impressions, because I believed at that time that personal detail might
make history more interesting, and I implicitly believed that there were
personal factors that helped explain human reactions even in a strictly
objective science. Wells, for example, was able to throw a little light on an
obscure New York psychologist who was deeply involved in psychoanalysis, Lydiard Horton. Wells characterized Horton as an amateur. Horton did
not care much for professional connections. He must have been independently wealthy, for he always had money to spend. "Talking with him was
like being smeared with Vaseline," Wells recalled, meaning he was over-
amiable. Horton was something of a recluse. He was a good looking man
and could have been successful socially. Beardsley Ruml, a social scientist
later very famous, was, when Wells met him in the World War I era, "a
matinee idol type." Or, to cite one other casual impression: David Shakow
knew he was smart but thought he was stuck where he was.

My attempt to gain insight from Wells on the 1920s attempt to organize
clinical psychologists on the whole failed. The founding of the American
Orthopsychiatric Association was subsequently written up,[29] but I did learn
from Wells that according to tradition, he had suggested the name of the
organization. He was at the organizational meeting, but he was too busy
at the time to be very much more active in it. He believed that the organ-
izers wanted an association in which psychiatrists, psychologists, and social workers operated on equal terms.

Wells was in charge of the committee to attempt to arrange certification
of clinical psychologists by the American Psychological Association. Papers
were issued, he recalled, to about twenty-five people on "a grandfather sort
of basis." But the whole effort did not work out well.[30]

Taken together, the foregoing impressions from my notes suggest a number of practical comments.

One, to which I have already alluded, is that inadequacies of the interviews often reflected my lack of preparation. I shall not try even to begin to talk about lost opportunities (not only Charlotte Bühler's new role in psychology but, for example, why did I not ask Mateer about her role in the functioning and breakup of Goddard's Ohio bureau in the 1920s?). Moreover, except in the case of the Freudians, I usually did not understand the theoretical problems sufficiently to ask questions of any depth. I was therefore reduced to looking for colorful, even gossipy information and memories, and for interpersonal relationships, implicitly emphasizing material that would reinforce a social constructionist point of view in the history of science and psychology.

Even that material does, of course, supplement printed materials. How else does one learn how not one, but a number of psychologists were put off by the smoking and drinking of a colleague who was supposed to have founded a school? How else does one learn about the ineptitude of a theoretician in the laboratory? How else does one find out about the linguistic and statistical strengths and shortcomings of leaders in the profession?

But having said that, one also has to ask how important such information is or will be. How important was it that I had further evidence of how Titchener valued his status and position? As far as it was relevant, the fact was already well known. Indeed, it is particularly significant that subsequent accounts based on written records rendered so much of my material redundant. That fact alone suggests to me that my work was not all that productive.

Yet in the end, I have to concede one thing that came out of the interviews. That was my personal understanding of the world of psychology as it existed in the first half of the twentieth century. I do not think that the history of early behaviorism is complete without understanding the extent to which Watson at various levels offended a number of his colleagues by his ostentatiously rebellious lifestyle, before such a lifestyle became more common in the 1920s. I do not think that I would have understood so early and so well that shamefully attractive sexual content really did get people to reading Freud had not both Woodworth and Wells, eminently sane men, called it to my attention. Certainly without Maier's obiter dicta about the implicit Yale conspiracy, I would have had a much shallower understanding of why American psychology evolved as it did in the 1940s, 1950s, and after. In short, I was able to imbibe a certain amount of wisdom from talking to some very astute and superior people.

But I wish to come back to the question that I raise in my title, the bottom line. The time and effort that I put into preparing for some of the interviews (Healy and Boring and one or two others), could have enabled me to publish articles, if not books. Indeed, people who have used my transcribed oral histories probably do not recognize the extent to which the product was the result of my scholarship. In other cases, my failure to prepare clearly wasted my time—but it seems doubtful that taking even more time would have produced proportionately more valuable material. I shall always treasure the experience of meeting and talking with many excellent people. But I am not sure but that what I did was not substantially recreational.

And so I return to my initial inquiry: what is the purpose of gathering the historical records of psychology? I do not think it is to do biography, which has a special focus and rationale. It is true that biography traditionally provides material for history, but history involves greater concerns than mere individual lives. Nor do we gather records for just the old-fashioned, often whiggish, history of ideas and techniques. We have publications that provide those materials.

I submit that we gather material—even material as dubious as that upon which I spent so much time—to leave as rich a record as possible within which future historians can search for what will be meaningful for their generations. This gathering of evidence is carried out as an act of faith, obviously a faith held by John Popplestone and Marion White McPherson. It is a faith shared by archivists, by historians, and by psychological investigators and practitioners smart enough to understand that their discipline has a past.

CHAPTER 3

Harry Hollingworth and the Shame of Applied Psychology

Ludy T. Benjamin Jr.

LIKE MANY OF THE INDIVIDUALS included in this volume, I owe much to the Archives of the History of American Psychology at the University of Akron and especially to the two people—John A. Popplestone and Marion White McPherson—whose foresight and hard work made this extraordinarily special collection what it is. For twenty-five years, since first introducing me to the archives, they have supported my work in history. They provided a scholarship that allowed me to make my initial visit to the Akron archives in 1975.[1] Although I worked in many collections in the three weeks I spent there that summer, I went in 1975 to work in the papers of Harry and Leta Hollingworth. Over the years I have published several articles on each of those pioneering psychologists.[2]

In looking over my curriculum vitae one will note other articles and book chapters that were largely based on information from the Akron collection, including several organizational histories: the Psychological Round Table (PRT), Midwestern Psychological Association, Eastern Psychological Association, American Psychological Association's (APA) Division on Industrial/Organizational Psychology (Division 14), and the industrial psychology that was part of the Association of Consulting Psychologists (ACP) and the American Association for Applied Psychology (AAAP) in the 1930s and 1940s.[3]

At Poppletone and McPherson's encouragement I wrote an article on the early psychology museum of David Pablo Boder, and with their help was able to contact many of the former colleagues and students of Winthrop Niles Kellogg for an article about his work in animal psychology, particularly the ape and child study. Other Akron-based articles I wrote were ones on the history of teaching machines drawing from the Sidney Pressey Papers and the Horace English Papers and another on B. F. Skinner's aircrib using the wonderful resources of the Cedric Larson Papers. One of the most recent products is an article that David Baker and I published on the history of the Boulder Conference, an article that drew heavily from the David Shakow Papers and several other collections there.[4]

I could list some other articles and book chapters that drew in part on the materials at Akron but I am sure that the message is obvious by now. I have benefitted substantially from the resources there, both from the collections and from the personnel.

In this chapter I want to return to the subject that took me to Akron for my first visit, that is, the work of Harry Levi Hollingworth. Specifically I am interested in understanding Hollingworth's lifelong career as an applied psychologist and the apparent paradox of his public denouncement of that career at the age of sixty.

Harry Hollingworth completed his doctorate with James McKeen Cattell, E. L. Thorndike, and Robert S. Woodworth at Columbia University in 1909 and stayed at Columbia's Barnard College for his entire career. In the thirty-year span between 1910 and 1940, he published twenty books and approximately one hundred research articles and reviews. Not included in that number are the technical reports provided by contract research with numerous companies. I have never been able to get a good sense of how many of those he may have written, but I am reasonably sure that it was more than forty.[5]

Hollingworth was well respected as an applied experimental psychologist. His work was recognized by his peers who elected him to membership in the prestigious Society of Experimental Psychologists and to the presidency of the American Psychological Association in 1927. He was acknowledged, even in his own time, as one of the pioneers in applied psychology, largely because of his caffeine studies and his early work on the psychology of advertising that resulted in three applied psychology books by 1917.[6] But he also wrote books on other applied topics including vocational psychology, educational psychology, clinical psychology, judging human character, and public speaking.[7] These applied books and his many contract researches made him famous. They also made him wealthy, wealthy enough that in 1944, after having had no raise in salary at Barnard for fifteen years, since before the stock market crash in 1929, he wrote a check to Columbia University for $51,000 to endow a scholarship in his late wife's name.[8]

In 1940, when Hollingworth was sixty years old and still five years away from his retirement at Barnard, he wrote his autobiography, a six-hundred-page work that was never published. The original manuscript is housed in the Akron archives.[9] The following quotation comes from that autobiography: "I might as well say once and for all to the undoubted amazement of my colleagues and professional associates, that I never had any genuine interest in applied psychology, in which field I have come to be known as one of the pioneers. It has become my sad fate to have established early in my career a reputation for interests that with me were only superficial."[10] That is a fascinating statement. To believe what he says one must conclude that Hollingworth spent his life working in a field that had no interest for him. Why would he do that? He offers us one possible answer in the last sentence of that quotation, that he felt trapped in applied psychology because of the early successes he had there, successes that somehow prevented him from doing other things.

Historians have written much about issues of objectivity in trying to reconstruct the past, what Peter Novick has called "that noble dream." On dimensions of objectivity, autobiographies and oral histories are especially suspect, not only because of what psychologists know about the fallibility of memory, but also because of what is known about the self-serving nature of such recall. Hollingworth also had this to say about his career as applied psychologist: "I became an applied psychologist in order to earn a living for myself and for my wife, and in order for her to undertake advanced graduate training. . . . Except for the revenue resulting therefrom, I found all these activities distasteful. There were plenty of interesting philosophical questions I wanted to investigate and researches I would have liked to undertake. It was disagreeable in the extreme to spend my time trotting down to these business clubs, talking the most elementary kind of psychological lore, and illustrating it with car-cards, trademarks, packages for codfish, and full color spreads. But I did it with such enthusiasm as I could muster."[11]

I want to challenge Hollingworth's claim of disinterest in applied psychology. I believe that the evidence is fairly compelling that he had ample opportunities to leave that field and pursue those subjects that he argued were of greater interest to him. To do this I first need to describe some of Hollingworth's work as an applied psychologist. I also will discuss some of his nonapplied work, contrasting the two in terms of their reception by his psychologist colleagues. Finally I want to address his disclaimer, suggesting reasons for what seems to me a clear case of denial. I want to begin with a description of Hollingworth's youth because I believe that it provides some context for understanding his interest in applied work.

Signs in Hollingworth's formative years, particularly his thirst for books, suggest that he might pursue an intellectual life. Yet family circumstances made such pursuits impractical. He was born in 1880 in DeWitt, Nebraska, a community of about five hundred people at the time. The town lies about forty miles south of Lincoln and is today about the same size as it was in Hollingworth's youth. His mother died when he was a little more than a year old, and his father remarried soon thereafter. The new marriage created a feud between Hollingworth's father and the parents of his former wife. When Hollingworth was still an infant he was kidnapped by his mother's parents, and his father had to go to court to secure the return of his son. It was only as an adult that Hollingworth learned the meaning of the capital letter "H" that appeared as a welt in the palm of his right hand. It had been burned there in his infancy in the aftermath of the kidnapping, no doubt as a means of identification. The brand persisted throughout his lifetime, reminding him, Hollingworth wrote, "of a troubled infancy."[12]

As a young man, Hollingworth's father had dreamed of a career in medicine, but he had a severe stuttering problem that ended that ambition. Instead, he chose carpentry as his profession and became what his son called the "village carpenter," building many of the houses, barns, and churches in the DeWitt area. Hollingworth began working with his father at the age of eleven and by the age of sixteen considered himself rather accomplished at the trade. At sixteen he graduated as valedictorian in his class, having completed the ten school grades offered in Dewitt. Evidently he had no plans for college. He worked for two more years with his father in carpentry. He did not enjoy the work but he was uncertain about what else he could do. His later success as a writer might have been predicted from several episodes in his youth, including his work in building houses. In his autobiography he wrote: "A favorite pastime while shingling a roof was to write short spontaneous verses on the under side of shingles before nailing them down, thus recording for posterity events of the day, incidents of the job, and bits of juvenile philosophy."[13] No doubt those shingles are long gone now, perhaps burned in stove boxes or fireplaces for the quick burst of warmth they would have provided in Nebraska winters. Of course, had they survived they might have ended up as part of the Hollingworth Papers at Akron, filling the Hollinger boxes of many shelves, each box containing three or four wooden shingles marked with the scribblings of a young psychologist-to-be.

Hollingworth clearly had intellectual interests as a child. He read and reread the few books in his home and the all too few books that were available in his school. His real education came, he wrote, from his discovery of the classic books listed in the catalog of Montgomery Ward and Company, ranging in price from seventeen to sixty cents. Eventually he ordered more than seventy of them, all of which were still on his bookshelves at the age of sixty when he wrote his autobiography. The works of Herbert Spencer, Thomas Carlyle, and Ralph Waldo Emerson were particularly impressive to the young Hollingworth. They awakened in him a longing for intellectual pursuits.[14]

At age eighteen Hollingworth applied for a teaching certificate for which he was eligible because of his ten years of formal schooling. He taught school for two years before he decided to pursue college. To get ready for college he entered the Nebraska Wesleyan University Academy for preparatory study of two years. Finally, at the age of twenty-three, he entered the University of Nebraska as a first-year student.

It was at Nebraska that Hollingworth began formal study in the new psychology, principally through the classes of Thaddeus Lincoln Bolton, a graduate of Clark University and a student of G. Stanley Hall.[15] It was also at Nebraska that Hollingworth met Leta Anna Stetter, who would become his wife and a psychologist of considerable accomplishments.[16]

As a young man, Hollingworth had been warned against the life of a scholar. He had had problems with his eyes and had worn glasses since the age of eleven. As he prepared to enter college he had consulted with an eye specialist in Lincoln who advised him "to get a red blanket, go to Oklahoma, get a job as a cowboy and drop all contact with books." He was warned that if he did not abandon reading, he "might lose such eyesight as [he] then had".[17]

Hollingworth ignored the advice and continued his contact with books, pursuing doctoral study in psychology at Columbia University, beginning in 1907. In his second year, while searching for a research problem for his dissertation, he decided to extend some psychophysical studies he had undertaken for an honors thesis with Bolton at Nebraska. Hollingworth's research sought to examine the differences in passive versus active movements, specifically whether one or the other produced more accurate discriminations in several perceptual and motor tasks. He speculated that establishing the superiority of active movements might have practical value. He wrote: "It seemed to me that this, if true, might have certain pedagogical implications. There was a slogan to the effect that 'Only activity educates,' but I could find no experimental demonstration of this faith." Hollingworth's studies on active and passive movements produced no measurable differences, but in the course of those studies he observed systematic errors in perceptual judgments. He developed those observations into a dissertation that was published in November 1909, shortly after his graduation.[18]

A year earlier Hollingworth had married his college sweetheart, Leta, who had been teaching public school in Nebraska while her husband-to-be worked toward his doctorate. The couple settled into a small apartment in Manhattan and tried to exist on the annual salary of one thousand dollars that Harry was making at his new job as instructor at Barnard College, Columbia University's women's college. Leta had hoped to teach school as she had done in Nebraska, but local laws prevented her from holding such a job because as a married woman, as it was reasoned at the time, she already had a full-time job as wife and was expected to expand that job as a mother.[19] Harry sought out extra employment to supplement their income, and they talked of the possibility of Leta pursuing graduate work. But each time they seemed to have a nest egg for that study a family emergency back in Nebraska would exhaust that money.

In his first year at Barnard, Hollingworth got the opportunity to offer an evening course in the extension division of Columbia University, essentially a curriculum intended for the working public, especially individuals in business. Not surprisingly, many of the courses were practical in nature. Hollingworth's initial course was titled "Applied Psychology." Like the other extension instructors, he was paid on a fee basis, that is, a fee from each of these students enrolled in the course but no additional salary from Columbia. Thus Hollingworth had plenty of incentive to make his classes popular. In this initial class he had five students from whom he received the total sum of seventy-five dollars.[20] A year later he also offered a similar course in the evening program of New York University.

His applied courses focused on the psychology of advertising. It is not evident why he chose that topic for emphasis. Perhaps it was dictated by the makeup of students in his evening courses, or perhaps because of their expressed interests. Or maybe it came from Hollingworth's familiarity with Walter Dill Scott's two books on the psychology of advertising. Through his contacts in these classes he was invited to offer, for a fee, a special set of ten lectures to the Advertising Men's League of New York City, which he did in the spring of 1910. Those lectures were eventually serialized in *Judicious Advertising*, a magazine for advertisers, and then published in 1913 in his first book on applied psychology, *Advertising and Selling*.[21]

Another event, however, in the beginning of Hollingworth's career had profound implications for his career as an applied psychologist as well as for his wife, the research he conducted in 1911 at the request of the Coca-Cola Company. In 1911 Coca-Cola was being brought to trial by the Federal Government under the recently passed Pure Food and Drugs Act of 1906 for marketing a beverage with a harmful ingredient, namely caffeine, an ingredient that the government claimed produced motor problems and impaired mental efficiency. As the Coca-Cola scientists and attorneys prepared for the trial in Chattanooga they realized that they had no behavioral or cognitive data on the effects of caffeine on humans. So they sought to contract for such research as quickly as possible given the closeness of the trial dates. The archival record is incomplete with regard to whom they may have contacted. We know that James McKeen Cattell was approached and he declined. Eventually the offer went to a financially needy Harry Hollingworth.[22]

In his autobiography he devoted more space to the caffeine studies than any of his other books or research projects. I think there is good reason for such attention, as I will indicate later. How enthusiastic was he to accept this contract? He was aware that other psychologists had turned down this opportunity. He certainly was aware of the tainted nature of this kind of work. Indeed, he reported that colleagues had made clear the lamentable nature of such work: "Applications outside the school were tacitly assumed to be unclean. Inquiries and appeals for help from businessmen, employees, manufacturers, lawyers, advertising men, were often either evaded by the seniors or at best referred to younger and more venturesome spirits in the laboratory, who had as yet no sanctity to preserve."[23]

Particularly problematic with the caffeine studies was concern about scientific integrity raised by a company spending large sums of money for research that it hoped would benefit its legal and commercial needs. Although Hollingworth may have had some concerns about his arrangements with the Coca-Cola Company,[24] I believe that he was eager to accept the task. He wrote that his willingness to undertake the work was both because of the scientific value of the studies as well as the financial rewards. I will address each of these in turn. Hollingworth wrote:

Here was a clear case where results of scientific importance might accrue to an investigation that would have to be financed by private interests. No experiments on such a scale as seemed necessary for conclusive results had ever been staged in the history of experimental psychology. . . . With me there was a double motive at work. I needed money and here was a chance to accept employment at work for which I had been trained, with not only the cost of the investigation met but with a very satisfactory retaining fee and stipend for my time and services. I believed I could conscientiously conduct such an investigation, without prejudice to the results, and secure information of a valuable scientific character as well as answer the practical questions raised by the sponsor of the study.[25]

Thus Hollingworth argued that the problem was one of scientific interest that offered the prospect of valuable scientific information, namely the effects of caffeine on mental and motor efficiency in humans. I do not doubt that assessment, but I am reasonably sure that Hollingworth would not have taken on the research at that time in his career had he not so desperately needed the money.

Hollingworth's autobiography is filled with tales of poverty in his family and especially that of his wife's family. They faced serious financial crises in the early years of their marriage, particularly surrounding the death of Leta's sister in Chicago and the expenses they incurred in transporting her body back to western Nebraska for burial. To survive financially during that time they borrowed money from several friends in New York, something that was very difficult for them to accept having to do.

As noted earlier, marriage barred Leta Hollingworth from some jobs, at least the ones in which she was most interested. She had a genuine desire to pursue her own doctoral work and the academic talents to succeed at that, partly evidenced by her graduation as valedictorian from the University of Nebraska. So one can imagine the frustrations they felt. They even considered the possibility of moving back to Nebraska where both of them could teach school. They reasoned that their financial situation could not be worse in Nebraska and that at least they would be closer to family. The offer from the Coca-Cola Company ended those family discussions.

The Coca-Cola funds were an economic windfall for the Hollingworths. I have never been able to determine the amount of the contract. In a 1912 letter from Leta to her cousin she wrote that the Coca-Cola Company had paid them "quite a neat little wad of money."[26] Harry noted that the funds paid completely for Leta's three years of graduate study at Columbia where she received her doctorate in 1916, plus paid for their spending most of the summer of 1912 on vacation in Europe. Harry was paid as director of the research project, which lasted for forty days using a six-room Manhattan apartment rented specifically for these studies. Of course, Harry was busy all day with his job at Barnard. So who ran the daytime research studies? Well, Leta did, of course, and she was paid to run those subjects. Thus much of that "wad" of Coca-Cola money stayed in the Hollingworth family.

The success of the caffeine studies, no doubt coupled with the success of the Coca-Cola Company in winning its case in Chattanooga, gave Hol-

lingworth considerable publicity within the business community. It resulted in a deluge of consulting opportunities from various businesses so
that by 1913 he was earning more from his consulting jobs than he made
from his Barnard College salary. Following is his account of some of the
kinds of applied questions that he was invited to answer.

> A federal department wants advice on how to interview farmers . . . a perfume
> manufacturer wants psycho-galvanic studies of the effect of his products; a silk man-
> ufacturer wants studies of the appeal of his fabrics; an evening newspaper wants to
> support its advertising columns by evidence that suggestibility is greater in the late
> hours of the day; a famous railroad wants advice and perhaps experiments to guide
> it in deciding what color to paint its box cars; a city planning commission requires
> data on the legibility of traffic signs; a manual trainer wants to know the psycho-
> logical height for work benches . . . an advertiser wants to know where on the page
> his return coupon should appear; several people want to know the differences in
> buying habits men and women exhibit; more than one question concerns . . .
> whether appeal to the eye is or is not better than appeal to the ear; a rubber com-
> pany wants tests made for the better selection of clerks and other employees; and
> a type foundry wants studies of the legibility of different type-faces.[27]

It is not clear how Hollingworth chose among the many offers he had.
Perhaps his decisions were based on how well these consultations paid. He
does not say that, but he does say that when requests for speaking en-
gagements became too great to accept them all that he accepted those that
paid a modest honorarium.[28] It is also not clear how long he pursued this
line of contractual research. Unlike the caffeine studies for Coca-Cola, most
of this work for such companies as Grinnell Sprinklers, Savage Firearms,
Gorton Codfish Company, and the United Drug Company was not published. The Hollingworth Papers contain unpublished technical reports, yet
information in the autobiography makes it clear that those records are
incomplete. My best surmise is that he accepted only a few of these contractual studies after 1925. By then the financial picture for the two Hollingworths was quite good considering two academic salaries, book royalties for both, and consulting income for both. However, the applied
research continued until at least the late 1930s.

To discuss all of Harry Hollingworth's applied research and writing
would be well beyond the space limits of this chapter. Instead, I will focus
on a few of the more important works that were principally applied in

nature. By 1920, in addition to the two books on advertising, Hollingworth had published a book titled *Applied Psychology* (1917) that dealt with the application of psychology to such fields as education, law, social work, medicine, and business. Another book, *Vocational Psychology* (1916), covered the existing literature on theory and methods of vocational assessment and counseling. His experiences as a psychologist at the army hospital in Plattsburg, New York, where he worked principally with what were then called shell shock victims resulted in his 1920 book, *The Psychology of Functional Neuroses*. These books not only demonstrate his interest in applied subjects but also his recognition of the diverse applicability of psychology.

Following the early work in advertising, Hollingworth moved into studies of selection, especially the selection of salespeople, creating the "Hollingworth Tests for Selection of Salesmen" in 1916.[29] This work coincided with his efforts to debunk the physiognomic systems that were then popular, and resulted in another book, *Judging Human Character*, published in 1923. Hollingworth was especially critical of the characterological system of Katherine Blackford that was used by so many American businesses.[30] In his own book on judging character, he promoted a mental testing approach to selection, drawing on the work pioneered by his mentor, Cattell. His book on vocational psychology also promoted assessment using mental tests.

After the First World War and Hollingworth's completion of his book based on work with shell shock victims, he received an intriguing invitation from the alcohol brewing industry. The year was 1919. The Volstead Act had just been passed, and the eighteenth amendment to the Constitution of the United States was just about to be ratified, prohibiting "the manufacture, sale, or transportation of intoxicating liquors."[31] Note that the amendment did not ban alcoholic beverages, but rather it prohibited "intoxicating liquors." Thus the issue became a matter of defining intoxication. The brewing industry was pursuing research of its own, specifically to produce a "near beer" that would have the taste and maybe some of the effect of a beer but would not produce intoxication. And to determine what constituted intoxication, specifically any significant impairment in motor or cognitive abilities, they needed a psychologist.

The invitation for that work went to Hollingworth, probably because of his success in the caffeine studies. And because of those studies, Hollingworth seemed eager to pursue the alcohol work, partly because he could use the caffeine research model for his new studies. The studies were begun in the Hollingworths' apartment but were moved when neighbors complained of the excessive frivolity. Apparently that had not been a problem in the caffeine studies. So the research was continued in the psychology building—Schermerhorn Hall—at Columbia University. The frivolity continued there as Hollingworth reported that one of the subjects delighted in sticking gummed labels on the top of Professor Robert Woodworth's bald head. It is not noted if Professor Woodworth found this amusing.[32]

The data from these alcohol studies were published in several articles.[33] Hollingworth was able to show systematic motor and cognitive impairment at specific dosages, taking into account assessments of body size and individual experience with alcohol. But the data were not helpful to the brewing industry in providing an absolute threshold for intoxication that might have permitted the manufacture of beverages with low alcohol content.

One could argue that these ventures were still principally based on the desire for money rather than any intellectual agenda spawned by Hollingworth's interests in psychology. But some of his works resulted from different motives, such as his research on the psychology of public speaking.

In 1915 Hollingworth was invited to address the Poor Richard Club, a Philadelphia men's advertising group, at its annual dinner. The banquet was held in the largest ballroom in the Bellevue-Stratford Hotel where some five hundred people were in attendance. At either end of the enormous room was a stage where comedians and other vaudeville acts performed throughout the meal. As soon as the dinner entertainment ended, the master of ceremonies introduced the first of the three invited speakers, Professor Harry Hollingworth. Here is Hollingworth's account of that speech: "... no one paid any attention to my presence. No one even seemed to know that I was talking. Everyone continued to joke with his neighbor, the waiters continued to rattle the dishes, and all eyes were on the vaudeville stages, where it was apparently hoped another clown or strip-tease would appear. . . . I struggled on with sentence after sentence, making just no apparent impression on the din. Finally in despair I sat down abruptly, in the very middle of my speech. . . . No one even knew I had stopped."[34]

Hollingworth's experience was bad enough, but the contrast with what followed made it even worse. The second speaker was a woman who was treated with a little more respect, but still the audience was rather inattentive. And then the third speaker was introduced. As he strode to the lectern, the audience cheered wildly. He was a large man, standing nearly six feet tall, clearly commanding in his presence. Like Hollingworth, he too was from Nebraska. He had been the Democratic Party's nominee for the presidency of the United States three times, the first time in 1896 when he was only thirty-six years old. At that July 1896 convention in Chicago he had won the nomination on the fifth ballot after delivering what is acknowledged by historians as one of the greatest speeches in the history of oratory. It closed with the famous words, "You shall not press down upon the brow of labor this crown of thorns, you shall not crucify mankind upon a cross of gold." The speaker was, of course, William Jennings Bryan, who was then serving as President Woodrow Wilson's Secretary of State. Hollingworth described Bryan's reception as follows: "Every one of his references to Old Glory brought down the house, and I was a little ashamed, in the light of my own dismal failure, of having announced to him earlier in the evening that I also was born in Nebraska."[35]

The experience had considerable impact on Hollingworth, who began to collect information on the psychology of public speaking and the nature of the audience. He conducted some studies on the topic in the 1920s and eventually published an entire book on the subject titled *The Psychology of the Audience* (1935), twenty years after his humiliating platform experience.[36]

Hollingworth published two other applied books in the 1930s, one on abnormal psychology (1930) that, interestingly, recalling his father's problem, contained a chapter on stuttering and stammering, and a second book on educational psychology (1933). Although he referred to his research in these books—for example, a chapter on drugs in the abnormal psychology book that drew heavily on his caffeine and alcohol studies—there was no research program specifically intended for them. They were written to serve as textbooks.

I have one final applied study to describe. It was about human motor automatisms. Such automatisms include head nodding, finger tapping, foot swinging, scratching, shoulder shrugging, and thumb twiddling. But, according to Hollingworth, no automatism is more common in humans than chewing. He observed that: "This activity has the special character of being an essential feature of a fundamental vital activity pattern—eating. But it is much indulged in . . . divorced from this fundamental pattern. Chewing is such a satisfying activity, in itself, that random masticatories such as straws, toothpicks, rubber bands, are utilized in order to support it. Most popular of all are the various chicle preparations. . . ."[37] Although the scientific jargon may obscure the meaning here, this was research about the effects of chewing gum.

This research was undertaken in 1934 and 1935 at the request of Bartlett Arkell, president of Beech-Nut Foods. Arkell was a friend of Hollingworth and had contracted with him for research on several earlier occasions. Apparently gum chewing was growing in popularity in the 1930s, and Arkell wanted to know what the benefits might be. The results of the studies were published in a ninety-page monograph that included investigations of the energy cost of chewing as reflected in pulse rate, the metabolic costs of chewing, the relationship of chewing to muscular tension, the effects of chewing or not chewing on various motor and cognitive tasks, and the influence of chewing on work output.

Hollingworth found that chewing gum does provide relief from tension and that the tension reduced is muscular. Not only is there motor evidence of tension reduction but subjective reports acknowledge the same, that is, subjects reported being more relaxed while chewing. The tension reduction was found to have little cost as measured either in pulse rate or caloric requirements. Tests of typing showed evidence that both speed and accuracy increased slightly, but other job tasks showed little evidence of benefit.

Arkell was evidently very pleased with the research results and modified his advertising for Beech-Nut Gum, proclaiming that chewing gum relieves tension. How did Hollingworth describe this tension reduction? The explanation was couched in terms of redintegration, a process by which a complex experience is generated by associations triggered by a single cue that is part of the larger experience. He wrote: "Our interpretation of the mechanism . . . is a very simple one. . . . The primary role of chewing is in the mastication of food. Eating is ordinarily a more or less 'quiet' occupation. When we eat, we sit, or otherwise repose. Random restlessness is at a low point. We rest; we relax; and the general feeling tone is one of agreeableness and satisfaction. An important item of the eating situation is the act of chewing. We suggest that, as a result of this contextual status, chewing brings with it, whenever it is sustained, a posture of relaxation. Chewing, in other words, serves as a reduced cue, and to some extent redintegrates the relaxation of mealtime."[38]

Like the alcohol studies fifteen years earlier, the chewing gum research received a lot of newspaper coverage.[39] Evidently it was Hollingworth's last contract research study for business and industry.

This chapter began with Harry Hollingworth's claim that he had no genuine interest in applied psychology. He followed that assertion with the following sentences: "My activity in the field of applied psychology was mere pot boiling activity, and now that it is over there is no reason why the truth should not be revealed. My real interest is now and always has been in the purely theoretical and descriptive problems of my science, and the books, among the twenty I have written, of which I am proudest, are the more recent ones which no one reads."[40]

The reference to the recent books is not clear. He wrote those words in 1940 when his most recent books would have been the monograph on gum chewing in 1939, the book on the psychology of the audience in 1935, and his book on educational psychology in 1933. Based on other passages in the autobiography it is certain the book he felt was his greatest contribution was his 1928 book, *Psychology: Its Facts and Principles*, a general psychology textbook. The book was derived from years of teaching the general psychology course and represented his attempts to systematize the field. Indeed, he referred to this book as his "system." Hollingworth noted that he always considered this book his masterpiece. He wrote: "This volume did me personally a lot of good. It straightened out my thinking in psychology, heretofore muddled and messy, and mapped out a path for all of my subsequent work to take. But it was never widely adopted as a text.

. . . One of my colleagues described the book as having been written for myself alone."[41]

The book was unusual in several ways; for example, it did not include any physiological material. Hollingworth wrote: "Since this is a textbook of psychology, it resolutely stands by its title. It has no chapters on neuro-anatomy, the physiology of the nervous or other systems of the animal body, or the structure of the sense organs. It finds plenty of honest psychological material at hand. . . . It is the writer's belief that the preoccupation of psychologists with hypothetical features of neurones, brain centers, synapses, and nerve tracts has impeded rather than advanced the science."[42]

In another way the textbook was unique, which quality likely ensured its commercial failure. It described most psychological processes in terms of the concept of redintegration. His utter satisfaction, indeed his joy, with his system is indicated in several places in the autobiography. He described it as bringing him an intellectual peace, allowing him to reach equilibrium in his thinking. Consider the following passage: "I had already formulated my 'system' and arrived at a satisfactory *Weltanschauung*. . . . My frantic intellectual fumblings had all represented the endeavor to alleviate the distress of doubt and uncertainty. To be in an intellectual muddle was always for me the strongest of irritants, that is, the most powerful of motives. I had now achieved, if you like, a formula which was in my experience so uniformly applicable and relevant that intellectual distress was almost wholly abolished."[43]

As one might imagine, the system was so idiosyncratic that few psychologists found it useful as a textbook or as a system of psychology. And the reviews of the book were certainly not what Hollingworth would have hoped for. He also claimed that the book was rarely cited. I have not done a citation analysis of the late 1920s and 1930s so I cannot verify that. What I can say safely is that his masterpiece, his system of psychology, failed to inspire colleagues in the way that it affected Hollingworth.

What is also clear from more than sixty published reviews of Hollingworth's books is that the applied books reviewed quite well compared to his books that were more theoretical in nature. Surely that was a source of considerable disappointment for him. Clearly this book was critically important to Hollingworth. With it he had achieved an understanding of psychology that had evaded him for the first twenty years of his career. The book afforded him a vision of psychology that bordered on certainty. Yet he seemed to be the only one who saw it that way. How would that affect his evaluation of his work?

He could draw the conclusion that his theoretical work was of little value and that the real contributions he had made in psychology were represented by his many applied works. That view might have been endorsed by many who knew his work. Or he could conclude that he had been so typecast as an applied psychologist in the early years of his career that it was impossible for his nonapplied work to be taken seriously. Or he could conclude that his system was misunderstood because he had failed to present his theoretical ideas appropriately. That is precisely the claim he made, that he resurrected a historical term, "redintegration," which carried historical baggage with it and led to misunderstanding; that he gave too much emphasis to the cue-reduction process in his theory, which was his use of a redintegrative idea; and that he should have devised a clever name for his system as some kind of "ism," rather than portraying the system as psychology.[44]

To maintain faith in his theoretical work, Hollingworth might have been inclined to devalue his commitment to the applied work. But what of his work did he consider applied? Consider the following passage in which he discussed the caffeine and alcohol studies: "Although both of these investigations were sponsored by industrial interests, I have never considered them to lie in the field of applied psychology. They were from the beginning straightforward efforts to discover the nature of certain facts and relationships, and the chief interest of the findings has never been in any industrial or commercial application of them."[45] Clearly he was interested in those studies. Further, he recognized them to be excellent experimental work. Yet this passage indicates his penchant for splitting hairs in arguing that they did not represent applied research. Those studies were done for specific applied purposes, and he took the money to work toward those purposes. He enjoyed the chewing gum research as well, and also his applied work in trying to solve the dilemma of what went wrong in his speech at the Poor Richard Club banquet.

Hollingworth came from a practical background, where he worked with his hands for more than a decade. As an undergraduate student he described the pedagogical applications of his honor's thesis. At Columbia he was educated in a doctoral program that spawned some of the applied psychology that would be characteristic of American functionalism, especially the use of mental tests for a multitude of practical purposes. He enjoyed the problem-solving nature of research, something that is evident in several autobiographical descriptions of his work, especially in his accounts of the work for Coca-Cola, the studies that proved to be a watershed event in his career.

Yet Hollingworth was educated at a time when pure versus applied distinctions in science were made evident to students, encouraging them to walk the path of academic truth doing "pure" research and to avoid the temptations of real-world riches from applied work, a distinction still evident in psychology and other disciplines. Academics in Hollingworth's time might have accepted applied work in educational and clinical settings, but when the work was funded by businesses with a clear agenda for the outcome of the research, then the work was open to serious questions about its scientific merit. Hollingworth's writings, both published and unpublished, indicate that he was well aware of what academic sanctity was about.

Perhaps Hollingworth felt himself to be a failure as a scientist because certain key markers of accomplishment had alluded him. For example, he was never elected to the prestigious National Academy of Sciences, whereas many of his contemporaries were, including eight of the twelve APA presidents surrounding his election year. Further, he never held a faculty position in a graduate research department. Although he was a member of the Columbia University faculty for his entire career, his assignment was to an undergraduate department at Barnard College, meaning that he could not leave a legacy of doctoral students he had trained.

In evaluating Hollingworth's autobiography it is important to remember that those words were written in the months after the sudden and tragic death of his wife at the age of fifty-three. By all evidence, Leta Hollingworth was the most important thing in his life. So perhaps his disclaimer about his interest in applied psychology could be attributed to his grief.

In conclusion, it could be argued that at the age of sixty, Hollingworth doth protest too much. If he became an applied psychologist to make a living and to aid his wife in going to graduate school, then he could have abandoned that work by 1925. Although it does seem that he stopped the small contract studies by then, he continued to publish books on applied topics and continued to work on other large-scale, commercially-funded projects until near his retirement. Why would he have continued that work for all those years if indeed it was of no genuine interest? If the theoretical and philosophical problems of his discipline interested him more, then why did he not work on those? Perhaps he followed the rewards, and not just the financial ones. That is, he continued to do the work that earned him good reviews and brought him attention, which was his applied work.

In summary, Harry Hollingworth was an excellent applied psychologist. He was an experimentalist who brought his science to bear on real-world problems in rigorous and imaginative ways. He was arguably one of the best of his day at what he did. Yet his comments at age sixty—and there is no evidence that he retracted those statements in the remaining sixteen years of his life—express dismay and maybe even shame about his applied work and perhaps about his career. It is disappointing that at the end of his career he could not be comfortable with his place in psychology's history as one of the individuals whose work expanded the domains of psychological science and practice beyond the boundaries of the academy.

CHAPTER 4

An Insider's Look at Experimental Psychology in America:

The Diaries of Walter Miles

C. James Goodwin

ONE OF THE ENDURING TRUTHS about doing research in an archival setting is that while searching diligently for X, one often stumbles upon Y, the end result being a paper like this one. Several years ago I was looking into the early history of maze learning and came across a 1930 article by the experimental psychologist Walter Miles, who was at that time head of the laboratory at Stanford.[1] The Miles paper concerned the history of animal research with mazes and included excerpts from letters he had received from some of the pioneers of maze learning research—Willard Small, for instance. I knew from conversations with John Popplestone and Marion McPherson that the Akron archives held the Miles papers, and I was excited to learn that the collection was a very large one; Miles seemed to be the type of person who didn't throw things away. Indeed, the collection includes material in 128 boxes and is described in a comprehensive (and daunting) 756-page inventory.

So I visited Akron, certain that I soon would be holding a letter written by Linus Kline or Willard Small and gaining some deep insight into the moments when the idea of maze learning first occurred to psychologists. Alas, it was not to be; apparently Miles did throw some things away after all. What I did find, however, and this was the Y found when searching for X, was a remarkable set of diaries that Miles kept over the years. Their contents, which occupy seven of the 128 boxes in the collection, eventually produced the chapter you are about to read.

The Miles diaries provide an absorbing insider's look at the state of experimental psychology, especially during the period beginning just before World War I and ending with World War II, and they yield some insights into the mind of an experimentalist of that era and into the various professional activities that occupied the time of a prominent researcher. My goals in this chapter will be to describe some of the contents of the Miles diaries as they relate to the state of experimental psychology during this period and to discuss some of the challenges that diary information poses for the historian. Before examining the diaries, however, let me introduce you to Walter Miles, who was born in 1885 and died ninety-three years later.

In an obituary for Miles, his close colleague Ernest Hilgard wrote that Miles "had a tremendous interest and curiosity about a great many topics." This is perhaps how a friend would describe the fact that Miles never became a leading figure in any particular area of research in psychology. He did not develop a systematic program of research, but drifted from one area to another, with the direction of the drift determined often by the presence of a particular type of apparatus or an apparatus-related problem that intrigued him. His penchant for apparatus is reflected in a portrait made for him in the early 1950s; it shows him in the lab, surrounded by equipment. That his colleagues perceived him first and foremost as a scientist is evident from a letter written during the drive to raise money for the portrait. Writing to Neal Miller, a Miles student and organizer of the fund, Harry Helson wrote that Miles was "one of the few psychologists who started out as an experimentalist and continued his interest in scientific problems all during his career, stopping neither to become a philosopher or a stamp collector or a huckster of psychological wares."[2]

Although he did not achieve the status of such peers as Karl Lashley, Clark Hull, Edward Tolman, or Robert Yerkes, Miles was a prominent enough figure in his day. His bibliography has impressive length (if not depth), he held several prestigious academic appointments, and he earned numerous honors. For instance, Miles was awarded the Warren Medal by the Society of Experimental Psychologists, he was elected to the National Academy of Sciences, and he served as president of the American Psychological Association in 1932. During the 1920s and 1930s, Miles would be on anyone's list of well-known and productive experimental psychologists.

Miles grew up in the Dakota Territory and the Pacific Northwest and graduated from Pacifica College in Oregon in 1906. Like so many others of his generation who became psychologists, the light first went on for Miles after he took a psychology course and read William James, *Psychology: The Briefer Course,* in this case. His family's Quaker background then brought him to Earlham College in Indiana for two additional years and a second bachelor's degree. His first job was teaching at Penn College in Iowa where, after just a year, he was recruited by Carl Seashore for Iowa's doctoral program in psychology. Already intrigued by laboratory psychology after a yearlong course at Earlham in which he worked his way through E. B. Titchener's famous manuals, Miles became fascinated by the apparatus he found in Seashore's lab and by the "build-your-own-apparatus" culture that Seashore fostered.[3] Miles quickly became, in the language of the time, a "lab man," and a fascination with laboratory apparatus and an aptitude for building apparatus became a lifelong trait.

After completing his doctorate in 1913, on the accuracy of human singing voices to hit specific pitch frequencies, Miles was offered a position as a one-year replacement for Raymond Dodge at Wesleyan University in Connecticut. The circumstances of the appointment appear to be a perfect illustration of the "old boys" network that surrounded Titchener and his fellow experimental psychologists. This much is known: (1) the young graduate student Miles was Titchener's guide and host when the latter visited Iowa in 1911, and the young man evidently made a good impression; (2) while on his way to a conference in Philadelphia in early 1913, Miles visited Titchener in his home at Cornell; (3) Titchener and Dodge were close friends; (4) the April 1913 meeting of Titchener's Experimentalists group was held at Wesleyan, with Dodge as the host. It isn't hard to imagine Dodge mentioning that he needed someone for a year and Titchener saying that he knew a bright young up-and-coming experimentalist from Iowa. I haven't been able to find correspondence between Titchener and Dodge that might confirm all this, but it is well known that job placement was a frequent consequence of the close camaraderie among the men in Titchener's circle.[4]

Mechanical aptitude was practically a job requirement for experimental psychologists in those days, and Miles easily fit the bill. I've mentioned how well he fit into Seashore's lab at Iowa, and at Wesleyan, he found himself in the laboratory of one of psychology's great apparatus inventors. He quickly familiarized himself with Dodge's tachistoscopes, devices for measuring eye movements, chronographs, and so on. Meanwhile, Dodge was on leave, spending the year at the Carnegie Nutrition Laboratory in Boston. When his leave was over, Dodge returned to Wesleyan and urged the Carnegie lab to take on young Miles. This occurred, Miles's debt to Dodge increased, and Miles spent the next eight years in Boston. He developed an almost devotional loyalty to Dodge.[5]

While at the Carnegie Lab from 1914 to 1922, Miles completed a number of applied research projects, including elaborate and sophisticated studies of the effects of alcohol and lack of adequate nutrition on a variety of behaviors.[6] He also collaborated with Dodge on a wartime project to improve gas mask efficiency (apparatus skills again). His work to this point in his career illustrates the point I made earlier about an apparatus focus, and reveals Miles as a researcher who could quickly adapt to the central features of the laboratory where he happened to find himself. Hence, at Iowa and in the presence of Seashore, Miles studied auditory perception; at Wesleyan as Dodge's surrogate, Miles became knowledgeable about eye movement research. Now at Carnegie, he found himself in an applied research environment and adapted accordingly.

Miles was forever grateful for the opportunity to work at the Carnegie lab, but he missed being around students; when another academic opportunity came, he jumped at it. This happened in 1922 and was a major position—director of the psychology laboratory at Stanford, working for Lewis Terman, the newly appointed head of Stanford's Psychology Department. Stanford originally offered the position to E. G. Boring, who was at the time becoming increasingly disenchanted at Clark University. Boring imposed a number of conditions that Terman found threatening to his own status, however, and the offer was withdrawn. Miles was a safer choice—he didn't have the stature of a Boring, so he wouldn't be as demanding, and he seemed to be eclectic in his choice of research topics, a trait that meshed nicely with Terman's philosophy at Stanford. Dodge again played a role, recommending his protégé to his friend Terman.[7]

Miles stayed at Stanford for ten years as director of the laboratory. While he was there, catholicity of interest was indeed the overarching theme, with his research topics ranging from eye movements during sleep to maze learning in rats to age-related changes in various cognitive and physical abilities. Most of his ideas for research, not surprisingly, were apparatus-driven, rather than deriving from a programmatic research strategy. As he later described the approach in an autobiographical essay: "A piece of apparatus designed to provide a task for a human subject and to give a score or measurable record of his performance seems to me to offer a standing invitation to research curiosity."[8]

As an example of how Miles's fascination with apparatus led to creative ideas for research, consider how he adapted reaction time methodology in an attempt to aid Stanford's football program. He called his device a multiple chronograph and described it in a letter to Dodge in early September 1927: "I expect to take a try at collecting some data from the football men in their fall practice. I have rigged up an arrangement by which I can measure the charging time from signal to first movement of body on seven men at once. My preliminary results on 28 football players gave a pretty good correlation with the speed rating which the coaches independently made. . . . Our head coach, 'Pop' Warner, has insisted that I canvas and rate the whole fall squad in this same manner." The three studies that Miles published on "football charging" might have established him as a pioneer in what we now call sports psychology. The research was done only a few years after Coleman Griffith set out to apply psychology to sport. Yet while Griffith made the topic the center of his professional life, Miles did what he normally did—he completed a few studies with a focus on developing a new apparatus or applying one in some creative fashion, then moved on to something else. I should point out, however, that in this case the "moving on" was partly the result of Stanford's coaching staff losing interest in the project; Miles later expressed some discouragement over this turn of events and might have pursued work along similar lines if encouraged.[9]

More traditional laboratory examples of Miles's ingenuity with apparatus concern his development of the ataxiameter, the pursuit pendulum, and the pursuitmeter. The ataxiameter was designed to measure head and body steadiness, while the pursuit pendulum and pursuitmeter evaluated hand-eye coordination, concentration, and fatigue. In brief, with the pursuit pendulum, a water-filled pendulum was put in motion and water flowed out the bottom. The subject had to catch the water in a small diameter cup. In the more elaborate pursuitmeter, the subject had to move a sliding dial to keep a visual stimulus within a type of crosshair that was constantly moving erratically. These two devices evolved into the rotary pursuit apparatus routinely found in laboratories today. Miles developed the devices, along with the ataxiameter while at the Carnegie lab; the instruments were ideally suited to help him investigate the effects of alcohol and reduced nutrition.[10]

A last example (and perhaps the most important) of Miles's apparatus-generated research projects concerned maze learning, his interest stimulated by a semester's leave spent at Berkeley in 1924, where he encountered maze heaven in the form of Tolman and his students. The outcome was a series of papers on maze learning, most being descriptions of new varieties of mazes, including an elevated maze that became perhaps Miles's best-known apparatus creation. Miles also became interested in the history of maze learning, as I mentioned earlier, and wrote a paper on the history of animal mazes. He also co-authored a brief history of human stylus mazes with one of his students, and two of his creations, the two story duplicate maze and the high relief finger maze, were marketed for a while by the C. H. Stoelting Co.[11]

One final area of interest for Miles during his Stanford years was a collaborative project with Terman, other department members, and several graduate students on what came to be known as the Stanford Later Maturity Studies. Funded by the Carnegie Corporation (Miles had the connections from his experience at the Carnegie Nutrition Lab), the project was a large undertaking, one of the first designed to examine developmental changes from early adulthood through old age.[12] Its importance for Miles is reflected in the fact that the studies became the topic of his APA presidential address in 1932. The overall conclusion of the studies was that abilities, both cognitive and motor, decline steadily with age. The Stanford Later Maturity Studies are sometimes mentioned to this day, but usually as an example of how the wrong conclusions can be drawn when using a cross-sectional design that compares age groups from widely different cohorts. As an aside, one of Miles's collaborators on the project was a former student of Terman's, Catherine Cox. Miles married her in 1927, two years after the sudden death of his first wife. Catherine Cox Miles became a distinguished psychologist, known for her collaboration with Terman on a project to estimate the IQs of famous historical personages (her doctoral dissertation) and for her work on gender roles and giftedness in children.[13]

Miles left Stanford in 1932, invited to become a permanent member of Yale's new Institute for Human Relations after spending a sabbatical there in 1930–31. The institute, an ambitious attempt to integrate all the disciplines at Yale that concerned human behavior, included researchers from such disciplines as psychology, sociology, linguistics, and anthropology. That Miles was invited was one final effect of his long friendship with Dodge. Close to retirement and suffering increasingly from Parkinson's disease, Dodge wanted to ensure that his laboratory and its precious apparatus would be in good hands. Miles was an easy choice for him, and he eventually convinced the Stanford psychologist to move east. Catherine was offered a position as clinical professor of psychology in the Department of Psychiatry at Yale's medical school.[14]

At Yale, Miles continued his lifelong pattern of shifting from one research topic to another. Some of his work was reminiscent of his earlier applied studies at the Carnegie Nutrition Lab, while other studies investigated basic perceptual processes, and still others described new or improved apparatus. His last notable contribution was once again apparatus related and made a contribution to the war effort in World War II. Studying dark adaptation, he noticed that wearing red goggles enabled pilots to work in normal light, while simultaneously beginning the process of dark adaptation. Being dark-adapted, pilots would be able to fly in the dark immediately if necessary, without having to wait in darkness for adaptation to occur. This creation earned Miles the prestigious Warren Medal from the Society of Experimental Psychologists in 1949.[15]

Miles remained at Yale for just over twenty years and retired in 1953 at the age of sixty-eight. Retirement for Miles, however, seemed to be just another word for career change. Within a year, he accepted a visiting professorship at the University of Istanbul. He taught in Turkey for three years, then became the scientific director for the naval submarine base in New London, Connecticut. He remained there for eight more years and finally retired for good in 1965, just before his eightieth birthday. He died in 1978. It might not have occurred to him that he was living disproof of the main thesis of his research on aging.

I have already mentioned the size of the Miles collection at the Akron archives—128 boxes and a 756-page inventory. The collection includes everything from the expected, such as correspondence and class notes, to the unexpected, such as a fingerprint card for Miles and an "electrocardiogram" printout for him. Seven of the 128 boxes contain diaries. Although not all of the pages of the diaries were counted during the inventory process, many were, so we know that there are at least four thousand pages of diary information in the Miles papers, and probably closer to five thousand. Although some of the booklets are little more than appointment books or calendars (valuable in their own right), and many of the diary entries concern topics unrelated to psychology (also of value, to the biographer), descriptions of several events of interest to historians of psychology can be found in the diaries, and in many instances the entries are quite extensive. At some of the professional meetings he attended, Miles must have done little but write furiously. So what do these diaries include that might interest the historian? Let me describe just a sample of the contents I have found helpful.

First, the diaries contain descriptions of three pre-World War I meetings of the group known as Titchener's Experimentalists. This group was a cohort of laboratory psychologists, mainly from the east, who met each spring, rotating from one member's lab to another. They would spend a long weekend discussing research in progress and tinkering with apparatus in the host lab. Except for the war year of 1918, the group met annually from 1904 until Titchener's death in 1927. In addition to the prewar meetings, the Miles diaries include an account of the 1928 meeting, the first one held after Titchener's death in 1927, at which the question of the group's future was center stage, and an account of the 1929 meeting, at which the future of the organization was decided; it became more formal and gave itself a name with capital letters: The Society of Experimental Psychologists. Lastly, the diaries include accounts of several of the society's meetings in the 1930s.

The descriptions of the early Experimentalists' meetings in the Miles diaries are noteworthy because one characteristic of the group's sessions was that virtually nothing was published about them. No minutes were taken, and reports of the meetings in the "notes and news" sections of journals are very sketchy at best and absent for most years. I know of only one formally printed program—the Dodge papers at Akron include a brief schedule of events for the 1913 meeting. This was clearly an aberration; the unwritten rules normally prohibited this kind of formality. But this was the tenth annual meeting, a milestone of sorts, and Dodge evidently felt the need to make note of it. The only published firsthand descriptions of the Experimentalists are to be found in two retrospective articles by Boring.[16] The failure to record the details of these meetings was in keeping with Titchener's strong desire to keep the group as informal as possible.

Considering the lack of information available about these meetings and my own interest in the group, I was naturally excited to discover that Miles had written about three of the early sessions. During the time he was at the Carnegie lab in Boston, Miles attended and made notes about the meetings held in 1915 at Yale, 1916 at Princeton, and 1917 at Harvard. The diary descriptions of these meeting are not nearly as elaborate as some of Miles's later entries, probably due to the nature of the meetings. Everyone was expected to participate, so a young experimentalist sitting in a corner writing away while others talked might not have been asked to return the following year. Nonetheless, the diary entries are informative and corroborate what is known of the group. Thus, in keeping with the group's informality and interest in apparatus, Miles mentions "being called upon" by the host to report on his research in progress, and in the 1916 meeting he demonstrated an electric counter that he was developing. The entry for the 1917 meeting is the most interesting of the three because even though it was held at Harvard, Miles noted that it seemed odd for Titchener to be serving as host. Titchener was always the dominant figure in the group, but the tradition was for the host to be the researcher in whose lab the meeting was held. As Miles wrote, "It [the meeting] was well attended. Titchener presided, I do not know exactly why except that Münsterberg's recent death and the fact that Titchener has been called to Harvard created a situation which may fully account."[17]

Miles later reinforced the impression of Titchener being in charge by writing that on the final day, "Titchener called upon me to report in the morning session."[18] Titchener in the end did not go to Harvard, of course, but presiding over the 1917 meeting suggests that he was considering it *and* that the possibility was known to the group. In his 1938 history of the Experimentalists, however, Boring listed Herbert Langfeld of Harvard as the host for this meeting, with Yerkes and Edwin B. Holt sharing the responsibility. This seems to conflict with Miles's account. The Harvard meeting was also marked by America's declaration of war on Germany, and Yerkes briefly took the chair and began discussions that eventually produced the army testing program. Unfortunately, Miles made no mention of the event.

So what else is in the diaries? As noted earlier, Miles spent most of the 1920s at Stanford. While there, he made several trips to the east, and because this was a major undertaking in those days, he tried to combine as much as he could into a trip. He would visit other laboratories en route, usually delivering paid lectures on his research, and he would center the trip on a major event, such as the annual APA meeting. He sometimes visited universities that were sending students to Stanford for graduate studies.[19] There are detailed accounts of two major trips in the diaries: one in the spring of 1928 built around a conference sponsored by the National Research Council (NRC) at Carlisle, Pennsylvania (considered below in more detail), and one in 1929, when Miles centered his visit on the famous IXth International Congress of Psychology at Yale.

Between March 24 and April 18 of 1928, Miles traveled east from Stanford to attend two events of importance for the future of experimental psychology—the NRC conference, held at Dickinson College in Carlisle, Pennsylvania, and the initial meeting of the Experimentalists after Titchener's death, held at Yale a week after the Carlisle meeting. In addition, the trip included visits to the University of Iowa (a homecoming for Miles), the Iowa Child Welfare Research Station, the Institute of Juvenile Research in Chicago, the University of Chicago, the Mellon Institute in Pittsburgh, the University of Michigan, and Clark University in Massachusetts. The diary records discussions at these locations, usually about apparatus and research, with a number of psychologists, including Lee Travis, Beth Wellman, Harvey Carr, Lashley, Louis Thurstone, Hull, and Walter Hunter. The trip is described in more than one hundred diary pages.

The Carlisle conference was sponsored by the NRC and funded by a grant from the Laura Spellman Rockefeller Foundation. The NRC, formed in the wake of World War I to provide government support for scientific research, contained divisions corresponding to the different sciences; psychologists found themselves in a unit combining anthropology and psychology. Although the bulk of this division's work in the twenties was in service of applied psychology (for example, one of the committees was the Committee on the Psychology of the Highway), the goal of the 1928 Carlisle meeting was to "consider the needs of laboratory psychology and to seek means of encouraging its growth," according to the invitation sent by Knight Dunlap, the Johns Hopkins psychologist who chaired the NRC's Division of Anthropology and Psychology at that time.[20]

Thirty-two research psychologists descended on the small Pennsylvania campus of Carlisle College for a two-day meeting on March 30 and 31, 1928. They included such luminaries as Karl Dallenbach, John Dashiell, Hull, Lashley, and Robert Woodworth. Not all the stars were there, however. Boring refused to go, writing to Miles that he was "not going to Dunlap's conference. I am getting very very tired of the N.R.C., which is always fixing up things that cost me time and money for somebody else's research." When Miles wrote back urging Boring to reconsider, especially in light of the fact that Boring was APA president that year, Boring grumbled in reply: "Nor had it occurred to me that I had any special responsibilities this year as President of the A.P.A. If I have, then I think that they are not the responsibilities of a slave, but the responsibilities to uphold wisdom and to denounce foolishness." These comments were not out of character for Boring, yet to the extent that his views were shared by those who went to the conference, and they were to a degree, the prospects for a successful meeting were in doubt from the start.[21]

Miles arrived in Carlisle on the evening of the twenty-ninth, after traveling from Pittsburgh on the same train with Hull. In his diary, Miles described him as being "much exercised in reference to theory of learning." Hull also complained about problems with his automatic correlating machine; it was apparently so delicate that it could not survive shipping, and an order placed by Miles had to be cancelled. Miles described Hull as "talkative, statistical, imaginative, gossipy, blustery." At Harrisburg, just north of Carlisle, Miles and Hull were joined by Margaret Washburn, the only woman invited to the Carlisle meeting. Miles noted that "W. is doubtful of the Carlisle Conference," a skepticism, apparently similar to Boring's, that turned out to be well founded.[22]

After settling in to the Molly Pitcher Hotel in Carlisle, Miles joined a group of colleagues (including Hull, Dashiell, Samuel Fernberger, and Woodworth) for an informal discussion of their ongoing research, a kind of mini-experimentalists meeting. Topics ranged from maze learning to drug effects. The official conference began at 10 a.m. the following morning. The psychologists first heard a seventy-five minute opening address by Dunlap, who detailed the problems confronting experimental psychology, as he saw them. Miles recorded the talk in seven full pages of his diary. Here are some of the points made by Dunlap, exactly as recorded by Miles and using his numbering system:

1. Lab. method has justified itself under difficult conditions during last 20 yrs.
2. Lab. method is academic, it is headed(?) to science for its own sake.
3. Lab. method is slow, expensive but must be waited for. . . . The outside wants social problems solved. . . . Application has been tried when there is nothing to apply.
4. Lab. man is pig-headed. He does not take the good problems given. He runs rats, works on children wetting bed, watches deaf and dumb man work his fingers while he thinks. . . .
8. The situation in lab. psych. is not satisfactory, it is in fact depressing.

—The war rush for application and aftermath
—vol. of research, great but question its quality
—too much teaching by our young men
—grad. students do Ph.D. then die on job; he has no time, he teaches or must organize

9. Unstable state of many psych. labs. . . . Staff, app.[aratus] and problems built up, then wreck the thing by bringing in a new man with new problems.[23]

In sum, according to Dunlap, the laboratory researcher was being pressured for quick, applicable results and had limited time to develop a solid program of research because of the pressures of teaching. He also argued that the research enterprise was inefficient because different psychologists would be working on the same topic in different labs, but not using quite the same methods; consequently, results wouldn't replicate and much effort would be wasted in trying to resolve differences. Finally, a lab would be developed and begin to be productive, then the experimenter would leave for a new job and the process would have to begin anew.

After laying out the scope of the problem, Dunlap proposed three solutions. First, analogous to the federal Bureau of Standards, he argued for a National Laboratory of Psychology. Its eventual creation was in fact the main reason why Dunlap organized the conference. The lab would be staffed by researchers on sabbatical and newly minted Ph.D.s working for a year or so before starting an academic career. Work would focus on a specific topic, and teams of researchers would work a problem through to its logical conclusion, even if it took several years and the membership of the team changed periodically.

Dunlap's second proposal was that the NRC promote the research of those young psychologists struggling under heavy teaching loads by funding summer research fellowships. The research could be done at the national lab or at the psychologist's home institution. Third, Dunlap proposed streamlining the publication process to increase its efficiency and the quality of the research published.

Dunlap had apparently sent a letter outlining his plans to conference attendees (although Miles didn't get one) and asking for written replies. He concluded his presentation by reporting on these replies, except the one from Washburn. Miles recorded Dunlap's statement in his diary, including a comment from Dodge, who was evidently sitting with Miles:

Washburn: Dunlap. "Dr. W. has written a full letter of criticism of my whole point of view. I [wish] that I had that letter here to read to you but it seems to have been misplaced." *Dodge*: "Freudian suppression."[24]

Lengthy discussion followed Dunlap's opening talk and, as one might expect with thirty-two psychologists in the same room, much of it was critical. The recording of this discussion is one of the best examples of Miles's Herculean effort to document the events he attended; eight full diary pages describe the series of comments and criticisms given by those in attendance. Many thought the idea of a national lab unworkable in practice, some objected to restricting fellowships just to young researchers, and some weren't sure what Dunlap meant by increasing the efficiency of publications. The group created committees to examine the proposals in more detail. These smaller groups worked through the afternoon and evening of the first day and presented their ideas the following day. More debate followed, resulting in the following three outcomes.

First, there was enough agreement on the national lab idea to pursue it further. The eventual outcome was the creation of the National Institute of Psychology in 1929, a federal organization designed specifically to promote basic research. Funding problems—remember, the Depression was just around the corner—and the strong individualistic (i.e., "pig-headed," to use the term from Miles's diary) tendencies of most researchers killed Dunlap's idea of a national lab, however, and rendered the National Institute little more than a paper organization. It went out of existence sometime during or shortly after World War II and, except for securing an invitation to the conference that led to the reorganization of the APA after the war, accomplished nothing of note.[25]

Second, there was agreement on the fellowship idea, but it was expanded beyond the summer and the beginning instructor level. During the 1930s, these NRC fellowships clearly improved the research lives of many psychologists, although once again, funding limits reduced their impact.

Third, the journal problem was discussed the least at Carlisle, but it actually had the most far-reaching consequences, starting a process that eventually led to the APA publication manual. At the recommendation of the Carlisle conference, the NRC sponsored a meeting of editors the following year which included a "Committee on Form of Manuscript," which produced the first uniform set of rules concerning the format of published papers. [26]

The week after the Carlisle conference, Miles went to Yale for the first meeting of Titchener's Experimentalists following the founder's death. He devoted thirty-one diary pages to the two-day event. For the most part, the meeting was actually a typical one—Miles wrote page after page of descriptions of research in progress, including sketches of apparatus. He mentioned the reorganization only briefly. What happened was that a group of nineteen "elders" appointed a five-man committee to decide the future of the group. This committee enlarged itself to fifteen (including Miles) and eventually decided to create the more formal group mentioned earlier, the Society of Experimental Psychologists, into which members would be elected.[27] The details of the reorganization make for an interesting story, and Miles was right in the middle of it, but space forbids the telling of it here. Instead, let me make some general observations about the use of diary information.

Several problems confront the historian faced with the task of extracting useful information from diaries like the ones kept by Miles. For example, there are the obvious practical difficulties that accompany the headache-inducing labor of working through hundreds of pages of semilegible handwriting. Many of the entries made by Miles were obviously written during the events in progress, so he had to write fast. But legibility is a relatively minor problem; it usually doesn't take long to become familiar enough with a writer's handwriting to read almost anything. Other problems for the historian are the same ones faced when studying correspondence—decisions about what to select, concerns over the veracity and overall value of the information, the difficulty of evaluating hearsay and gossip, and the overall issue of how to interpret the contents.

A difficulty more likely to be found in diaries than in correspondence is what could be called the "looking over one's shoulder problem." This occurs when the diarist writes with history in mind. Believing that the diaries will be read by historians, the writer tailors the entries to put himself or herself in a favorable light. I don't think this phenomenon characterizes the Miles diaries, however, for two reasons. First, the diaries are so encyclopedic, especially when he was recording presentations at conferences, that he could not have given much thought to shaping a phrase to benefit himself in the future. Second, Miles says very little about himself in the diaries, and virtually nothing in them could be characterized as reflective or introspective. When he does talk about himself, it is to give an account of his research. Even when he had the opportunity to be self-congratulatory, he wasn't. A case in point is the IXth International Congress at Yale in 1929, when Miles was clearly the center of attention at what he called in the diary the "Cattell-Pavlov Party," held during one of the evenings. The fifteen people there included Pavlov and three other Russians; James McKeen Cattell, Wolfgang Köhler, and Harold Weld. The event centered on some films Miles had taken of his elevated maze studies. Rather than emphasizing the importance of his research and how impressed the great Pavlov was, the diary gives the typical mundane and detailed account that characterizes most of the diaries, focusing on the questions asked and the issues discussed by those who were there. In this case Miles must have written much of the entry after the session, because he was clearly in the middle of it when presenting his films, and as he recorded in the entry, he even served as the good host; in his words, "Between films I served iced ginger ale, etc.," It set him back $3.50.[28]

Despite the problems associated with interpreting diary information, such data can be of great value to the historian. Specifically, they can do five things.

First, diaries can reveal the precise details of the kind of world inhabited by the writer. Thus, for Miles, life centered on the laboratory, and many of his entries yield insights into the nuts and bolts of operating a laboratory. For example, consider the Miles diary description of a conversation with Karl Lashley, recorded during the 1928 trip. By reading it one learns such details as the methodological danger of assigning rats to groups as a function of "randomly" grabbing them out of a colony. The problem is that the tamer rats will be selected first and consequently a two-group experiment might have tamer rats in one group and wilder groups in another, a classic confound. Also, Lashley pointed out a fact known to rat-runners: the tamest rats are white; hooded rats or rats with more gray in them tend to be wilder. As Miles quoted Lashley: "the more white, the less bite." Finally, Lashley advised Miles to buy a "small chicken marking punch" from Sears/Roebuck and showed him a system for notching holes in a rat's ear so as to identify a colony with a population up to 999. A page in the diary includes sketches of rats' ears with notches drawn to illustrate the system.[29]

Diaries can also provide a look at the modes of thinking and ways in which individuals organize their worlds conceptually, even if the writer is not very reflective, and Miles wasn't. Hence, in the Miles diaries, one gets a good idea of how an experimental psychologist thinks, both then *and* now. For instance, in the account of Miles showing his films to Pavlov and others, the bulk of the diary entry was a set of questions he was asked about the research; they nicely illustrate the empirical what-if thinking one might expect from a room full of positivist scientists. Here's what Miles wrote that evening:

—What is the effect of new wood?
—What is the effect of turning the maze?
—What is the effect of changing an animal to a maze of increased size but no change in pattern?[30]

A third strength of diaries is that like other sources of information, they can serve as data to support or question assertions made by other historians. For instance, the Miles diaries lend support to the belief that Titchener exerted firm control over the Experimentalists, even in the 1920s when his own system was crumbling around him. As another example, Franz Samelson's argument about the slow growth of Watsonian behaviorism would clearly be supported by a content analysis of Miles's descriptions of the mainly nonbehavioral research he encountered during his travels.[31] Indeed, Miles's entire research career is a good indication of how our old tendency to describe psychology's history mainly in terms of work done within the context of the "schools" of psychology was an over-simplification. Like many other experimental psychologists, Miles worked on problems of interest to him, without regard to whether the problems supported the claims of one "school" of psychology or another.

As an example of an entry that calls historical description into question, or at least would lead one to look more closely at the record, consider Miles's account of the 1916 APA meeting. Münsterberg had just died, and most history texts give the usual, "He's only been rediscovered recently, because he was hated when he died, due to his misinterpreted pro-German views." Yet in his diary, Miles wrote this about the sentiments expressed at a banquet commemorating the APA's twenty-fifth birthday: "Much mention was made of Hugo Münsterberg's warm friendliness and wide hospitality; like the New Testament host he did not invite just those who would invite him."[32]

Diary information can also convey a sense of how one psychologist views another. Thus Washburn, Titchener's first doctoral student, had this to say about him in 1934, apparently in a conversation with Miles at a meeting of the Society of Experimental Psychologists. Miles wrote this in his diary: "Washburn's attitude toward T. He never discovered anything, he did not create any apparatus, or methods, he was simply not an experimenter. Was always playing to an audience, usually G. E. Muller. T said that a postcard from G. E. M. was his best reward. In the last years he in some way lost the audience. His great points were his learning and his ability to give a lecture. The theses which came from Cornell were doing over the things of Hering and others. Miss W. was his first grad student, he gave her but little according to her; they were too near the same age. Miss W. says that her loyalty, admiration, and devotion are all to Cattell."[33]

A fifth and final point about the value of diary information is that because the contents raise more questions than they answer, they can be a rich source of future projects. Hence, the Miles diaries provide a launching pad for the historian interested in such topics as the Carlisle conference, the reorganization of Titchener's group, and the origins and evolution of research apparatus.

In closing, let me point out that I believe the greatest strength of diary information, especially when the diaries have the level of detail that characterize those kept by Miles, is that they give the historian a close look at the day-to-day life of a person who is living in a specific historical time and place. I must confess that when I first ran across the diaries and started reading them, I was not especially appreciative of the level of excruciating detail that Miles included. I wanted him to concentrate on the big events, the ones that most critically shaped the psychology of his era. Who cares about whether he served ginger ale to Pavlov? But then a historian colleague of mine pointed me in the direction of a remarkable Pulitzer Prize-winning book by historian Laurel Ulrich, titled *A Midwife's Tale: The Life of Martha Ballard, Based on Her Diary, 1785–1812*. Ballard's diary is a bit like the Miles diaries—full of detail about seemingly trivial day-to-day life and often repetitive. For that reason historians have often disregarded the Ballard diary, but Ulrich saw its mundaneness as its strength. In her words, "Yet it is in the very dailiness, the exhaustive, repetitious dailiness, that the real power of Martha Ballard's book lies. To extract the [dangerous] river crossings without noting the cold days spent 'footing' stockings, to abstract the births without recording the long autumns spent winding quills, pickling meat, and sorting cabbages, is to destroy the sinews of this earnest, steady, gentle, and courageous record."[34]

I cannot think of a more eloquent way to sum up the value of the diaries of Walter Miles. In much the same way that the Ballard diary informs readers intimately about the life of a midwife at the turn of the eighteenth century, how better to understand what life was like for a prominent experimental psychologist in the 1920s and '30s than to be almost literally by that person's side day after day.

CHAPTER 5

Contextualizing Documents, Data, and Controversies:

Working With the Henry Herbert Goddard Papers

Leila Zenderland

WITHIN THE HISTORY OF PSYCHOLOGY, few subjects have generated as much controversy as the creation and dissemination of intelligence tests. Almost from its inception, this type of testing has sparked battles that were not merely about mental measurement. Intertwined with these psychological debates were battles over broader issues, including the scope and significance of class, race, or ethnic differences, the shaping of educational policies, and the efficacy of social reforms. As a result, the intelligence testing controversies have long suggested the need to explore the relationship between psychological knowledge and social contexts. As a graduate student exploring American cultural history, I first became intrigued by this relationship after reading psychologist Leon Kamin's fascinating study, *The Science and Politics of I.Q.* The early history of such testing, I concluded, would make an excellent topic for a dissertation. To reduce my subject to manageable proportions, I decided to focus on the life and career of the very first American intelligence tester, Henry Herbert Goddard.[1]

I thought it would be possible to study this subject precisely because psychologists concerned with the development of their own profession had themselves moved so far towards cultural history that the two fields had begun to intersect. By the 1970s, many psychologists and historians had agreed that the emergence of intelligence testing needed to be examined within a historical context emphasizing the political and social debates of the day.[2] Moreover, the broad contours of this contextualization were usually explained in ways that were relatively easy for a non-psychologist to follow. The intelligence testing debate, most accounts explained, was essentially one component of a much larger battle that pitted scientists emphasizing the power of heredity against those stressing the importance of the environment. Intimately linked to this scientific dichotomy was a political one, for hereditarians most often tended to be political conservatives who usually defended the status quo, while environmentalists were more likely to be political liberals promoting social reform. Thus, in this instance, scientific conflict was also political conflict, thinly disguised but nonetheless discernable.

Of course, this conflict, I learned from psychologists, did have an intellectual component, an internal history of ideas about mental measurement. Ideas about how to measure minds were usually traced from Francis Galton's anthropometric laboratory to Charles Spearman's theories about the existence of "general intelligence" ("g") to Alfred Binet's early intelligence scales to Lewis Terman's Stanford-Binet Revision. Yet these technical innovations, much of this literature emphasized, mattered less than the political predispositions of the psychologists themselves. Far more significant in explaining their work were many of these scientists' commitments to the eugenics movement, for instance, or their efforts to justify widening class disparities, or their desire to bolster American nativism or racism. In fact, these were the concerns that made Goddard's work important, for while this psychological tester had hardly been a theoretical innovator, he had gained fame largely as a eugenics popularizer. Seen within this broader cultural context, the history of intelligence testing offered a classic illustration of the interrelationship between psychology and politics, a textbook case in the sociology of science. Such a project, I expected, could be both interesting and relevant. I also hoped it could be completed relatively quickly, once I had examined the primary sources that would document Goddard's life and work.

Examining these sources ought to constitute a pretty straightforward task, I believed, for Goddard certainly seemed to be, as Stephen Jay Gould put it, the "most unsubtle hereditarian of all." From his laboratory at the

Vineland Training School, Goddard became a world-renowned authority on the condition then known as "feeblemindedness," later labeled "mental retardation" and now called "developmental disability." His most famous book, *The Kallikak Family*, linked a feeble inheritance to just about every important social question of the day, including crime, poverty, prostitution, and alcoholism. Once a respected work of science, by 1940 this study had been, in psychologist Knight Dunlap's words, "laughed out of psychology."[3] Having read much of Goddard's published work, I anticipated few difficulties in placing his version of psychological science within a historical context that linked hereditarian theories concerning intelligence to both political conservatism and to widely held popular prejudices of his day.

It was with such a framework in mind that I first came to the University of Akron to study the Henry Herbert Goddard Papers. And it was there that I met and began to work with and learn from John Popplestone and Marion White McPherson, two remarkable psychologists who had founded the Archives of the History of American Psychology and who were willing to share with me their own extraordinary knowledge of the history of their discipline. After too many years and far more visits to Akron than I had anticipated, I finally completed my dissertation. What I had begun as a graduate student in Philadelphia I would finish as a new professor in Southern California. After several more years of researching my subject, I published *Measuring Minds: Henry Herbert Goddard and the Origins of American Intelligence Testing* in 1998.

In countless ways, working with the Goddard Papers proved to be a set of experiences full of surprises. These experiences offered me an invaluable education, for they allowed me to explore firsthand both the enormous potential as well as the frustrating limitations of working with archival materials. In order to reconcile the published data produced by Goddard with the unpublished documents found in his papers, I soon discovered that I would have to place both sets of materials within a richer and more multidimensional historical context. And while I cannot summarize all that I learned from these efforts, I will try to suggest some aspects of how this process of historical reconstruction worked, for it was this process that ultimately led me to situate Goddard's life, the work he produced, and the controversies his work inspired within a framework quite different from the one I had in mind when I began.

Among the many things I learned when I began working in Akron was that while no biography of Goddard had yet been published, I was not the first person to undertake this task. Among those who had tried, in fact, was Goddard himself. By the end of his life, this psychologist had clearly become more introspective, for his late-in-life letters to friends and relatives were increasingly filled with anecdotes about his past. In trying to explain his own life, Goddard had also planned to produce an autobiography; toward this end, he had begun to write reminiscences from his childhood, education, and early career. He had also apparently started to gather materials that he would need for such a project, for scattered throughout his papers were various outlines and lists (for example, a list of summer vacations) that he had evidently hoped to use. By this time, however, Goddard was in his eighties and beginning to suffer from memory loss; many of these efforts were incomplete, sketchy, and often indecipherable.

More potentially promising were the initial efforts of Goddard's devoted student, psychologist Robert Fischer. Over the years, Fischer had become something like a surrogate son. By 1948 he was contemplating the task of explaining Goddard's work as well as his role within the history of psychology. What he would need in order to do so, Fischer told Goddard, was "any or all of the correspondence you carried on with the men that counted in the field in your time. . . . I know you may consider perhaps your early correspondence personal, but since I am working on a biographical study of you and am trying to put you in your proper place in the ontogenetic development of . . . American psychology, I do need your help . . . ," Fischer explained. "I want to write a decent and an intelligent biography—not eulogistic, but factual . . . but I am working without tools," he confessed. "Will you please send me . . . what correspondence you can spare at the present time," he asked.[4]

The reply he received from Goddard, however, was hardly encouraging. "Now as to correspondence . . . ," he responded to Fischer, "I have never kept any correspondence because I never had enough that was worth keeping. 'The men that counted' in the field in my time never wrote to me—

probably because they realized that I *didn't count*. I have not a single letter, of the kind you have in mind . . . ," Goddard declared. "I am going to run through some scrap books and other places where letters would be likely to be stored, if saved at all," he continued. "Should I find anything at all I will surely send it to you. My suggestion would be that you forget about the biography, wrap up what little you have on the subject, and mark it 'Dropped for Lack of Sufficient Data.' "[5]

Goddard's answer was not very promising—either for Fischer or for me when I read it in Akron years later. Were it to prove true, my own idea of writing a biography might also have to be "dropped for lack of sufficient data." Yet even a cursory glance at the dozens of boxes of Goddard materials housed in Akron suggested otherwise.

My own attempt at producing a biography had been made possible by the very different approach to the history of their field adopted in the 1960s by Popplestone and McPherson. Like Fischer, Popplestone and Mc-Pherson too had reached the conclusion that American psychologists interested in the history of their discipline had largely been working without enough tools. Perhaps their own backgrounds in clinical psychology had led them to understand that the history of psychology needed to be more than just the history of the most famous or the most successful—the history, that is, only of "those that counted." Clearly they were influenced by other psychologists of this decade who had begun to reexamine the history of their field in new ways. Equally apparent were Popplestone's and McPherson's sensitivities toward new trends in historiography, for they were working at a time when the writing of history was itself undergoing a major transformation. During this decade, a new generation of historians had begun to pay attention to a range of new sources in order to produce more inclusive versions of American social history—writing "history from the bottom up," as contemporaries called it.[6] Whatever their inspiration, Popplestone and McPherson approached their new project with a clear conception in mind: they would try to document how psychologists actually worked by establishing an archive for the papers of practitioners. One of their greatest early coups was persuading Henry Herbert Goddard's niece, Alice Whiting, to give them all his papers.

It was this vast collection that I now confronted in Akron. Deciphering just what I had before me, however, proved no simple task. On one point Goddard was apparently right—his papers contained relatively few letters from psychologists whom most of his contemporaries would have considered "famous." Instead, his boxes were filled with large amounts of more routine correspondence, including countless letters from unknown teachers, doctors, lawyers, parents, civic organizations, old schoolmates, and Quaker friends and relatives. Equally evident, and often mixed in with scattered professional correspondence and occasional bits of research material, were the accumulated miscellanea of a lifetime—old bills, contemporary advertisements, pictures of unidentified companions, and a very large number of newspaper clippings, some chronicling his own career and others simply reflecting subjects he had apparently found interesting. Moreover, in following the traditional practice of historical archivists—trying to preserve materials in the order in which their subjects kept them, if possible—Popplestone and McPherson had preserved much of Goddard's rather unique filing system (a system that he had probably devised while suffering from what were apparently the early stages of Alzheimer's disease). Making sense of such a collection, I gradually realized, would prove a challenge in itself.

To suggest a sense of the confusion I initially encountered in trying to work with Goddard's papers, I have cited below only a few of the many thousands of items included in the Goddard inventory. Among the items listed in the first few pages of this inventory (which itself runs to more than one hundred pages) are the following:

- MS. on High School Psychology
- An undated handwritten manuscript containing a description of Mary Paine (feebleminded)
- Correspondence regarding assistance in gaining entry into U.S. for a Miss Krenberger
- Untitled two page typed document regarding the role of different sensory modalities in teaching children
- Lowell Thomas letter
- Letter to Editor of the *Friend* complaining about the introduction of Spiritualism into Quakerism—author unidentified

- Folder labeled "Ephemeris." Contents taken from a loose-leaf note-book bearing this label. A picture of the New Royal Hawaiian Hotel was glued inside the front cover and Currier & Ives American Home-stead Winter inside the back
- A typed list of the states in the order of admission [to the United States]
- Letter to "Mr. Pastore," of 4/3/48 in which Goddard replies to criticisms of his hereditary interpretations
- Receipt for a coal bill, Oct. 19, 1889

What Popplestone and McPherson had collected, inventoried, and made available to historians, I gradually came to realize, was less a guide to the past than a complex and very jumbled set of clues. The Goddard Papers offered clues to a long and complex individual life, to the formation of an emerging profession, and to a bygone era. My task as a historian would be to make sense of these clues by placing them in some kind of meaningful order. At times I felt like I was working with a very large jigsaw puzzle, trying to reassemble small pieces until a recognizable picture came into view. At other times, I felt like a detective tracking down leads, with one clue leading to another—or to a dead end.

In order to discern what many of these documents signified, I came to see, I would have to situate them within a context. Sometimes the significance of a whole set of clues would suddenly become clear; at other times, however, it would be years before I would understand the significance of a single document. At times, this process would require diligence; on other occasions, it seemed to involve luck as much as skill. In some instances, for example, letterhead might prove far more revealing than a letter, for while the text told me little, the stationery might identify an individual's institutional affiliation and organizational memberships; it might also list the names of other members of the same organization, thus showing how Goddard was embedded within a particular social network.

In order to more fully understand and identify the names, episodes, and controversies I was uncovering in reading Goddard's correspondence, I had to immerse myself not only in the history of psychology, but also in the histories of medicine, biology, education, sociology, criminology, and religion. Equally crucial, I had to gain a richer understanding of what it meant to be a New England Quaker in the last half of the nineteenth century, a middle-class reformer in the Progressive era, or a practicing clinical psychologist in the first half of the twentieth century. Finally, I had to become far more familiar with the general culture of this era—that is, with what people in these decades were most likely to be reading in their newspapers or hearing on the radio about the world around them.

This process of working with archival materials can be illustrated to some extent by considering what can be gained from an analysis of just three items included in the very abbreviated list of inventory items cited above. Among these items are three letters: one from Lowell Thomas, one regarding Miss Krenberger, and one to Mr. Pastore. Each of these items tells a story of its own; each says something as well about both Goddard and his era. Each also makes the most sense when interpreted within the broader context of the times.

Of the three persons mentioned, certainly the most famous in Goddard's day and the most familiar to an American cultural historian would have to be Lowell Thomas. An immensely popular reporter, filmmaker, world traveler, and author, Thomas was one of the most widely recognized media figures of his day. (Even in my own day, this name was recognizable, for I myself had vague childhood memories of an old television show that featured Lowell Thomas.) During World War I, I learned, Thomas had become famous by taking a motion picture camera crew to cover every front. While covering the Near East, he had met T. E. Lawrence, and in the 1920s Thomas produced a traveling film lecture presentation that made "Lawrence of Arabia" a household name. In 1930, Thomas became radio's first news reporter. He also wrote more than fifty popular books chronicling his adventures around the world, among them *Goodnight, Everybody, With Lawrence in Arabia,* and *Pageant of Adventure.*[7] Why should a letter from such a celebrity be listed in the Goddard inventory?

Even a cursory look at the correspondence between them makes the "relationship" clear. Their communications began with a letter from Lowell Thomas (on stationery that depicted a camera and identified him as "The News Voice of the Air").[8] Dated January 10, 1933, it stated:

Dear Mr. Goddard:

Last night, Ralph Hitz, President of the Hotel New Yorker, told me that he was anxious to have you stop at The New Yorker when you are in New York.

So I volunteered to drop you a note in his behalf, because, first, Ralph Hitz is the kind of chap one likes to help. And secondly, I'm enthusiastic about the New Yorker and the unusual attention and service they always give you.

You probably have heard that the New Yorker has been strikingly successful right though the depression, largely because Mr. Hitz has been able to provide his guests with ten-dollar a day service and luxury at less than half that price. You can even get a room there for as little as $3.50 a day!

I hope you'll try the New Yorker the next chance you have. I'm enclosing a card of introduction—just present it to the Assistant Manager or the Room Clerk when you register and you'll get every possible attention.

Sincerely,

Lowell Thomas

Of course, the significance (or rather, insignificance) of such a letter became obvious as soon as I read it. In the midst of the Great Depression, the New Yorker Hotel had mounted an advertising campaign promising luxury service at bargain prices; they had secured the endorsement of Lowell Thomas to be used in their promotion. This letter, in short, was largely an example of 1930s junk mail—the kind of mail that most persons, then and now, would quickly throw away.

To my surprise, however, Goddard had kept this letter. Even more surprising, he had answered it.[9] His answer, moreover, suggests something as well.

My Dear Lowell:

I was overjoyed to receive your letter. I was much pleased that you should remember me. Our meeting tho short was, of course, highly exciting. In fact I have seldom had such an enjoyable experience as that which gave me the opportunity of knowing you. You may not remember all the circumstances, tho you would if I had time to recall them to your mind.

I am greatly pleased that you remembered me after all these years. Your memory is so much better than that of our mutual friend Ralph Hitz. He seems not to remember me at all! Why, I have never stayed anywhere else in New York since the New Yorker was built! While it is remarkable that you remember me, I of course, feel very familiar with you being one of the millions that carry on a conversation with you almost every evening of our lives. Of course it is a somewhat one-sided conversation because you do not hear what we say. But we talk to you just as tho you heard. When you say "Good evening everybody" Mrs. Goddard always says "Good evening Lowell." You see you are just one of the family. Well, "So long" until we meet at the New Yorker.

Yours as ever Henry Herbert Goddard

Goddard's ironic response soon brought a personal reply from Lowell Thomas. "Many thanks for that cheery letter you wrote me," Thomas wrote back (on stationery, by the way, from New York's Waldorf-Astoria Hotel). "This time you are hearing from me under my own signature. That other was a little stunt trumped up by a publicity friend of mine." Thomas ended his letter with one of his signature lines. "As they say in Arabia," he concluded, "may your shadow never grow less."[10]

What was I to make of Goddard's lighthearted exchange with one of the most famous celebrities of the 1930s? Such correspondence was certainly not of much significance for a biography of the kind I was planning to write, for my study was designed to explore the origins of intelligence testing. Still, even an irrelevant exchange such as this one could tell me several things about my subject. At a most basic level, it told me that Goddard was prosperous enough, even during the Great Depression, to be a regular guest at the New Yorker Hotel, and that he often spent his evenings with his wife learning about the world by listening to Lowell Thomas's radio adventures.

Upon more reflection, I could see some striking similarities between some of Goddard's lifelong interests and those of Lowell Thomas. In fact, like Thomas, Goddard too was something of an outdoorsman, for since his youth this psychologist had also been an athlete, a camper, a hiker, and above all a mountain-climber; during his lifetime, he would eventually scale a number of dangerous peaks, including the Matterhorn. Moreover, in an age when travel was far more difficult, expensive, and rare than today, Goddard had made numerous trips—to California in the 1880s, to Hawaii in the 1920s, and to see the Soviet Union, the catacombs of Rome, and the pyramids of Egypt (where he was photographed riding a camel) as part of a world tour in 1931. Thus, Goddard the psychologist probably shared at least some of Thomas's love of "adventure."

Finally, this exchange illustrated Goddard's understated and often self-mocking sense of humor—a trait that would frequently surprise me while I was working with his papers. Of course, since none of these things had much to do with the main emphasis I had chosen for my study—Goddard's role as a disseminator of intelligence testing—this exchange with a famous figure did not even merit a mention in my biography. Even so, the very act of reading it allowed me to understand my subject in a more nuanced way, for it helped me to set Goddard within his own era.

If letters from famous figures such as Lowell Thomas often provided little that I could use directly, letters from unknown persons could be far more revealing—once I had established a context for understanding their meaning. Among the most haunting of all the items I eventually found in the Goddard Papers were those suggested in the inventory by the item that states "Correspondence regarding assistance in gaining entry into U.S. for a Miss Krenberger." This item was actually a copy of a letter. The original had been sent on September 28, 1938, by someone identified only as "SCK" (the signature didn't appear on the copy) to a Mr. Edwin J. Schanfarber of Columbus, Ohio. In this letter, "SCK" told Schanfarber that Goddard, his former professor, had sought his assistance in helping Miss Krenberger emigrate to the United States.[11] At first, the item made relatively little impression on me, for it seemed to have little to do with my main focus—exploring Goddard's work as an intelligence tester. Moreover, none of these persons—Krenberger, Schanfarber, or "SCK"—were immediately recognizable (nor could I identify them by using secondary sources on the history of psychology). Only after I had pieced together clues found throughout the Goddard Papers would I begin to see the complex story suggested by this document, with all its historical and human drama. In relation to the larger story that I was trying to tell in my book—a story that I struggled to keep focused on the central issue of "measuring minds"—this poignant episode would prove something of a tangent. As a result, I would eventually have to summarize it in a few paragraphs in a manuscript that was already growing far too long.[12] What lay behind those paragraphs, however, was a complex tale that deserves to be told in its own right, for it is particularly valuable in illustrating the enormous power of archival materials to allow historians to recapture the past on a human scale.

In going through Goddard's papers, I had come across a number of letters signed "Krenberger." Some were written in German and signed "S. Krenberger"; others were in English and signed "Selina Krenberger." Apparently there were two Krenbergers. Dr. S. Krenberger (first name never used) was a Viennese scholar who had maintained a very warm professional relationship with Goddard. Selina was his daughter. The letters in German had been written by the father, those in English by the daughter.

The letters between Goddard and the father are from the 1920s. Dr. Krenberger (according to his letterhead) was the director of the Israelitisches Taubstummeninstitut in Wien (Jewish Institute for the Deaf and Dumb in Vienna). He was also the editor of a small Viennese journal of "Heilpädagogik" (medical pedagogy) titled *Eos* (Greek for "sun") focused on what were then called deaf, dumb, and feebleminded children and later of a journal on the same subject titled *Levana* (Hebrew for "moon").[13]

Goddard had met Krenberger on one of his trips to Europe. Such a meeting would hardly have been uncommon, for on these trips Goddard usually paid visits to institutions, special classes, or individuals with particular interests in handicapped children, special education, or abnormal psychology. Krenberger clearly shared these interests, and the two continued corresponding once Goddard returned home, exchanging not only letters but also books, journals, or articles they had written. (On one visit to Europe, Krenberger had taken Goddard to meet his world-famous Viennese Jewish colleague, Sigmund Freud.)[14] Krenberger's letters to Goddard indicate both personal warmth and professional admiration. "Your picture hangs over my writing table," he told Goddard in one such letter.[15] This correspondence, which apparently continued until Krenberger's death in 1930, indicates the need to place Goddard's scholarship within a world-wide context, for it suggests the existence of an international community of psychologists, physicians, and special educators who shared their interests and experiences.

The correspondence between Goddard and Krenberger's daughter Selina, which begins in 1938, must be placed within a very different context. On March 12, 1938, Nazi troops crossed the Austrian border; a day later, Austria became a part of the German Reich, thus opening a nightmarish chapter in the history of Vienna's Jewish community. Facing the sudden passage of brutal anti-Jewish measures that radically restricted occupations, income, and basic civil rights, as well as a rapidly escalating campaign of orchestrated antisemitic violence, tens of thousands of Jews tried desperately to escape Nazi Austria. (That June, the Gestapo allowed Freud, then eighty-two years old, to depart Vienna after twice searching his home.)[16] Among those seeking a way out was Selina Krenberger.

In 1938 Selina Krenberger was an attractive, unmarried forty-three-year-old writer who lived on a small pension. (In one of his letters, her father had told Goddard that her ten-year engagement to a doctor in the army had ended.) While she had helped her father on some of his projects, she had also published her own work. In fact, some of her short stories had appeared in a New York German-language newspaper, the *Staats-Zeitung und Herold*. By August of that year, Selina had contacted her father's professional friend, Henry Herbert Goddard, to see if he would sponsor her emigration to the United States.[17]

Goddard, then seventy-two years old, was clearly willing to help, but he wasn't sure how to go about sponsoring a refugee—no easy process in this era. Seeking assistance, he first contacted an old acquaintance, Samuel Fels. A Philadelphia Jewish philanthropist who had made his fortune manufacturing Fels-Naptha soap, Fels had also been a major contributor to the Vineland institution and had funded Goddard's Kallikak research in 1912. (*The Kallikak Family* was dedicated to Fels.) By 1938 Fels had been approached about many such cases. "The letter from Selma [*sic*] Krenberger is just another case among the thousands," he told Goddard.[18]

In order to come to the United States, Fels explained, Krenberger would need "an affidavit made by someone here who guarantees that she will not become a public charge." If Goddard wished to do this, he could supply him with an application form. Of course, Krenberger would probably lose her only means of support if she left, Fels informed Goddard, for her pension would be confiscated by the German government and she would be allowed to keep only the money for her passage. However, if she were able to get to the United States, Fels promised Goddard, he and his wife would "do what we can to smooth her way," particularly in helping her find a job.[19]

Fels himself continued to believe that the situation would soon change due to international pressure. "It is possible and not unlikely, I think," he wrote Goddard, "that the International Committee now sitting in London which was called together by President Roosevelt, may have enough influence with the German government to, in some way, ease the fate of those unfortunates who for the time being can see nothing open for them except to leave the country." Such hopes, historians now know, proved wishful thinking, for a series of international conferences focused on the refugee problem ended as disastrous failures.[20]

More immediately helpful than Fels was another of Goddard's Jewish contacts. In September 1938, Goddard wrote to "SCK," whom I gradually realized had to be psychologist Samuel C. Kohs. Through my research, I had become familiar with Kohs's writings, for he had been an active participant in the early I.Q. debates. He had also been one of Goddard's Vineland assistants. With Goddard's help, Kohs had secured a job as a psychological tester at the Chicago Municipal Court. Apparently, however, this Jewish psychologist had had difficulties finding academic positions in his field, for he would later write that "narrow prejudices" had induced him to leave psychology; even so, he always expressed very warm feelings toward Goddard. By 1938, Kohs had become national field director of the National Coordinating Committee for Aid to Refugees and Emigrants Coming from Germany (a fact which I learned from his letterhead).[21]

"Just now, I am troubled about the daughter of a good friend of mine in Vienna," Goddard wrote Kohs that September, for "like the thousands proscribed by Hitler," she "wants to leave Austria-Germany. In desperation, she has written me," he added. "I would be glad to help her if I could and if I knew how. I understand that there are many Jewish organizations in this country, doing all they can to relieve the situation," he continued. "It occurred to me that you would know all about them. . . ."[22]

That same day, Kohs ("SCK") sent parts of Goddard's letter to Edwin Schanfarber. "Dr. Goddard is a sort of godfather to me," Kohs told him, "and I will be most grateful to you for any assistance you can give him." Kohs also told Goddard to have Selina apply for a visa at the American consulate.[23]

On October 3, 1938, Goddard received a letter from Samuel Luchs, an attorney with the law firm of Schanfarber and Schanfarber. "Our Mr. Schanfarber is President of the local Jewish Welfare Federation," Luchs explained, and "we have helped quite a few people prepare the necessary papers. At Mr. Kohs' request, therefore, we are writing to put our services at your disposal," he told Goddard. Thus, the meaning of the letter from "SCK" to Edwin Schanfarber was now clear: Kohs had arranged for a Jewish law firm experienced in such matters to handle the Krenberger case for Goddard. Moreover, Luchs, apparently an Ohio State graduate, knew Goddard as well, for he ended his letter with "sincere personal regards from one who had the good fortune to be enrolled in one of your classes a number of years ago."[24]

What followed next, as reconstructed through Goddard's papers, was a complex struggle to extricate Selina Krenberger from Nazi Austria—a struggle that would last for more than a year. On one side was Goddard, now helped by Luchs's law firm, with assistance from Fels. They would have to fight an ever-tightening series of Nazi regulations as well as the bureaucratic hurdles that the United States government in general and the State Department in particular used to discourage immigration (especially from Jewish refugees).[25] Caught in this struggle would be Selina Krenberger, whose situation grew more dangerous by the day, and whose letters to Goddard would alternate between hope and despair. Missing from Goddard's papers are his letters to her (perhaps because he didn't keep carbons of personal correspondence), but from her responses, it is clear that he had tried to keep her spirits up in what was obviously a race against time.

By September 1938, Selina had registered with the United States consulate. "How glad my father would be if he knew what interest you are taking in the lot of his child," she wrote Goddard that October. Yet the struggle to survive was growing more difficult, she conceded. If more than a month passed without her hearing from Goddard, she would plead desperately for his advice, or send a short note merely as "a sign of life," only to apologize for such behavior in later letters. Moreover, her isolation increased as friends left the country by any means possible. "All my friends are already abroad," she told him that December.[26]

By January, Selina's spirits were raised. "Today I received my affidavits [from two strangers secured by Luchs's law firm who each vouched for her financially]. This is your work," she wrote Goddard, and "I thank you ever so much." (Luchs also had Goddard write a letter to the United States consul in Vienna in support of her application.) By February, however, Selina's situation had again become precarious. "I lost my little rent," she informed Goddard. "Each day another question: how to go on?" In a March letter, she told Goddard that the Krenbergers's family physician had "returned from Buchenwald after 8 months." With his "Arian" wife he had quickly left Austria for France, she explained, and now had a visa to enter the United States. Selina asked Goddard to give him a recommendation that would help him find a position in America. "Your name alone opens possibilities," she added. Her own situation, however, was looking bleaker, particularly as other Jewish refugees flooded into Vienna. "The question of how to emigrate is getting more and more difficult," she reported in March. "The U.S.A. Consulate in Vienna is closed for three months to be able to work up thousands of affidavits," she added. "The quotas are exhausted and I was told that my turn would be in January or perhaps in March 1940."[27]

Seeking any way out, at one point Selina suggested an "absurd" possibility: an arranged marriage to an American. "Many sham-marriages or name-marriages take place nowadays to overcome the difficulties and to open an outlet," she wrote. "If anybody were kind enough to offer this possibility to me, I should be saved," she explained, for "I should be on the preference quota and I might soon get to the land of freedom and liberty." In even suggesting such a solution, she hoped that Goddard would not judge her too harshly. "My dear fatherly friend, you know my father's noble character. I am my parent's child, I have the moral qualities which guarantee my inner decency. I talk to you, the psychologist who sees and judges the world and men from a higher point of view," she told Goddard. "You know that an intellectual woman, not old enough to resign herself, will struggle for the possibility of living to the last. . . . don't laugh at my letter, better weep about it. You are my last resource. Is it to be understood that I wish to go on living?"[28]

Whatever Goddard may have thought about such a suggestion, the law firm handling her case apparently expressed no interest in pursuing it. Instead they continued the process that would make legal emigration possible. Meanwhile, Goddard evidently put Selina in contact with Quaker relief workers then operating in Vienna. After meeting with one such Quaker woman, however, Selina reported that she had been unable to offer much help.[29]

By July 1939 Selina was once again hopeful, for she had finally received a registration number from the American Consulate indicating that she could probably leave by December or January. In response, she sent a poem to Goddard. It was her very first poem written in English, she explained, and in it she tried to express what her life was like.[30] As written in Selina's imperfect English, it stated:

> I paint my heaven quite alone
> In clear and brilliant colours
> If shrill intricacy of earth
> Spends wants and thousand dolours.
> The colors mixes fantazy—
> Only I pay for them—
> The receipt reads as: "poetry
> Is paid with martyrdom."

By October 1939 bureaucratic complications once again made emigrating seem a nightmare. "The first medical examination I missed, because my passport was not at time ready. And just as it was ready, the day before the second, I got your letters," she told Luchs. "It seemed light in darkness and a good sign," she explained. "But as I was at the Consulate I was told together with many others that everybody must have not only before his visas, even before his medical examination a booked ship ticket. . . ." To get such a ticket, she was told to wire a shipping company in Italy. "That

I did," she reported. But "tickets are only to be paid in dollars" and "it is here not possible to buy dollars."[31]

Luchs's law firm, however, was clearly used to such complications and immediately assumed the task of arranging her ticket. "We are attempting to get a booking on the *Vulcania* which sails from Trieste," Luchs now notified Fels (with copies sent to Goddard). "If the necessary preparations cannot be concluded in time, the next available sailing is the *Saturnia*," he reported. Fels agreed to take it from there. "I will arrange to have her met on arrival," he replied, ". . . and also see that she is taken care of for a month or two to give her an opportunity to find a position."[32]

By mid-October, Luchs, Fels, and Goddard were exchanging letters almost daily as they tried to complete arrangements.[33] Finally, Luchs had good news to report, for he included a copy of a letter that Selina had asked him to forward to Goddard.[34] Dated October 26, 1939, it too is worth quoting in its entirety:

Dear Sir:

With great joy and thankfullness I received the letter from the Italian line about the booking of the ship ticket and your wire. The letter came yesterday, your wire today. I have still to bring many things in order and if all goes well hope to sail with the *Saturnia* the 6th of December, arriving as very doubtful "Christmas gift" in U.S.A.

It was feared that the wires did not reach you. Many acquaintances of mine, in the same situation, got after few days answers. Don't be angry with me. I'll tell you once, what hard times we experience. Sometimes I am so tired of heart, soul and body, that I fear to loose my strength and never come to see you and your country. Please excuse me by your and my friends. With this ticket you gave me back the right of self-destination.

For ever to you all thanks and many kind regards.

Sincerely yours,
Selina Krenberger

This was the very last letter that I found from Selina Krenberger in the Goddard Papers. Thus, the correspondence apparently ends with Selina receiving the good news of the booking of a ship ticket and with her long-awaited arrival in the United States now within sight. Yet the absence of any letters from Selina once she arrived in America proved troubling. Of course, Selina Krenberger might simply have landed safely in the United States and written no more such letters—or at least not any that Goddard had preserved. On the other hand, her apparent silence might mean more. Perhaps she hadn't arrived after all, I began to think. Once again, here was an episode in Goddard's life that made both the man and his era seem all too real. And while this episode was clearly tangential to the main story on which I was focusing—Goddard's key role in the early history of American intelligence testing—I found it hard to ignore.

To determine the fate of Selina Krenberger, I first tried to find out if she had actually arrived on the Saturnia. I could do so by checking this ship's passenger list. Historical records of this type can be accessed through the National Archives; they are also available in the invaluable collections gathered by the Church of Jesus Christ of Latter-Day Saints (the Mormons) for genealogical research. At the Mormon Library in Los Angeles, I found the massive index that contains the names of all passengers who entered the port of New York by ship prior to 1945. Searching these lists, however, I could find no record of a Selina Krenberger entering the country.

Of course, such a finding was not in itself conclusive. After all, Selina Krenberger might have entered on another ship through another city, particularly since her plans had still been somewhat tentative. Or perhaps she had found some other way to escape Nazi Austria. To answer my own questions, I would have to look further.

Through contacts with the German consulate in Los Angeles, I learned that the best way to find out the fate of a wartime Jewish refugee would be to write to two agencies, the International Tracing Service of the Red Cross and the Israelitische Kultusgemeinde Wien (the Jewish community organization of Vienna). Writing to both, I included a copy of Selina's final letter (cited above) as well as one that showed her last known address. I also told both agencies that based on my research in the Mormon archives, I feared that she may never have arrived in the United States.[35]

The response from the Red Cross offered little immediate help. "As far as your request to receive information about Ms. Selina Krenberger is concerned," they wrote me in February 1997, "we wish to inform you that the International Tracing Service, for the reason of the protection of individual rights, is entitled to provide with information of the kind that you requested only the persons concerned themselves or their direct relatives."[36] They did institute a search to try to find any living relatives; however, since I feared that the entire Krenberger family might well have perished in the war, I held out little hope for information.

Fortunately, however, by this time I had already received an answer from the Israelitische Kultusgemeinde Wien. It too is worth quoting, for it is from this letter that I learned not only of Selina's fate, but also something of the history (and the first name) of her father.[37]

Dear Madam:

Acknowledging receipt of your letter dated April 23, we have to inform you that we have found this mentioned Miss Krenberger. As you suppose she really had not any good luck inspite of the existing affidavit.

Selina Rosalie Krenberger was born in 1893, Dec 13 in Wien. Her father was Salomon K., Dr. phil. (medical pedagogue) from Triesch in Moravia (now Czechia), her mother was Laura Paschkes. The parents married in 1891, May 17 in Wien. She stayed single. In 1941, Jan. 29 she deceased in a little Jewish hospital because of heart, liver, lungs and jaundice, it is to guess that she was ill already when arrived the attempt at rescue. She was buried at our cemetery and if you are interested in her death certificate you may demand it. . . .

We hope we could tell you what you wanted and remain

Israelitische Kultusgemeinde Wien

Department of records

(Mrs.) H. Weiss

Thus, due to the generous investigation conducted by the Viennese Jewish community in order to provide answers to my questions, I learned a few more pieces in the larger story of the Krenbergers. The apparently hopeful final letter found in the Goddard Papers actually offered a clue to a tragedy, for Selina Krenberger had never been able to escape Nazi Austria.

By 1941 this bright, determined, and talented woman—a woman who had come alive to me through her letters to Goddard—was dead. All the available correspondence had suggested a story with a happy ending; the real ending, however, was actually quite different.

Yet even with these answers in hand, questions still remained. Had Selina really been ill in 1939? Perhaps she had failed her medical inspection, thus ending any attempts to gain legal entrance to the United States. On the other hand, how much faith should any historian put in the causes listed on a death certificate prepared at a Jewish hospital under Nazi occupation in 1941? Was it possible that something else had befallen her? By this time, moreover, any delay would have greatly reduced her chances of ever escaping Nazi Europe.

Whatever questions lingered in my mind about Selina Krenberger's tragic fate, the episode once again told me something about Goddard. Then in his seventies, this psychologist had made a concerted effort to save his foreign colleague's daughter. For more than a year, he had offered her his advice and comfort. Far more important, by using his Jewish contacts, he had secured financial support for her in America and had acquired a law firm specializing in such subjects to handle the complex paperwork involved with wartime immigration, including producing the necessary affidavits and arranging her passage. In the end, all these efforts had failed. In fact, it is not even clear to me if Goddard himself ever knew what had ultimately happened to Selina Krenberger.

This story, which emerged from the archives, had captured my attention. Still, I realized that in a book focusing on "measuring minds," the heartbreaking story of the Krenbergers would have to be told in a very abbreviated way. Of course, on a deeper level, this story was both suggestive and ironic, for it raised the far larger subject of the Second World War itself, and this subject was crucial to any analysis of Goddard's legacy. After all, eugenic ideas had certainly found a welcome home within the Nazi movement; thus, while the Nazis had burned other books, they had reprinted a new 1933 edition of *Die Familie Kallikak*. In the wake of this war, the very connotation of the word "eugenics" would be forever changed in ways that would profoundly affect Goddard's reputation, his own antifascist views (or private actions) notwithstanding.[38] Yet in analyzing this legacy, I realized, I would have to consider not only the contexts in which Goddard's ideas had later been used by others but, more importantly, the contexts in which he himself had created and disseminated them. This meant focusing most of my book on Goddard's years at the Vineland school and on his influential work as the first American intelligence tester.

The item I found in the archives that would ultimately help me to shape the issues at the core of my book are cited in another entry listed in the partial inventory cited above—the one that states "Letter to 'Mr. Pastore' . . . in which Goddard replies to criticisms of his hereditary interpretations."[39] Here at last was an inventory entry that my secondary readings had prepared me to recognize.

Nicholas Pastore was a respected historian of psychology. He was the author of a highly influential 1949 monograph titled *The Nature-Nurture Controversy*. "The object of this study," his book explained, "is to investigate the relationship between the outlook of scientists on controversial nature-nurture problems and their attitudes toward social, political, and economic questions." Originally Pastore's dissertation, this research had been supervised by social psychologist Goodwin Watson. In the book's foreword, Watson argued that recent developments in the postwar world, including the growing influence of cultural anthropology, changing ideas about the significance of race, and the rise of Lysenkoism in the Soviet Union, all indicated that the nature-nurture debate was closely linked to contemporary political concerns. For Watson, this meant that the positions advocated by past participants probably reflected their politics as well, for "the question remains whether even these very superior men had learned how to free their research from the limitations of their social frame of reference." By focusing on the connections between scientific and political views, Pastore's text would become an early classic in the sociology of science.[40]

To document these connections, Pastore had prepared short summaries of the political views of twenty-four scientists most active in the nature-nurture debate, largely based on their writings. Apparently, to check his work, he had sent copies of his summaries to those still alive. The 1948 "letter to 'Mr. Pastore' " was evidently Goddard's attempt at an answer. Of course, it was hard to discern precisely what Goddard was answering, for

Pastore's initial letter to Goddard was missing. Serendipitously, however, I later found a critical clue in the Lewis Terman Papers at Stanford University, for this collection too contained a letter from Pastore and an answer from Terman written in 1948. Judging from the phrases used in Goddard's reply, it quickly became clear that Terman and Goddard were both answering the same letter.[41]

"I have prepared the first draft of a doctorate," Pastore's letter began, "dealing with the following question: 'Is there a relationship between the outlook of scientists on nature-nurture problems and their outlook on social, political, and economic issues?' (That is, does the hereditarian assume a conservative orientation and the environmentalist a liberal orientation?)"[42] Based on their publications, Pastore's initial summaries concluded that both Goddard and Terman were scientific hereditarians and political conservatives who would oppose most efforts at social amelioration.

Judging from their responses, however, these conclusions were deeply disturbing to both Goddard and Terman. While Terman was apparently willing to accept the term "hereditarian," he protested vigorously against being labeled a "conservative." His own political views, Terman replied in a detailed response, were decidedly left of center, for Terman had been a strong advocate of Roosevelt's New Deal, a supporter of the Spanish Republicans, an early opponent of European fascism, and an outspoken critic of McCarthyism. (Terman's reply was so adamant that Pastore reclassified him as a hereditarian "liberal"—one of only two exceptions to his overall argument.)[43] Goddard (who by then had also become an avid New Dealer, an antifascist, and an opponent of nuclear proliferation) was also troubled, but he struggled against both labels as descriptions of his work. "Had you been writing in 1910–1920 you would never have written that," he tried to explain to Pastore.[44]

For a historian, such documents were invaluable, for they allowed me to see how two prominent testers responded to what would largely become the dominant historical explanation of their writings in the postwar period. Of course, the fact that both objected so strongly to Pastore's interpretation certainly didn't mean that Pastore was wrong. After all, most psychologists of this era preferred to think of themselves as objective scientists. Most (then and now) would certainly have protested against a theory that linked their work to their politics—or worse, their prejudices. Even so, the vehement objections produced by Goddard and Terman and the arguments they mustered to support them proved provocative, particularly in light of what I was finding in both the published record and in Goddard's unpublished papers.

It was not that I failed to find science and politics (and prejudices) deeply intertwined in this literature. This very intertwining, however, called into question just what one meant by "hereditarian" or "environmentalist," or what distinguished a "liberal" from a "conservative," for the meanings of all these terms, I discovered, changed subtly from one decade to the next. A framework pitting conservative hereditarians against liberal environmentalists seemed particularly problematic for the decade prior to the First World War, when Goddard's work proved most influential. In this decade, Goddard certainly did prove to be, as I had expected, an outspoken proponent of the power of heredity and a promoter of the eugenics movement (although he later changed many of his views); yet unexpectedly, his earliest supporters and opponents did not seem to fall neatly on opposite sides of a single heredity-environment divide. This dichotomy proved equally unhelpful in explaining the wide range of issues being debated in the massive body of literature generated by the early testing movement—more than 700 articles published during this decade alone.[45]

In order to explain the diverse responses to Goddard's work that I was finding, I gradually realized that I would have to reconceptualize the testing debate. Instead of a single, two-sided debate, I came to see the earliest testing controversies as a series of debates taking place simultaneously within different communities. In addition to psychologists, participants also included members of the medical community, the educational community, the community of social and political reformers, and the community of religious activists. Such a framework allowed me to situate Goddard's work within multiple historical contexts; at the same time, however, it also required me to reconstruct each of these contexts by recovering the questions, issues, and answers that each of these groups found most compelling.

Reconstructing the medical debates of Goddard's day proved immediately fruitful, for this allowed me to understand not only Goddard's but also Alfred Binet's arguments in a new light. In his earliest articles on intelligence testing, Binet did not cite any of the psychological pioneers who are now most closely associated with the history of testing. Absent, for instance, is any mention of Francis Galton, Charles Spearman, James McKeen Cattell, or Edward Thorndike. Among those individuals Binet did cite specifically, however, were Edouard Seguin, Jean Esquirol, William Ireland, and D. M. Bourneville—in short, some of the most prominent doctors of France and Britain who had studied the medical condition then known as "mental deficiency." Fortunately, by working in the archival collections of the College of Physicians of Philadelphia, I was able to read many materials written by these doctors and thus to discern their answers to a controversial question perplexing the medical community of Goddard's day: what is a "feeble" mind?[46]

The medical literature of the pre-World War I decade, I found, was filled with discussions of heredity and environment. Such discussions, however, were not sharply polarized, largely because most physicians still held on to a Lamarckian understanding of what heredity meant, scientific proofs to the contrary notwithstanding. In particular, while most of these doctors repeatedly emphasized the power of heredity, they also believed that almost anything done by or to a pregnant woman could affect her child. For example, Dr. Martin Barr, the most prominent American medical expert on feeblemindedness in Goddard's day, ardently advocated sterilization to stop hereditary degeneration; in the very same article, however, this influential doctor also warned expectant mothers to avoid reading French naturalist novels, for they were filled with "frightful moral monstrosities" that might take their toll on an unborn child.[47] During this decade, many American institutional doctors began using Binet's tests; they did so, however, not because these tests told them anything particularly new about heredity, but because Goddard had convinced them that Binet's psychological tests could be useful in classifying different degrees of mental deficiency, whatever their cause.

In examining how these doctors worked, I also realized that data derived from testing could have different meanings if interpreted within different contexts. For instance, psychologists considered intelligence tests scientific precisely because they produced data that could be quantified. Psychiatrists, however, usually paid scant attention to quantification. Many even failed to determine a mental age when using Binet testing; instead, they often asked Binet's questions and simply took the answers into consideration when making what was still a subjective diagnosis. Moreover, such doctors had few qualms about dropping some of Binet's questions or inventing new ones whenever they wished. For example, Dr. E. H. Mullan, a physician employed by the United States Public Health Service, advised doctors to develop their "own made machine" in testing the mentality of patients. After examining 250 black prisoners, this doctor found that none could pass a Binet item written for eleven-year-olds: rearranging the words "A—defends—dog—good—his—master—bravely" into a sentence. Their failure, he hypothesized, was probably due to poor reading skills as well as "environmental conditions," for these men rarely used words such as "defends" or "bravely" in their daily lives. Such a finding, however, did not cause Dr. Mullan to label himself an "environmentalist" or to eschew testing. Instead, he simply rewrote Binet's question using new words: "Eggs—supper—boys—the—for—eat—and—bacon." This time, he reported, his results were "uniformly good." In this doctor's mind, he too was using Binet testing, and he too found it valuable.[48]

If the medical responses to intelligence testing defy a simple dichotomy linking acceptance to hereditarianism and rejection to environmentalism, a similar complexity is evident in the responses of the educational community. Here too both unpublished correspondence and published literature suggested a complicated interaction between psychological theories and educational practices. While many in the medical community tended to resist "objective" procedures as a threat to their professional prerogatives, many educators longed for them. Reliable measurement, they believed, held the hope of transforming pedagogy into a science. Yet teachers too raised provocative questions when it came to testing. Some criticized Binet, for instance, for paying too little attention to specific school skills, such as reading and writing. Others, by contrast, saw Binet's tests as too academic, for they placed far too much emphasis on the use of language. Marking the answers to Binet's questions as simply right or wrong, moreover, raised problems as well.[49]

Among the Binet questions measuring "abstract thinking" among twelve-year olds, for instance, were several asking for definitions of abstract concepts such as "justice," "goodness," or "charity." For older adolescents, Binet had focused on the differences between words with similar sounds, such as "event" and "prevent." According to teachers, the answers to such questions often reflected more linguistic complexity than they had anticipated. One student, for instance, defined justice as follows: "When a man does wrong, he is brought before a justice and asked why he did it and how he did it." Goodness, another wrote, "is when a man says 'Goodness! you're [*sic*] house is on fire.' " "Charity," one student replied, "is a place that begins at home." "An event is a circus," another child explained. "Prevent is to stop you from going to it." Questions about the relative importance of nature and nurture clearly played a role in these debates; so too, however, did other questions, including those concerning the types of aptitudes the school ought to be measuring, the role played by language acquisition, and the relative powers that teachers, doctors, and psychologists ought to exercise in determining classroom placements.[50]

Surprisingly, the model pitting conservative hereditarians against liberal environmentalists proved especially weak in explaining the reactions of reformers to Goddard's science in the decade preceding World War I. Here too, discussions of heredity and environment abounded; yet many activists involved with the most important reform movement of this decade, progressivism, saw no problem in paying attention to both factors. For instance, among the materials I found in the archives of the Children's Bureau, a new government agency headed by progressive reformer Julia Lathrop, was a seven-page speech on mental deficiency delivered to a Washington Jewish women's club in 1913. In its first three pages Lathrop offered a detailed recounting of Goddard's findings from *The Kallikak Family*. She followed this, however, by praising Maria Montessori's discoveries in advancing special education, psychiatrist William Healy's work with Chicago juvenile delinquents, and sociologist Katharine Bement Davis's efforts as head of the Reformatory for Women at Bedford Hills, New York. All were crucial advances, she suggested, in safeguarding the well-being of American children. Thus, Lathrop situated Goddard's work within a broad spectrum of progressive efforts that evidently blended hereditarian with environmental reforms.[51]

Perhaps the most overlooked context which helped explain much of Goddard's psychological science proved to be the religious. In going through Goddard's papers in Akron, I found a large number of items that concerned the Society of Friends (Quakers). There were letters from Goddard's mother, a Quaker missionary; lots of reminiscences about his days in Quaker boarding schools; catalogues from Quaker academies where Goddard had been a principal before he became a psychologist; and correspondence with persons who still used the words "thee" and "thou" (a Quaker practice) well into the twentieth century. There were also many cryptic references to "RMJ"—Rufus M. Jones, Goddard's former schoolmate who became a very prominent Quaker theologian and a founder of the American Friends Service. To understand Goddard's social and political views, these materials suggested, I would have to learn more about the history of the Quakers. I would also have to explore the ways that this religious community had reacted to the Darwinian debates of the late nineteenth century.

Such findings should not have been surprising, for this generation of psychologists clearly had been affected by the struggle to reconcile science with religion. After all, the psychological heroes of Goddard's day included William James, author of *Varieties of Religious Experience*, and G. Stanley Hall, author of *Jesus, the Christ, in the Light of Psychology*.[52] Even so, I was surprised, for the intelligence testing debate had never been framed as part of the larger religion/science debate. Yet the more I examined Goddard's papers alongside his writings, the more this framework came into view. The link between the two, I gradually realized, had little to do with the idea of mental measurement per se; instead, it involved the deeper relationship between the psychologist and those deemed needy—in this instance the institutionalized children at the Vineland school. I would have to explain Goddard's work within a context shaped not only by psychological innovations but also by older traditions of Quaker social activism and missionary paternalism.

Particularly striking in much of Goddard's psychology, I discovered, was its potent blend of modern science with Christian mission. Such a framework allowed me to see Goddard's most famous (and now infamous) work, *The Kallikak Family*, in a new context, for this study too blended new eugenic theories with traditional religious admonitions about the sins of the fathers being visited upon succeeding generations—a fact recognized and appreciated by contemporaries, if not by historians. As one 1913 reviewer noted, Goddard's book was simultaneously "the most convincing of the sociological studies brought out by the eugenics movement" as well as an "impressive lesson of the far-reaching and never-ending injury done to society by a single sin." Many reviews emphasized precisely this combination, which helps explain much of this book's early popularity.[53]

In fact, it was only by paying attention to Goddard's Quaker background that I was able to solve another piece of this puzzle: the meaning of the opening paragraph of Goddard's first professional paper on mental deficiency. Goddard had given this paper in 1907, after completing his first year at Vineland, to an organization made up largely of physicians then meeting in Philadelphia. Titled "Psychological Work Among the Feeble-Minded" (a title, I eventually realized, which itself had missionary overtones), it began with the following sentences: "Carlyle says that perhaps the most remarkable incident in modern history is George Fox's making for himself a pair of leather breeches. He finds in this outward act the expression of a mental resolution which was the beginning of religious freedom in England and in the world."[54]

While these opening lines were evidently understood by Goddard's audience, they were largely meaningless to modern ears (or at least to my ears). Nothing I read in the history of psychology helped me decipher them. I knew George Fox had been the founder of the Quakers, but to which "Carlyle" was Goddard referring? It was common practice in this era to use last names only in professional citations; thus, the name Carlyle might in fact refer to another psychologist, or possibly a physician, or perhaps another Quaker leader. How was I to identify him? And what did a pair of "leather breeches" have to do with religious freedom? More to the point, what did any of this have to do with Goddard's psychology?

It would be years before I would stumble upon the answer. In order to understand the religious context within which Goddard had been raised and which the Akron materials had led me to see as important, I had begun working in the library of Whittier College, a Los Angeles Quaker institution. There I came across a schoolbook describing famous episodes in

Quaker history. It included a story about George Fox's leather breeches and a reference to a famous quotation by the well-known Scottish historian Thomas Carlyle. This clue proved crucial, for I could now search Carlyle's writings to find out what Goddard was alluding to in his paper.[55]

I now also understood why Goddard had felt comfortable using such an allusion. Thomas Carlyle was one of the most widely read historians of the day. His acclaimed work, *Sartor Resartus,* included a stirring paean to George Fox. This passage had found its way into Quaker textbooks; it would thus surely have been familiar enough to an audience of Philadelphia doctors, many of them likely graduates of this city's numerous Friends schools (including Goddard's alma mater, Haverford College).

In particular, Carlyle had lauded the extraordinary courage of this seventeenth-century shoemaker turned charismatic preacher. To prepare for preaching outdoors in England's rainy weather, Fox had designed for himself a practical but unorthodox article of clothing—a pair of pants made from shoe leather. In so defying the stifling social conventions of the day, Carlyle saw Fox as doing something of tremendous significance.

"Perhaps the most remarkable incident in Modern History," Carlyle had written, "is not . . . the Battle of Austerlitz, Waterloo, Peterloo, or any other Battle; but an incident passed carelessly over by most Historians . . . namely George Fox's making to himself a suit of Leather." Fox, Carlyle continued, was "God-possessed," and his "shoe-shop, had men but known it, was a holier place than any Vatican. . . ." To Carlyle, this small act of independent thinking illustrated the "outflashing of man's Free will, to lighten more and more . . . the Chaotic Night that threatens to engulf him." Such incidents often seemed "the only grandeur there is in History." In this one small act of free thought, Carlyle wrote, Fox had become a prophet. Moreover, by the nineteenth century, many of Fox's followers had become the most outspoken opponents of the slave trade. "Stitch away, thou noble Fox," Carlyle had exclaimed, for "every prick of that little instrument is pricking into the heart of Slavery, and World worship . . . were the work done, there is in broad Europe one Free Man, and thou art he."[56]

Henry Herbert Goddard had chosen to begin his career as a psychologist studying mental deficiency by paraphrasing Carlyle. Apparently, he identified his own efforts to use psychological techniques in working with institutionalized children with Carlyle's account of Fox stitching his unusual outfit. Both, he implied, were unconventional acts that would ultimately free the mind of man. In his next few sentences, Goddard extended this Quaker allusion, for he again cited Fox's leather breeches as well as the "quakings" associated with his passionate preaching style. "Some one more familiar with the history of institutions for the feeble-minded, must locate the event which marked the beginning of the newer view of defectives," Goddard argued. "The leather breeches may be just completed, and not much preaching done and no quakings apparent," Goddard exclaimed, "but the movement is on." Much like a new religion, Goddard's metaphor implied, the "quakings" of a new psychology would soon be felt.[57]

Thus, by closely exploring Quaker materials, I had come to understand one of Goddard's psychological papers. Other explorations led to similar insights, particularly in documenting the responses of physicians, teachers, and social reformers to Goddard's work. These responses led me to reconsider the 1948 exchange between psychologist Henry Herbert Goddard and psychological historian Nicholas Pastore. Like Pastore and Goodwin Watson, I too had come to appreciate the enormous impact of extrascientific factors on psychological science. At the same time, I could also understand why Goddard had written to Pastore that his work was being interpreted out of context. Only by recreating a much richer context, or more precisely, a series of contexts, would it be possible to regain more of the meanings that contemporaries found in Goddard's writings. Only by moving beyond a two-sided debate pitting conservative hereditarians against liberal environmentalists could the complexities evident in the earliest testing controversies be recaptured. Goddard's papers had required me to search for new explanations in order to make sense out of what I was finding.

It is of course impossible to summarize all that I learned from reading Goddard's unpublished correspondence with Lowell Thomas, Selina Krenberger, Nicholas Pastore, and with hundreds of others whose letters, both important and unimportant, somehow found their way into his papers. Working with these materials led me to challenge many of the assumptions I had held when I first came to Akron. They also offered me an intangible feeling for a past world—a world that expressed its ideas, feelings, and fears in language subtly different from our own. Integrating these insights with those gained from reading Goddard's publications, I came to see this psychologist, the controversies generated by his work, and the era in which he lived in new ways.

It was Goddard's papers—with all their confusion, their richness, their incompleteness, and their suggestiveness—that led me to develop a more complicated multidimensional context in order to fit the pieces of this particular historical puzzle together. It was the Archives of the History of American Psychology that gave me the opportunity to reconstruct such a context by offering me a unique entrée into Goddard's world. And it was the determination, dedication, and vision of John Popplestone and Marion White McPherson that had made such an archive a reality. All those who share their deep interest in exploring the historical development of American psychology and in understanding the role that psychology came to play within American society are in their debt for the invaluable gift they have given us.

CHAPTER 6

Three Decades of Historical and Archival Research on Psychology and Religion

Hendrika Vande Kemp

I BECAME A FRIEND of the Archives of the History of American Psychology for two reasons—first, because of repeated personal encounters with John Popplestone and Marion White McPherson at regular meetings of Cheiron[1] and Division 26 of the American Psychological Association; second, because I've been helped in my various research projects by literally dozens of archivists, reference librarians, and curators of collections who took the time to answer focused research questions or to photocopy the signature page of a dissertation when I was engaged in tracing the intellectual roots of my faculty colleagues.[2] Popplestone and McPherson embody the archival spirit that dwells within the archival corners of libraries everywhere.

In his invitational letter to the participants in this volume, David Baker indicated that John Popplestone was "interested in process aspects of doing history, similar to much of the discussion in the summer 1999 issue of *The Journal of the History of the Behavioral Sciences*" (*JHBS*). In preparation for my presentation, I've immersed myself in the 1999 section of the *JHBS* focused on "Assessing Historical Research in the Behavioral and Social Sciences" and in the section of the 1975 issue of the *JHBS* focused on archival history, and I've revisited Ludy Benjamin's spirited account of his archival adventures.[3] In addition, I've reflected on my own career as a historian of psychology specializing in the psychology of religion and the interdisciplinary connections between psychology and theology/religious studies. I will address here four separate but interrelated processes manifested in my career as a historian of psychology: (1) choosing an area of specialization; (2) defining specific research topics; (3) describing the scholarly processes that are typical of my historical research; and (4) incorporating archival data into and involving archivists in my historical research. I will discuss the last two processes, which are of necessity interwoven, in tandem.

My interests in both religion and history took root during my undergraduate years at Hope College. I wrote a review paper on Milton Rokeach's *Dogmatism Scale* for my "Tests and Measurement" class,[4] and found myself immersed in the debates on religion and psychopathology that date back at least to the middle of the nineteenth century.[5] I chose to write about the University of Minnesota's Paul Everett Meehl when I had to write about a great psychologist for my "History and Systems of Psychology" class. I discovered that in addition to his outstanding contributions to learning theory, clinical psychology, and philosophical psychology, Meehl was also a Lutheran layman who addressed the integration of psychology and Lutheran theology.[6] Frustrated in my efforts to enroll in a scheduled course in the "Psychology of Religion," I participated in an independent study with the biblical and philosophical theologian Robert Palma, who assigned me to read Paul Tillich's *The Courage to Be,* a volume based on Tillich's Dwight Harrington Terry Lectures.[7] In my clinical work I frequently return to Tillich's discussion of the meaning of nonbeing and the related existential anxieties of fate and death, emptiness and meaninglessness, and guilt and condemnation, and I count this volume among the essential "classics in the integration of psychology and theology."[8]

For a world literature class, I pursued "the definition of the Greek concept of the soul and the modern concept of the self," and explored the historical connections between these concepts. This research provided background for my later publications on the relationship between soul and spirit as well as *psuchē* and soul, and equipped me to chair a dissertation on the place of the soul in western psychology. For my senior seminar paper, I wrote a survey of the American pastoral counseling movement, a literature review that undergirded several later research projects and inspired a seminar on "Historical Contributions to Pastoral Counseling."[9]

After I began graduate studies in clinical psychology at the University of Massachusetts/Amherst, I flirted with several other research interests before I chose to focus on religious issues. In my interview-based master's research I applied William Perry's framework for ethical and moral development in college students to their religious development.[10] This research awakened my postmodern consciousness: I gradually realized that Perry's stage theory—like the recapitulation theory of G. Stanley Hall before him, and various theorists of religious development who followed him—appeared to privilege as "more mature" that which is merely an alternative epistemology.[11]

I had my first taste of "archival" research in a graduate seminar on naturalistic research with the social psychologist J. William Dorris. For this research, I perused 507 college catalogs to see if they offered "courses in psychology *of, and,* or *in* religion, and/or courses in mysticism, religious experience, and phenomenology of religion." These data were used to help determine "if contemporary liberal arts curricula and courses in academic psychology reflect the spiritual trends of the 1970s . . . which implicitly unite religion and psychology in a concerted effort at their understanding."[12]

For my predissertation comprehensive project I wrote a lecture series on psychology and religion which I taught at the University of Massachusetts/ Amherst as an undergraduate senior seminar. I read many classics in psychology and religion, and developed an appreciation for the idiographic method, the notion of "state-dependent sciences," and Paul Pruyser's ego-psychological analysis of religion.[13] My dissertation originated in a desire to link my interest in religion with Howard Gadlin's inquiry into changes in identity formation in the nineteenth century. From this research I gained an increasing comprehension of steps involved in the historical emergence of the unconscious in psychological theory, the link between death and the unconscious, and the association between dreams and philosophy.[14] Under the direction of Gadlin and historian Barry F. O'Connell, I also gained extensive knowledge of historical research methods and of the resources necessary for research on the nineteenth century.

During my predoctoral internship year at Topeka State Hospital I participated in a seminar on theology and personality taught by Kenneth Mitchell and John Dillingham of the Menninger Foundation. The other participants were two clergymen and a clergywoman who were completing a year of clinical pastoral education at the foundation. Our reading list included Seward Hiltner's *Theological Dynamics,* and with this textbook as a model we learned a process of theological construction around practical issues of pastoral care.

These experiences prepared me well for my position at Fuller Theological Seminary, where I joined the faculty in the Graduate School of Psychology in order to teach "History and Systems of Psychology," the "Psychology of Religion," seminars in the integration of psychology and theology, and various clinical psychology courses.[15] Faced with the fact that my teaching would be in the liberal arts tradition of interdisciplinary scholarship, I chose to focus my historical interests on the psychology and religion movement so that my historical scholarship might inform my contributions to the ongoing integration of psychology and theology.

Like other historians of psychology, I've discovered that history resembles mystery.[16] Beginning with one small, tantalizing question or clue, the historical sleuth relentlessly pursues a trail of potential facts, undeterred by dozens of fruitless leads, rewarded by occasional confirmation of details that accumulate to build a case. Perhaps the most fruitful question of my early career as a historian arose from reading Franz Delitzsch's *A System of Biblical Psychology*, published in 1866. I soon ascertained that Delitzsch's footnotes were full of citations for books whose titles included the word "psychology." I confirmed that these citations had not been included in François Lapointe's historical articles, and subsequently unearthed numerous previously unreported uses which I documented in two short reports. My curiosity about the biblical psychologies as a genre led me to place an inquiry in the Division 26 newsletter.[17] This inquiry elicited no answers to my historical questions, but it did inspire Robert H. Wozniak to invite me to compile an annotated bibliography on psychology and religion in his series of *Bibliographies in the History of Psychology and Psychiatry.* As I studied the biblical psychologies in order to write annotations, I was surprised to find that many of the nineteenth-century authors distinguished between spirit and soul, regarding human nature as tripartite. This is an uncommon position in Christian theology, prone to lead the theologian into various heresies in the domain of Christology,[18] and I suspect that its prevalence during the late nineteenth century resulted from a need to save the spirit for the theologians after the "New Psychology" claimed the soul for its domain—a hypothesis that deserves further study.

Wozniak's invitation to work on the annotated bibliography was truly a boost to my scholarly career. The background research exposed me to one thousand integrative books, and I continually return to works encountered during that period of immersion in the historical literature. Historical curiosities and clues are scattered through the bibliography, which was published in 1984,[19] and they have inspired both my own research and student dissertations. One such clue was the publication, in the early 1950s, of a twenty-four-page booklet by the psychological phenomenologist Robert Brodie MacLeod on *Religious Perspectives of College Teaching in Experimental Psychology*. This authorship struck me as a curiosity, and I added MacLeod to the list of great psychologists who remained "unknown" as psychologists of religion.[20] I am still completing a book chapter on these psychologists, and my students and I have completed projects devoted to several of them. I have published articles or book chapters focused on the religious contributions of G. Stanley Hall (1824–1924),[21] Gordon Allport (1897–1967), Virginia Staudt Sexton (1916–97), and Alfred Adler (1870–1937).[22]

My doctoral students have also written dissertations on individuals contributing to the psychology of religion or the integration of psychology and theology. Three of these involved extensive archival research. Anne Coughlin explored the psychological contributions of the libertarian attorney Theodore Schroeder (1864–1953), who founded the Free Speech League in 1911 and later developed a complex theory on the erotogenesis of religion.[23] John Steigenga investigated the psychology of Henry Burton Sharman (1865–1963), a liberal New Testament theologian who founded the Student Christian Movement and developed the "Sharman method" for studying the life of Jesus as a means of learning to surrender the individual will to God.[24] David Johnson investigated the work of Fritz Künkel (1889–1965), whose We-psychology blended the theories of Freud, Jung, and Adler with existentialist and interpersonal ideas and a unique interpretation of Christianity.[25] As these projects progressed, various interconnections became clear to me. I discovered that MacLeod's booklet was a reprint of a 1952 book chapter which was a formal follow-up to Gordon Allport's previously completed study of religion in psychology textbooks published in 1948, both projects having been commissioned by the Edward W. Hazen Foundation. I also discovered that MacLeod had studied Sharman's *The Records of the Life of Jesus* at Camp Minnesing and that he taught informal seminars on *The Records* at Swarthmore College.[26] During the 1940s, Künkel and Elizabeth Boyden Howes (who later was a co-founder of the Guild for Psychological Studies) led many Sharman *Records* seminars at The Pines, a retreat center they established in the San Bernardino Mountains.[27]

Another set of curiosities was connected with two early journals. The first, *Psychotherapy: A Course of Reading in Sound Psychology, Sound Medicine and Sound Religion*, was published in 1908–9. At this time "psychotherapeutics or psychotherapy" was defined as "the treatment of disease mainly or wholly by direct and indirect appeal to or utilization of the influence of mental conditions upon bodily states." Allen Fleming wrote a dissertation on this journal.[28] The second, *The Journal of Psychotherapy as a Religious Process*, appeared in the reference section of one book I reviewed. Securing a copy of the journal, I embarked on an extensive research project described in detail below.

To investigate *The Journal of Psychotherapy as a Religious Process* I relied heavily on both personal and institutional archival materials. Photocopies of the *Journal* sat on my desk for several years as I wondered how to answer my many questions about its history and that of its publisher, the Institute of Rankian Psychoanalysis in Dayton, Ohio. I was intrigued by the title of Künkel's 1954 inaugural article on "The Integration of Religion and Psychology," and suspected that this constituted one of the earliest uses of the term "integration" for the interdisciplinary work of psychologists and religious scholars.[29] My research on the naturalization of the term "integration" was included in a 1996 book chapter on religion and clinical psychology.[30] I knew from a *Journal* footnote that the editor, the Rev. William Rickel, was a Harvard graduate, and eventually I remembered how useful the alumni records at Amherst College had been for a research project on the 1833 "phrenological lecture tour" of Amherst students Henry Ward Beecher and Orson S. Fowler.[31] The Harvard University Alumni Records

Office provided copies of Rickel's fifteenth, twentieth, twenty-fifth, and thirty-fifth anniversary reports, along with his current mailing address in France. I wrote to Rickel, who provided me with an original set of *Journals* (now shelved in McAlister Library at Fuller Theological Seminary) and his file of correspondence relating to its history. Rickel's personal archive contained 198 letters written to or by Rickel or his wife, Doris Mode, with seventy-five different correspondents.[32] Rickel's most extensive correspondence was with Künkel, and it was this correspondence that first aroused my interest in Künkel as a potential subject for more extensive research. I have published an overview of the *Journal* and am currently at work on an extensive book chapter.[33] Here, I will comment on some of the benefits I derived from access to Rickel's letters.

First, I was able to assess the extent of Rickel's network and to judge its adequacy through his professional correspondence. Rickel was in fact connected with most of the significant contributors to the dialogue on psychotheological integration, but the time had not yet arrived for a journal like this to succeed.[34]

Second, I uncovered several types of politics that affected the success of the institute and the *Journal*. The interpersonal psychotherapist Harry Bone took Mode to task for "using Dr. Rank's name for an enterprise whose outlook includes ideas to which he would never subscribe, and without the permission of his heirs." Bone also suggested that the group "eliminate the term Psychoanalysis from your title: it is a trade name with definite restrictions and you are in serious danger of serious inconvenience from the American Psychoanalytic Association."[35] The institute was, from the start, plagued by this "question of lay analysis." Rickel described himself variously as a "pastoral-analyst; i.e., Psychoanalyst with a basic religious orientation to psychology," a "psychoanalyst," a "lay psychoanalyst," and "a religiously oriented psychotherapist."[36] One might diagnose him as suffering from an identity crisis, but these various labels resulted from Rickel's efforts to deal with the controversy around lay analysis. In the mid-1940s Mode requested the Ohio Bell Telephone Company to open a new heading of "Psychoanalysts" in its yellow pages. On the advice of the American Medical Association, Ohio Bell denied her request, and Mode and Rickel— who were both actually clinical social workers—were listed as "psychologists." Rickel felt this listing was misleading, creating a false impression of staff credentials.[37] He also argued that psychoanalysis was "not exclusively a medical matter: for historically and currently, both in America and in Europe, there are many psychoanalysts in practice who are not physicians. . . . there is no law or legal reason to prevent our having a correct listing." The logic of Rickel's request appealed to officials of the L. M. Berry Company, which handled the directory advertising. Their representative indicated that, "we, after some discussion, are inclined to agree with your point of view." However, he had no choice but to defer to the judgment of Ohio Bell, whose response encapsulates the attitude of the psychiatric power structure: "The only directories using this heading are located in California. Psychologists whom we contacted agree that 'Psycho-analysis' was the function of a Psychiatrist." Letters in Rickel's files indicate that this position was also espoused by Seward Hiltner, who was at that time the foremost pastoral theologian in the United States and the editor of *Pastoral Psychology*. Künkel in fact regarded Hiltner as the most formidable opponent of lay analysis by clergy.[38]

Psychiatrists at the distinguished Menninger Foundation were more sympathetic to the lay analysts. The psychologist Rudolf Ekstein documented that the Menninger Foundation was permitting "some selected non-medical people training in therapy or analysis for work within a clinical setting." Karl Menninger privately supported Rickel's work. He wrote to Rickel in 1954: "I have read Volume I, Number 1, of your JOURNAL, and liked it, and actually commented on it in my privately circulated Reading Notes. I will be glad to send you these with the provision that you not reprint them or publish them in any way. I think this would do us both harm."[39]

Another interesting letter hints at the internal strife that occurred within the Vienna Working Circle for Depth Psychology, which included Viktor Frankl, the founder of logotherapy; Igor Caruso and his student Wilfried Daim, who both creatively blended personalism, existentialism, and psychoanalysis; the social psychologist Peter R. Hofstätter; and the pastoral theologian Albert Niedermeyer.[40] Daim and Caruso had both criticized Frankl in published *Journal* articles. Caruso felt that Frankl's logotherapy was a form of "spiritualistic propaganda." To Rickel he wrote: "Certainly the underlying concept of Dr. Viktor E. Frankl, that every psychical disturbance has a meaning, is right. But this insight is smothered by so many theological, anthropological and psychological misconceptions and errors and is stated with so much demagogic accessories, and moreover, the personal character of Dr. Frankl is so disagreeable, that I have vowed to myself since some time, not to enlarge the personal animosity against him and to speak and write about him as little, as there is possible."[41]

Caruso's comments on Frankl in his 1952 book were gracious, and he incorporated many of Frankl's ideas into his existential psychology, in which he argues that "analysis and synthesis are the two poles of every psychotherapy." Only Viennese "insiders" and those with access to archival correspondence would know about the tension in the relationship between these two innovative contributors to the understanding of psychotherapy as a religious process.[42]

I started my research on Robert Brodie MacLeod in 1984 by placing an inquiry regarding MacLeod's involvement with the Hazen Foundation in the *History of Psychology* newsletter. The only response to this inquiry was a discouraging letter from a psychologist who insinuated that to suggest that MacLeod "become involved in" religion implied "something shady." She did provide an address for MacLeod's widow, Beatrice, and I put my question to Mrs. MacLeod. Bea MacLeod knew nothing about the Hazen Foundation Project, but she informed me that as a student MacLeod "had been strongly influenced by Henry Burton Sharman, and through the years of his professorship at Swarthmore College he regularly held volunteer seminars which led scholarly-minded students through Sharman's 'Records of the Life of Jesus.' " She also wrote that MacLeod's "interest in religion was widely known through his membership in the 'Society for Religion in Higher Education.' "[43]

I had been rather thoroughly demoralized by the original response to my simple inquiry, and despite the leads provided by Mrs. MacLeod, I tabled the MacLeod project for nearly four years, until it occurred to me that Swarthmore graduates might be able to tell me something about the *Records* seminars. An inquiry in the *Swarthmore College Bulletin* in February 1988 turned out to be extremely productive and proved to me the worth of the archival records maintained by individuals. Six Swarthmore alumni responded to my inquiry, and they connected me to several more student seminar participants. Three of these persons were afflicted by the archival urge. John Nixon, a self-proclaimed "pack rat," confessed that he still had his handwritten notes from ten meetings of the MacLeod *Records* seminars during the winter and spring of 1935. Nixon, who now lived in Los Angeles, drove to my Pasadena office for an interview and lent me his notes so that I could make a transcript.[44] Mary McDermott Shideler participated in the Swarthmore seminars from 1935 through 1938 and also attended the Minnesing summer conferences in 1937, 1938, and 1942. Shideler couldn't sort through the boxes in her barn until the snow cleared, but she eventually provided me with copies of her typed notes on the Swarthmore and Minnesing seminars,[45] her correspondence with MacLeod and with Sharman, and MacLeod's correspondence with Sharman. Since 1988, Shideler and I have exchanged more than one hundred letters about MacLeod and the Christian writers Charles Williams and Dorothy Sayers; I've visited her at High Haven, her home in Boulder Heights, Colorado, for extended conversations; and she has provided me with copies of her books in which she pays tribute to MacLeod.[46] William Matchett, who led *Records* groups at Swarthmore in the late 1940s, provided me with a copy of a *Records Leader's Handbook* based on a three-week seminar sponsored by the Alpha Psi Zeta Foundation in 1946. That seminar took place at Pendle Hill, the Quaker conference center in Wallingford, Pennsylvania.

From information provided by Nixon, Shideler, and Matchett, and from letters from various other Swarthmore graduates, I now know that MacLeod led two *Records* groups, "one for beginners and the other for advanced students." MacLeod was apparently an amateur textual critic who enjoyed the challenge of the higher biblical criticism that had also appealed to G. Stanley Hall when Hall studied in Germany.[47] MacLeod indicated in a 1941 letter to Sharman that he never used *Jesus as Teacher: Student Edition* "as the basis for discussion . . . because my students have always found the task of untangling sources both exciting and rewarding."[48] MacLeod turned the seminar over to Harold March, a colleague in the Department of Romance Languages, to clear time for work with the National Defense Research Commission in late 1940. After MacLeod left Swarthmore for Cornell, occasional seminars continued into the early 1950s.[49]

It was gratifying to learn about MacLeod's connection with Sharman, but these discoveries brought me no closer to understanding why Mac-Leod, who had no standing as a psychologist of religion, would be chosen by the Hazen Foundation to write about *Religious Perspectives of College Teaching in Experimental Psychology.* I wrote to the Hazen Foundation in 1984 and 1987, but received no response. In 1989 I presented a paper on MacLeod at the annual convention of the American Psychological Association (APA). In a last-ditch effort to acquire information, I wrote to the Society for Values in Higher Education (SVHE), the organization that grew out of the Society for Religion in Higher Education (SRHE); again I received no response. I was distracted from this research for several years after suffering a head injury in a car accident,[50] but in the mid-1990s I attempted to prepare the MacLeod materials for publication. I wrote to the Danforth Foundation in 1995 and was told they had "not kept any systematic, categorized historical background data on its programs." In the meantime, Dorwin Cartwright had read my APA paper. Cartwright was convinced that the SRHE "played a larger role in [MacLeod's] development than [I had] been able to show." Cartwright was a member of what was in its early years the National Council on Religion in Higher Education (NCRHE), an institution founded in 1922 that "awarded fellowships to graduate students who were headed for a career in college teaching." Recipients of these Kent Fellowships automatically became members of the NCRHE, which lobbied "for the inclusion of religious experience as a proper subject in the curricula of our colleges and universities." Later, Danforth Fellows also automatically became members. I knew from Michael Wertheimer's MacLeod obituary that MacLeod had been a Kent Fellow. Ernest Hilgard also reported that, "When Rensis Likert was called upon to assemble a group to deal with civilian morale problems during World War II, he immediately selected a number of Kent Fellows to work with him—among them Cartwright, Hilgard, and Robert MacLeod."[51]

At this point, I had little doubt about the fact that MacLeod had been a Kent Fellow and a member of the NCRHE. The curious fact remained that MacLeod did not list the Kent fellowship on his vita, which some would account for by the fact that "in the 1920s and 1930s holding a Kent Fellowship and membership in the National Council on Religion in Higher

Education were one and the same thing." However, the professional activities section of MacLeod's published curriculum vitae included neither NCRHE nor SVHE. It is unlikely that the modest Kent Fellowship supported MacLeod's dissertation studies, as there is no mention of it (or of the NCRHE) in the foreword or vita included in his dissertation, a copy of which was provided by the archivist at Columbia University. The Cornell archives were no more useful, as the MacLeod collection at Cornell included only materials from the years after 1948. I decided to write one more letter to the SVHE, and this time I "hit pay dirt." Executive Director Kathleen McGrory verified that MacLeod was a 1928 Kent Fellow. She also sent materials that clarified the relationship between the SVHE and the Hazen Foundation: during the early years, NCRHE activities were funded "largely by New Haven's Edward W. Hazen Foundation, which also provided free office space from 1948 through 1972." NCRHE published proceedings of two sets of conferences related to religion and college teaching during this period. Between 1945 and 1948 several Faculty Consultations on Religion were sponsored by the American Council on Education, the Hazen Foundation, and the NCRHE. Between 1951 and 1962, numerous Conferences on Teaching Religion to Undergraduates were sponsored by the Hazen Foundation and the Danforth Foundation. MacLeod and his wife regularly attended NCRHE meetings in part because the society had a " 'social gospel emphasis,' "[52] and MacLeod must have emerged as a natural candidate to discuss ways to address religion in the teaching of psychology.

The MacLeod project has taken me on a fascinating journey. One lesson I learned in the process is that in many cases personal archival collections are of more value than are institutional archives. In the future I hope to benefit from MacLeod's journals, which his daughter Alison is now transcribing.[53]

My research on Gordon Allport represents a more traditional use of archival materials, although I broke tradition by not traveling to Harvard. Provided with a list of archival holdings and assisted by the onsite monitoring of Eugene Taylor, I hired a Harvard work study graduate student to locate, photocopy, and mail the relevant items for me, a strategy that suited both my budget and the demands of my clinical practice.[54] I perused many of Allport's unpublished manuscripts, portions of which were incorporated into his 1950 book, *The Individual and His Religion*. I was able to compare the manuscript and published versions of his book chapter on religion in college textbooks and his chapel sermons. And I studied two different manuscripts on *The Psychological Roots of Religion* that formed the basis for his later essay in *The Advent Papers* series published by Boston's Church of the Advent.[55]

The Allport project constituted a potent lesson on the difficulty in using archival materials for later publication. Notes in the archives suggest that Allport had the assistance of his wife, Alma, when he prepared the detailed and accurate reference lists that accompanied such published projects as the chapter on religion in textbooks. For his many guest lectures, Allport generally prepared complete typewritten texts. At best, these manuscripts included parenthetical names and dates, without complete references. At worst, these typescripts lacked all information about Allport's sources. His chapel sermons were filled with undocumented references to scripture, hymns, poetry, literary classics, credal statements, and the psychological literature. I will not discuss here the tedious process involved in tracing Allport's undocumented citations, but I do want to comment briefly on the challenge of determining whether plagiarism has occurred.

The question of plagiarism intruded into the Allport research in a totally unexpected fashion. I was fascinated by several ideas expressed by Allport in a wartime lecture given March 1, 1943, on "The Clergyman as Mind Raid Warden." Allport offered several techniques for arousing the conscience of parishioners. He recommended that clergy preach on a variety of relevant topics, such as scapegoating, race relations, the evil of war and Christian ideals, guilt, fear, death, participation in the war effort, trust of allies, and planning for peace. But I was most intrigued by Allport's psychology of hymns. Allport suggested that clergy use hymns to break down resistances and render persons receptive to the pastor's message. Allport also emphasized the "striking parallels between Christian hymns and Nazi *Parteilieder*—in spite of utterly different ideologies." Nazi songs about "dead heroes and saints" were matched by such Christian hymns as "For All the Saints, Who from Their Labors Rest." Allport asserted that America's "patriotic songs tend to be footballish. Church hymns come closer to the

American morale building songs." He suggested that clergy "use [hymns] widely and planfully."[56]

I decided I should place Allport's comments in the broader context of the psychology of religion and, more specifically, the psychology of hymns. I was also curious to see whether there existed at this time a psychology of hymns. Searching the PsycInfo database, I found four relevant articles, one of them by Roland L. Warren on "German *Parteilieder* and Christian Hymns as Instruments of Social Control," published in the *Journal of Abnormal and Social Psychology* early in 1943.[57] I was shocked to find that Allport's remarks in his talk to clergy were lifted, essentially word-for-word and without attribution, from Warren's article. Allport, as editor of the *Journal of Abnormal and Social Psychology* from 1937 to 1949, no doubt had access to a prepublication copy of Warren's manuscript. It is possible that Allport had written or oral permission from Warren to use the material. I have not inspected the archives relating to Allport's period as editor of the *Journal of Abnormal and Social Psychology* or searched the Allport archives for Warren correspondence; nor do I know what informal remarks prefaced Allport's formal presentation. Obviously there are a number of alternatives to my plagiarism hypothesis, and I would like to believe that Allport gave full credit to Warren. Yet the episode tarnished my image of Allport: with little extra time and effort he could have included Warren's name in the typescript and indicated that the work was recently published or currently in press.

In any case, the possible plagiarism was an aberration: Allport generally was guilty only of the sin of incomplete documentation, and my research in the Allport archives illustrates that archival records may, because of textual incompleteness or inaccuracy, require extensive followup research.

As I've reviewed the files related to various projects described here and several other historical research projects which are in progress, I am intensely aware of the fact that the research process is one that underlines our interpersonal interdependence and interconnectedness. I have exchanged hundreds of letters with librarians, archivists, church historians, fellow historians of psychology, and laypersons in order to obtain answers to my historical research questions. Rickel's file concerning *The Journal of Psychotherapy as a Religious Process* held nearly 200 letters; my file relating to this journal contains approximately 90 letters. My file on Künkel contains more than 50 letters. My file on MacLeod contains more than 150 letters. I have exchanged over 100 letters with Mary McDermott Shideler. The Allport file contains about 80 letters, many of them concerned with *The Advent Papers* series, about which I hope to write a future paper.

These many letters document not only interdependence, but also the many puzzles and curiosities that are part of the historical research process. After my papers are sent to the Archives of the History of American Psychology, a future generation of researchers will assess the adequacy of *my* networks, the thoroughness of my research methodology, and the significance of my contributions to the history of psychology and religion. And they will either thank or blame John Popplestone and Marion White McPherson for making it all possible.

CHAPTER 7

Whatever Happened to the Brass and Glass?

The Rise of Statistical "Instruments" in Psychology, 1900–1950

Ryan D. Tweney[1]

IN 1930, THE YEAR the C. H. Stoelting Co. of Chicago published what was to be the largest-ever catalog of psychological apparatus, there was virtually no use of inferential statistics in psychology, in spite of the fact that William Sealey Gosset had long since presented the *t* test and Sir Ronald Fisher had presented the general logic of null hypothesis testing. Only after Fisher's epochal introduction to analysis of variance procedures did psychologists even notice the procedure.[2]

By 1950, however, the use of null hypothesis testing was frequent in psychology journals, and nearly every graduate program in psychology was requiring training in analysis of variance and related methods.[3] Why was the shift so rapid, and what did the new techniques of statistical methodology replace? Answering this question requires attention to the cognitive nature of the "instruments" of statistics and their relation to more traditional kinds of instruments, as well as attention to the context of American psychological research before, during, and after World War II.

The present paper seeks to open inquiry into this issue, in part by using a "history of instruments" approach. John Popplestone and Marion White McPherson noted that "visuals," that is, photographs of people, documents, and apparatus, frequently tell a different story about psychology than the narrative text that is usually the sole source for the historian.[4] In the present context, treating statistical procedures as if they were "instruments" akin to the brass and glass sort allows deeper insight into the practices of psychology during a critical period.

Oddly, to present-day eyes, the use of inferential statistics did *not* replace the use of correlational statistics in psychology. Instead, correlational techniques, which were in use by psychologists almost from the establishment of the discipline in America, showed no change in their relative use in American psychological journals between 1935 and 1952. As Anthony Rucci and Ryan Tweney found in their survey of six American journals, the use of correlational techniques remained steady at around 30 percent of all journal articles; during the same period, the use of ANOVA increased from 0 percent to nearly 20 percent, and the use of the *t* test increased from 0 percent to 32 percent. Thus, the simplest possible explanation, that psychologists simply took advantage of a new statistical tool to substitute for a less adequate one, will not work, at least not if we restrict our attention to the now-standard claim that correlational techniques are "softer" than ANOVA techniques. Instead, I urge the claim that statistics replaced brass and glass, and that the shift had no effect on the use of correlational methods. In making this argument, I confirm a claim made by James Capshew, that interest in the specifics of laboratories and instruments declined after World War II, in spite of the continuing ideological strength of experimentation.[5] In fact, statistical analysis strengthened this ideology to a degree that instruments alone had not been able to do.

In the present paper, I first characterize the nature of instruments in general, drawing upon recent work in the history and philosophy of science and arguing for a parallel cognitive function of physical brass and glass devices and of statistical procedures. Next, I describe some aspects of the use of statistics and of other scientific instruments prior to World War II in America. I then attempt to understand the shift by which inferential statistics displaced brass and glass instruments as the primary "epistemic things"[6] used by American psychologists.

Instruments are crucial in all of modern science; the popular image of the scientist emphasizes a cluttered laboratory filled with bubbling flasks and sparking coils, and the reality of science is in fact dependent on a variety of sophisticated devices that extend the sensory and cognitive capacity of the investigator. Thus, as part of the recent emphasis upon the practices of science (not just its ideas), instruments as cognitive tools have begun to attract the attention of historians and philosophers of science. Psychology as a fledging discipline in the United States was similarly dependent upon instruments. Its earliest journals were filled with articles about instrument design and construction, while glowing reports of laboratory design and construction make clear the important iconic value of instruments and laboratories to a science trying to establish its credibility in an academic and public milieu.[7]

Interest in scientific instruments among historians of science had been limited until relatively recently, partly because of a tendency to avoid what is sometimes described as "antiquarianism," the mindless cataloging of devices without analysis of their functional role as aspects of material culture and without insight into their relationship to other cultural and social forces. However, some outstanding work has been (and continues to be) carried out in the form of museum catalogs and the like; at its best, such work forms an impressive body of documentation, rich in possibilities for further analysis.[8] Unfortunately, one difficulty in understanding the role of apparatus in psychology is the relative *absence* of such exhibition catalogs for psychology;[9] there is a need for more extensive description of collections of instruments, especially the very large one held by the Archives of the History of American Psychology. The present paper can perhaps serve to encourage further scholarship among historians of psychology in this regard.

Instruments serve many functions in science. They extend human sensory capacity (microscopes, for example, or, within psychology, apparatus for detecting galvanic skin response). They permit recording of observations (kymographs, say), and they enable measurement (meter sticks, reaction time apparatus). Beyond these direct and obvious functions as devices that aid *representation*, however, instruments also serve as a means of *intervention*.[10] Instruments can "stage" phenomena that otherwise are awkward to observe (cloud chambers, operant chambers), bring untidy phenomena under control (regulated power supplies, memory drums), or even create the phenomena themselves by bringing about events that would not occur except for the actions of apparatus (cyclotrons, or the many illusions that fill psychological texts). And, in a function that is the focus of this paper, instruments can *make inferences*. In the physical sciences (even aside from the increasing use of computers to intelligently explore data sets), we can see this in the myriad demonstration devices used to make phenomena clear to others and in automated "discovery" systems. In psychology, we can see the making of inferences from data as the principal instrumental use of statistical procedures. Whether we regard instruments as "epistemic things," following Hans-Jörg Rheinberger, or as "inscriptions," following Bruno Latour,[11] we can easily regard statistical procedures and brass and glass as parallel "devices."

Instruments in this broader sense (broader, in that I include statistical procedures) suggest a comparison with the use of figures and tables in psychology. The most obvious difference, given the list of functions above, might seem to be that figures do not normally permit intervention; instead, they serve as merely representational devices. From a cognitive point of view, however, this is too simple, since figures can and do manifest properties that permit users to manipulate information. Serving as a prime example are such computational devices as nomographs, figures that can be used to perform calculations explicitly, say by holding a straight edge in position along the axis of a chart and reading off the answer closest to the edge crossing of an index line. In the precomputer age, these were common in engineering, and some were developed specifically for psychology.[12] More generally, viewing a figure is an active process that may require fairly sophisticated thinking—as anyone can attest who has tried to teach undergraduates to recognize the presence of an interaction by visually noting the relative parallelism of two line graphs on a common scale. In fact, much of the debate about the role of graphical methods in presenting information centers on the ease with which such "computational extension" is possible for a given graphic representation. Jiajie Zhang has constructed a taxonomy of graphical representations based on the extent to which aspects of the representation cue internal representations, as opposed to being present externally in the graphic (and hence available perceptually). He argued that the best graphics are those that present all of the implicit scale information in the representation, while the worst graphics are those that present more information in the graphic than is implied by the scale being represented (for example, using bars of differing length to represent nominal variables).[13]

Suggesting that an instrument (or a statistical procedure) is an epistemic thing is consistent with recent cognitive psychological views that cognition can be understood by characterizing the computations carried out upon specified representations, a position advanced by Herbert Simon and well articulated by the late David Marr.[14] This approach can be extended to include both *external cognition* (manifested in instruments) as well as *internal cognition*. The external device can serve as a means of providing successive representations (as with a kymograph), or it can subsume some of the computational manipulation of those representations (a cumulative recorder, say, which provides a record that would otherwise require a long and tedious series of summing and plotting operations).

Things can "make us smart," to use Donald Norman's phrase. In a series of papers, Zhang and Norman argued that an external representation can change the kinds of computation that a human thinker uses in solving a problem; in effect, the external representation does some of the thinking.[15] In the Roman numeration system, for example, addition is much simpler than in the Arabic numeration system. To add two Roman numbers, one simply concatenates all the symbols of both and employs a handful of concatenation, reordering, and recoding rules to simplify the result: VII + V = VIIV (by concatenation) = VVII (rearranging) = XII (recoding). There is less to learn than with the Arabic system, which requires a much larger memorized addition table. For multiplication, however, the advantage is reversed; Arabic multiplication is much simpler because there is a natural way to reduce the labor involved in combining across the differing powers of the base. (Try multiplying XX by XL, to see how complex the Roman system makes this operation!) The Roman system externalizes the hardest parts of addition, whereas the Arabic system externalizes the hardest parts of multiplication.

From this point of view, the notion of "representational determinism" easily applies to scientific devices such as instruments, graphics, and statistical tools. In an examination of the physicist Michael Faraday's experiments in acoustics, I was able to show how similar considerations account for some of his strategies of experimentation. In trying to determine the dynamics that underlie the regular patterns induced on the surface of a vibrating fluid (as when "crispations" are generated on a glass of water by tapping the rim of the glass), Faraday had to deal with the need to detect and represent rapidly moving events that were "smudged" by the human visual system. Thus, the first step was to conduct experiments on the movement illusions generated by repetitive sequences, exemplified by the "false spokes" seen when two carriage wheels are turning rapidly in front of each other. By constructing apparatus to manipulate these phenomena, he developed a dynamic account of the illusory appearances, then used the account to construct models of what might be causing the appearances of the vibrating fluids. For example, in an elegantly simple experiment, he took a piece of tin, "dimpled" it with a punch, then explored its visual appearance under different lighting conditions, thus confirming what he had inferred about the changing appearances of vibrating fluid surfaces. Faraday's papers on this work provide many similar examples of devices constructed specifically to serve as representations of phenomena in the cognitive-perceptual domain and in the physical domain. These then allowed him to distinguish between "observer dynamics" and "physical dynamics." Across both papers, we can track the development of his thought from perceptions, through "inceptions" (perceptual-like internal cognitions that serve as semi-abstract test beds for his theories), to the final construction of publicly disseminated mental models and their physical realizations. In this instance, we can watch Faraday's transition from externally perceived phenomena, through internally manifested models, returning finally to the construction of external representations (apparatus). Of course, the externalization of representation was concrete and immediately present to Faraday; his intended audience of other scientists had to rely upon yet another externalized representation, namely, his translation of the results into a published or spoken record. In other instances, Faraday externalized his thinking in the form of theoretical claims, rather than apparatus; here, members of his audience had to rely upon the published or spoken record to reconstruct their own internal representations.[16]

The representational functions of instruments have sometimes been accorded a revolutionary role in science. Galileo's use of the telescope to confirm Copernican accounts of the solar system is perhaps the most famous example. Some historians of science have argued that the explosive growth of physiology at the end of the nineteenth century was in large part based upon the extensions made possible by the "graphic method" of Etienne Jules Marey and others, that is, by devices like the kymograph that produced records of changing events that were either too slow or too fast to perceive directly.[17] In this instance, externalizing the temporal phenomena of physiology was seen as the touchstone of a discipline that quickly institutionalized its success.

Instruments were important from the earliest days of "physiological psychology" in Germany and, by the time of the "great migration" of young Americans to obtain their education in European laboratories, had an established place at the center of the new discipline. In fact, physiology's success in America played an important role in the decision by early American psychologists to deploy instruments and laboratories (many of them modeled after those of their physiological counterparts) as the primary step in establishing the credibility of the new science. The function of externalized cognition transcended the immediate scientific function of sharing and persuading an audience of other scientists. Instead, the objective of achieving other social interests and purposes became paramount: encouraging funding, establishing status, and defining standards for comparison with other disciplines.[18]

The precise measurement of time was especially important to early experimental psychologists. However, obtaining precision in this domain was a problematic issue requiring extensive "negotiation" over construction of apparatus, procedure, and calibration. For example, reaction time measurement was central to Wilhelm Wundt's program of research, not surprisingly, for one who spent much of his early professional career in Hermann Helmholtz's laboratory in Berlin.[19] Wundt's earliest contributions to science were actually in experimental physiology, and he is still cited for his studies of the electrical stimulation of nerve and muscle preparations. His close acquaintance with apparatus is indicated by, for example, his detailed description of Helmholtz's myograph in Wundt's massive *Lehrbuch der Physiologie des Menschen* published in 1865, studies which used a kymograph designed by Carl Ludwig.

Wundt's involvement with apparatus was passed on to many of his students. James McKeen Cattell, for instance, while still a student at Leipzig, claimed to have found and corrected an error in Wundt's use of Hipp chronoscopes. Wundt had assumed that the onset (or offset) of a current resulted in the instantaneous generation (or instantaneous collapse) of a magnetic field. In fact, there is a "rise time" and a "decay time," both of which need to be corrected for in order to obtain accurate measurements.[20] Michael Sokal gave an account of this episode, noting that Cattell later softened his early (exaggerated) claim about the deficiency of Wundt's apparatus. It is unlikely that Wundt himself was deficient in understanding either the physics involved or the complexity of calibration required (as Cattell had hinted), since he had earlier written a fairly substantive text on medical physics, a work which contained a sophisticated discussion of electromagnetic induction (without, however, noting the temporal properties of the phenomena). Further, Wundt himself was the designer of a control apparatus which came to be accepted as a necessary adjunct for any laboratory using a Hipp chronoscope.[21]

Ernest Hilgard suggested that part of the reason Wundt's influence declined in the United States may have been a growing gap during the early twentieth century between the apparatus used for teaching and lecture demonstrations on the one hand, and that used for research on the other. Brass and glass with a Leipzig flavor dominated the instructional side of psychology long after the research apparatus had moved on to newer (perhaps less dramatic) instruments. Even today, it is not unusual to find apparatus that is essentially a century and a half old used in the undergraduate teaching laboratory, even though it has been a long time since pursuit rotors, say, were actively part of any research program in psychology! More to the point, while early psychology had its proponents of a Leipzig-like precision in experimentation (most notably, Edward Scripture and Edward Bradford Titchener), for most American psychologists, the need for precision seems to have declined after 1900—even to the point of being actively disdained by some, such as Hugo Münsterberg, who argued that mental states could not be "measured" in the same sense as physical or physiological variables.[22]

Early American laboratory texts often contained suggestions to instructors for the apparatus needed for the teaching of psychology, and almost all of the apparatus recommended in these texts was directed at measuring and demonstrating perceptual phenomena. Only some of which was originally intended exclusively for psychological research and teaching. For example, tuning forks were almost always included, but they were a staple of the physiological laboratory as well. Even so, a large variety of other apparatus, reaction time instruments, say, were unique to psychology, and many of these carried the name of their developer: "Wundt's Demonstration Chronometer," "Mueller's Memory Apparatus," "Ewald's Reaction key," and the like. Further, attention to the limited budgets of instructors in a new field often meant that the expensive commercial instruments would be modified to permit a cheap, home-built, apparatus instead. In this sense, accounts like those of Edmund Sanford's manifest a "wood and nail" approach to instrumentation![23]

At least in the elementary texts (and perhaps partly because of cost), the kind of dynamic instruments that were so central to the physiology laboratory were absent; instead, the beginning student was usually introduced to static "one shot" measurements of single-stimulus performances. In fact, dynamic instruments (such as kymographs) were commonly used only as research instruments in the study of human movement and of the emotions, rather than of sensation, perception, or the cognitive processes. Initially, both sensory processes and motor processes were of equal concern to physiology as well as psychology. Indeed, the young Titchener, as an undergraduate student of the great English physiologist J. S. Burdon-Sanderson, was first exposed to Wundt's work in Burdon-Sanderson's lab, later moving to Leipzig for his doctoral work.[24] Even so, physiology remained much more oriented toward the temporal dynamics of both motor and sensory processes than did psychology.

The influence of the physiology laboratory as a model for psychology was reflected in many aspects of the incorporation of instruments into psychology. Thus, the C. H. Stoelting Co. of Chicago began its existence as a purveyor of primarily physiological apparatus. As early as 1895, Christian Hans Stoelting himself supplied apparatus specifically tailored to prominent psychological laboratories, such as Titchener's at Cornell, Joseph Jastrow's at Wisconsin, and Scripture's at Yale. Further, physiology had been Stoelting's first major market (the firm had earlier been known as the "Chicago Laboratory Supply and Scale Company"). When the firm was incorporated in 1903 under the Stoelting name, its catalogs and lists almost invariably referred to its stock as offering "Psychology *and Physiology* apparatus."[25] Indeed, browsing through these catalogs still suggests that much of the equipment was indistinguishable from that used by the physiologists as late as 1937.

The advent of behaviorism put a special premium on the study of human and animal movement, and this was reflected in yet further instrumentation unique to psychology (for example, the animal learning maze). An unusual example can be found in the attempt of one of John B. Watson's associates, Anna Wyczoikowska, to measure tongue movements while subjects were asked to "*think* of a word or sentence." For this study, a "flattened wine glass as a receiver" was connected to a Marey tambour fitted with a pen, and a kymograph was used to record the movements. Little description of the apparatus was given in the article, although a manual of psychological apparatus published by Charles H. Judd in 1907 gives an extensive description of such equipment and its use; presumably Wyczoikowska was using similar devices. However good the apparatus may have been, the study was actually a rather poorly conducted one, since little attempt was made to control the many obvious potentially confounding factors. Thus, in spite of its optimistic conclusion that subvocal movements were detectable during "thought" (a conclusion which confirmed Watson's hypothesis about the behavioral nature of thinking processes), one cannot conclude much of anything from the study. Watson discussed the study in his 1914 book, but concluded that tongue movements are not the definitive test; instead "we need to get some direct way of observing the vocal cords, throat formations, etc. It will be extremely difficult to get evidence either for or against the present theory." In spite of its inadequacies, Watson included five graphs from Wyczoikowska's study, each a kymograph tracing of tongue movement during the task. Even so, Watson's later books make no reference to the study, nor do his later statements of the tongue movement theory.[26]

The growth of psychology's instruments in the traditional sense (optical, mechanical, or electrical devices) was paralleled, of course, by the emergence and growth of paper and pencil instruments, particularly intelligence tests. These included the Army Alpha and Beta, as well as the huge variety of tests described in Guy Montrose Whipple's influential manuals. Given the generality of our claim—that instruments are epistemic things—such tests must also be considered instruments. While a complete treatment is beyond the scope of this chapter, it is worth noting that paper and pencil tests, superficially quite unlike the brass and glass instruments of the laboratory, were eagerly adopted by many of the "clients" of psychology, particularly in education, engineering, and management.[27] For many psychologists, they thus served as a distinguishing characteristic of the new science of psychology. Further, their use was *not* affected by the introduction of statistical methods during World War II, making for an interesting possible comparison to the brass and glass instruments. For the present purpose, we need only note that statistical significance testing did not displace tests.

The instrument cabinet of psychology filled quickly before World War II, as did the test cabinet, and in the early years the proudly displayed gleaming devices were frequently invoked to warrant psychology's status as a science. Tests do not "display" so well, but they too were invoked, giving psychology a unique hold on the prediction and control of human behavior, an aspect that endeared them to many.[28] Both were included in the Stoelting Co.'s "Great Catalog" of 1930, which offered thousands of each kind, many with extensive descriptions of their use. The range of devices in the catalog makes clear the overall "landscape" of psychology's reliance upon brass and glass, as well as paper and pencil tests, and of apparatus appropriated from other fields. When Stoelting's catalog appeared in 1930, then, the place of the instrument was secure; even in 1937, when Stoelting published a shorter "Supplement" in lieu of a promised new edition of the full catalog, the reason was "merely" economic: the Depression had affected the psychology market, but there was no hint that the impetus for instrumentation had lessened (whether tests or physical devices). What happened during the 1940s that led to the sudden emergence of statistical tests and the consequent decline of the brass and glass side of psychology's instrumental base? Answering this question demands some attention to the history of statistics.

Statistical analysis was an important part of even the earliest endeavors of scientific psychology in the nineteenth century. Gustav Fechner, for example, relied upon statistical concepts to characterize variability in his seminal work on psychophysics, as did Charles Sanders Peirce and Joseph Jastrow in what, incidentally, is probably the first psychology experiment published in the United States, and, as Stephen Stigler notes, perhaps the first use of a blind randomized experimental procedure. Most such psychological uses of statistical methods relied heavily upon methods derived from the physical sciences and were used to characterize the error of a set of observations, most often from repeated measurements on a single individual. Such "physics-like" research continued in psychology for some time, reflecting a concern with the systematic error—the accuracy—of each piece of equipment or of each measurement procedure. Less attention was paid to random error, that is, to the precision of a procedure or instrument. In effect, the major concern was whether or not the indicated mean values were close to the true values, rather than whether the spread of measurements around a mean was large or small.[29]

At times, the variation in measures of a single individual was itself the object of interest and was not dismissed as "error." For example, George S. Fullerton and Cattell attempted to rethink the basis of psychophysical determinations of the threshold of sensation.[30] They argued that instead of looking for *the* threshold, a statistical definition of the detection of low intensity stimuli should be adopted, in effect treating variability as an inherent property of sensation. Their claim that the "error" in detection varied in proportion to the square root of the stimulus intensity is one of the earliest attempts to incorporate intraindividual variation within the province of psychological law.

In what Kurt Danziger has characterized as the "Galtonian" tradition,[31] statistical analysis was also prominent, but the emphasis was upon the measurement of interindividual differences. The initial focus was upon variation, a key concept for the post-Darwinian functional approach of the Galtonians. Yet, within psychology (as within eugenics) interest in variation was soon displaced by interest in the mean value, or central tendency, a change that Danziger attributed to increasing bureaucratic pressure to characterize aggregates of people (as in school systems). Early in the twentieth century, the use of descriptive statistical techniques thus spread rapidly in educational psychology, generating texts written specifically for that market.[32]

The dominant psychological use of statistics in the United States reflected a statistics "without *p* values". Such statistical applications were closely related to those prominent among sociological and economic users of statistics.[33] Significance testing, as such, was not used in psychology prior to the adoption of Fisher's approach,[34] which happened quickly after the publication of his 1935 book. Nonetheless, precursors to significance testing did exist, the most common being use of the "critical ratio" for comparing two means, defined as the difference between the means divided by the "standard deviation." The latter sometimes represented a *pooled* value across the two groups, although with N instead of N-1 in the denominator.[35]

Correlational statistics were heavily used during World War I, the U. S. Army mental testing effort led by Robert M. Yerkes producing some of the largest data sets ever gathered in the name of psychology! Mental testing of this scope depended upon statistical analysis of the results, and the statistics used—Pearsonian "large N" analyses—were an essential part of the endeavor. In fact, brass and glass proved notoriously poor in the realm of mental assessment, as Cattell found to his chagrin. Contrary to his expectations, the results of various traditional laboratory measures of performance (reaction time, sensory span, thresholds, etc.), failed to show any statistical correlation with measures of school performance.[36] Despite Cattell's disappointment, however, and the emergence of mental tests as instruments of a different character than the traditional brass and glass, the use of brass and glass did not appear to decline after World War I; instruments much like those used in physiology continued to be important, especially to experimental psychologists. That would soon change.

The demands of war research in World War II exposed many psychologists to new problems, new techniques, and a need to face the limitations of accepted psychological methods. In contrast to the first war, there was much less of the huge "measure everyone" emphasis that characterized the Yerkes-led mental testing project of World War I. Instead, a large variety of projects used the research abilities of psychologists, often in collaboration with scientists from other disciplines. War research also affected the nature of statistical analysis itself, and, in fact, provided an opportunity for statisticians to establish their autonomy as a distinct profession. Many of the common uses of statistical inference that characterized postwar use by psychologists were being extended by statisticians and mathematicians during the war. Thus, Jerzy Neyman led a research group at Berkeley which studied bombing and fire control, sequential analysis was developed by Abraham Wald and others, and W. Edwards Deming and his associates were extending quality control statistics. More to the point, significance testing began to find its way into the specific applications upon which psychologists were working. At the time, the use of statistics of the Fisherian sort was not entirely new to psychologists. Rucci and Tweney found seventeen articles in psychology journals that used ANOVA between 1934 and 1939, although most of the applications were, as A. D. Lovie noted, rather unimpressive.[37] Yet the wartime experiences of psychologists drove home the utility of these procedures, led to many more psychologists learning the new procedures, and provided paradigmatic exemplars of their use.

Under the leadership of John C. Flanagan, the experiences of the Army Air Forces Aviation Psychology Program are illuminating. Founded in 1941, the program eventually included hundreds of psychologists whose work was carried out to develop and extend personnel training and assessment programs. In one of the largest reports to result, J. P. Guilford summarized the research on printed classification tests developed and used during the war. A separate chapter by Lloyd G. Humphreys used and defended factor analysis. The report mentions significance testing only incidentally, in several footnotes, although several tabular presentations of data give the probable error! The body of the report sometimes included the significance of validity coefficients, but, again, only incidentally, and without discussion.[38]

A somewhat more "modern" appearance is suggested by the approaches adopted by a team of psychologists headed by Arthur W. Melton at the School of Aviation Medicine in San Antonio beginning in 1941.[39] Tasked with developing psychomotor tests for the selection of pilots, bombardiers, and gunners, Melton and his colleagues, like Guilford and his colleagues, adopted a "classical" test theory approach based upon the assessment of the reliability and validity of pursuit rotor tasks, specially developed eye-hand coordination tasks, and the like. However, one senses that they were unwittingly drawn into what had become an unusual domain for a psychologist, namely, assessing the *constant error* that could underlie a given test administration. This factor loomed large because the need for multiple copies of the test apparatus administered at widely separated testing bases forced them to pay primary attention to the constancy of the physical apparatus and its manufacture; there is a hint here that the old error-assessment procedures of physics, once prominent in psychology, were beginning to resurface.

Statistically, Melton's group relied upon traditional psychometric devices, centering on correlational methods and factor analysis, but they also used some informal significance testing (e.g., results that varied by more than one standard deviation from the mean were occasionally referred to as "significant"). Still, for the most part, the analyses could be construed as "Galtonian" and were in full accord with those recommended by Guilford.[40] A similar comment can be made about Neal Miller's report on the use of psychological tests to assess pilot potential and pilot training programs. Again, the report presents much statistical analysis, nearly all of it consistent with prewar psychometric assessment approaches, but "significance tests" also appeared in scattered contexts. And the glossary appended to Miller's report defined the term "statistical significance," along with "standard deviation" and "correlation coefficient." In the text itself, both critical ratio tests and the analysis of variance sometimes made an appearance, but sporadically and without explanation in either case.[41] Clearly, we are looking at a transitional stage, in which significance testing was beginning to appear but was still being applied inconsistently and was still unusual enough to call for some explanation.

A more principled use of both physicalistic statistical procedures and post-Fisherian statistical testing is manifested in the report prepared by Paul Fitts in 1947, describing the psychological research carried out at Wright Field on the design of equipment. In his introduction, Fitts was explicit about the role of significance testing in the program he directed: "Experimental psychologists will agree that much of the research in psychology has been concerned with establishing qualitative differences. The most commonly used statistics in psychology are those employed in testing the null hypothesis. In the field of equipment design, however, it is usually not sufficient to be able to say that one design is preferable to another or that a statistically significant difference exists between two alternative designs. Most engineering problems require the expression of psychological findings in quantitative terms and the determination of functional relationships over a wide range of conditions." Indeed, the report reveals many uses of significance tests (no critical ratios!) and even more graphs showing quantitative relationships. In fact, although one of the shortest reports in the series, Fitts's is also one of the most heavily illustrated, suggesting confirmation of the claim that relative "hardness" of a scientific field is positively correlated with the use of graphs depicting data.[42] Of course, Fitts's claim that null hypothesis tests were the "most commonly used" is, as we have seen, simply not true for this period.

Flanagan's 1948 summary of the entire program contains a revealing section on statistical analysis. In general, Flanagan was more consistent than either Melton or Miller in reporting significant differences where those seem relevant to a psychologist today. Still, in a section on the implications of war research for general issues in experimentation, his focus was mainly on correlational methods and the ways in which they could be improved, for instance, by careful attention to suppressor variables in the interpretation of regression coefficients. Most interesting in the present context, however, are Flanagan's comments on experimental design: "A common fallacy in interpreting experimental findings is to assume that failure to eliminate one hypothesis in a particular situation means that this hypothesis must be accepted as being true."[43] He noted that this could lead to the premature rejection of studies that detected only small effects, even when those small effects were replicable. While Flanagan did not directly mention significance testing in this passage, it is clear that he was referring to the dangers of placing too much trust in significance tests, particularly those that are nonsignificant. Clearly, the Fisherian logic of hypothesis testing, suitably modified by what sounds like a "hybrid model" concern for Type I and Type II error, was spreading among psychologists engaged in the war effort.[44]

Psychiatrists were also extensively involved in military research and professional projects during the war, and it is interesting to note the absence of quantitative and statistical methods in the reports prepared by psychiatrists, in contrast to reports by psychologists such as those noted above. In one notable project, a group of psychiatrists assessed the impact of the very dangerous bombing raids carried out by the Eighth Air Force during its first operational year—raids so dangerous that only 10 percent of the air crews survived a normal fifty mission tour of duty.[45] The psychiatrists conducted extensive interviews and surveys of crew and officers. Their report gives only the most primitive tabular summaries of data, and the survey questions used betray a complete lack of statistical or psychometric awareness. This is not to suggest that the work was in any sense lacking in value, nor that the participating psychiatrists were shirking the task! Most notably, one psychiatrist, "D. G. W." (presumably David G. Wright, one of the authors) flew along on several missions to observe directly the behavior of a crew under stress. On one harrowing raid, the plane was repeatedly hit by enemy fire and barely made its return to base. Wright's cool observations of the crew's behavior give new meaning to the term "grace under fire"!

Some of the most influential activities of psychologists were directed at questions that, while directly relevant to military applications, were close to basic research concerns as well; it is these efforts that most directly involved psychologists in the new statistical methods. During the war, experimental psychologists sometimes worked closely with physical scientists, and some of their major achievements depended upon "physicalistic" mathematical techniques. The highly secret and highly productive "Psycho-Acoustic Laboratory" at Harvard exemplifies one such program. Founded in 1940 under the sponsorship of the Office of Naval Research, scientists here carried out studies on the reception and transmission of acoustic signals under varying conditions of noise, in an effort to improve range-finding and detection, as well as to facilitate acoustic jamming of communication signals. After the war, Harvard took over the laboratory, and its work continued, producing important results on the understanding of speech and language.[46]

George A. Miller was one of the young scientists recruited as a graduate student at Harvard to work in the Psycho-Acoustic Lab. His work during the war involved the reception and transmission of acoustic signals, including speech, under conditions of noise. His postwar publications based upon this work reflect few, if any, uses of statistical inference. Instead, there are multiple figures showing parametric relationships, and the statistics that are used are primarily those that assess error, rather than those that attempt to make inferences. Shortly after the war ended, Miller became aware of the information theory developed by Claude Shannon and his associates at Bell Labs (work that had previously been classified). His later applications of this new approach to language and cognition in general similarly reflect his physicalistic approach to statistical measurement.[47]

It is now possible to see why the institutionalization of statistics was so rapid after the war. Rucci and Tweney noted that, by the 1950s, nearly every graduate program in psychology in the United States required a course in statistics,[48] and this remains true today. What has not been noted is that statistics displaced another mode of externalizing cognition, the instruments that were otherwise dominant until the 1930s. And, if instruments were displaced by statistics, we can ask how statistical tools served functions that had previously been carried out by the brass and glass, and in what manner their use was justified.

As psychology expanded rapidly after World War II, experimental psychologists were entrusted with ensuring the scientific credentials of a predominantly clinical field, and the training of graduate students (most of whom had little background in mathematics or the physical sciences) required special attention. In this climate, the adoption of analysis of variance training in American graduate programs is less surprising. Such training permitted a new generation of psychologists access to a set of tools of perceived scientific status and value, without demanding additional training in mathematics or physical science.

In a recent book, Peter Galison argued that the history of experimental particle physics in the twentieth century reflected the interaction of two distinguishable "material cultures" of physicists. One group, the "imagists," emphasized a pictorial tradition in which events in bubble chambers and the like constituted the fundamental data, and another group, the "logicists," relied upon counting procedures subjected to statistical analysis.[49] It is not clear whether the history of American psychology's "material culture" can be usefully divided into two such camps, but it is clear that

Galison's concept of a "trading zone," in which ideas, concepts, apparatus, and techniques move across interdisciplinary and inter-subdisciplinary boundaries, has much to offer our understanding of psychology. In effect, then, my argument is that the exigencies of war research led to the creation of such a trading zone; for the first time large numbers of psychologists were exposed to procedures and modes of research from other disciplines which rendered moot much of their earlier reliance on brass and glass, while giving them new opportunities for acquiring and using new statistical skills.

The postwar environment of American psychology permitted those psychologists who had acquired new respect for statistical procedures to implement and institutionalize their skills. After 1945, graduate training programs in psychology expanded rapidly, driven in large part by a perceived societal need for more clinical and counseling services, but also by the needs of cold war military, corporate, and governmental bureaucracies. Experimental psychologists newly apprised of Fisherian statistical testing and measurement-oriented psychologists who had had their psychometric and statistical skills sharpened by war research were thus able to join in recommending that statistical training in *both* domains be a requirement for doctoral-level education in psychology. Far from a "two psychologies" split, in which correlational and experimental psychologists diverged,[50] interests converged, and the rapid institutionalization of ANOVA training was the result. In turn, the emphasis on apparatus inevitably declined; instruments did not vanish from the scene, but they did become invisible. Ironically, the most popular instrument currently held at the Archives of the History of American Psychology is not actually an instrument! Stanley Milgram's "shock apparatus" is, to all intents and purposes, a stage prop; the real tool of the famous obedience studies was the statistical analysis of the results.[51] Statistical procedures had become psychology's favored tool, and its badge of scientific rigor as well.

By the end of the twentieth century, the dominance of statistical significance testing was essentially complete; the presence of p values, indicating acceptance or rejection of a null hypothesis, is a characteristic of nearly every empirical study published in psychology. The association is so strong that presence of a p value can, in fact, be used to reliably date an article in an American journal—if there are none, then it dates from before 1935; if present, it is probably after 1950. Indeed, Raymond Hubbard, Rachel Parsa, and Michael Luthy, who extended Rucci and Tweney's 1980 study by examining the appearance of *p* values in randomly sampled volumes of the *Journal of Applied Psychology* from its founding in 1917 through 1994, found that significance tests increased, from single-digit percentages (counting probable errors and critical ratios as "tests") in the 1920s, to 94 percent in the 1990s. At periodic intervals, this practice has come under criticism, but its strength, as of the year 2000, showed little prospect of weakening.[52] Statistical analysis remains the favored "instrument" of psychology.

Much more needs to be done to elaborate the change in question. If it is fair to conclude that "brass and glass" instruments were replaced by statistical instruments, it is clear as well that psychology, like all sciences, used such artifacts in a two-fold fashion: as epistemic artifacts in the service of knowledge, of course, but also as warrants for its status as a science. Each is a necessary function, and each suggests that more is to be learned through the careful study of all of the epistemic artifacts of psychology.

CHAPTER 8

Archival Adventures in the History of Comparative Psychology

Donald A. Dewsbury

I WOULD LIKE TO USE my career of research in the history of comparative psychology to illustrate the value of archival collections, offer some thoughts about how they can be used, and suggest some responsibilities for the users of archival collections. Although placing people into a limited number of pigeonholes is always dangerous, there seem to be at least three kinds of workers in the history of psychology, the dabbler, the retread, and the straight liner.

The *dabbler* is well trained in other fields of psychology but has an interest in the history of psychology as an adjunct to his or her other work. The dabbler may teach a course in the field, read some literature, and occasionally publish an interesting article in the field. However, for the dabbler, historical studies remain a secondary interest, and time simply does not permit serious study.

The *retread* starts out like the dabbler but, at some point, gets so consumed by an interest in the field as to become impatient with the time demands of his or her primary research. A critical point is reached at which one realizes that historians have methods and approaches that are just as important and difficult as those used in the psychology laboratory. One cannot be properly engaged in the discipline without making it a primary concern. The retread then shifts interests away from a career that may or may not have been successful and/or rewarding previously to focus on historical studies and attempts to become as sophisticated in the new methodology as possible within a limited time frame.

The final category is a relatively recent innovation, the *straight liners*. With graduate programs in the history of psychology in departments of psychology, such as those at the University of New Hampshire and York University, in departments of history, history of science programs, and various science and technology programs, some individuals, who identify their interests in the field at a relatively early age, proceed directly into the history of psychology. With the professionalization of the history of psychology, and indeed history of science in general, a cadre of younger historians has emerged well versed in historical literature and methodology from their graduate study years. This is just a part of the overall professionalization of the history of science as has been noted by various scholars.[1]

The work of these different historians is all useful. The retread often has a familiarity with the field that is difficult for the straight liner to achieve. The straight liner, on the other hand, may be versed in methods and literature that are hard for the retread to grasp. The straight liner can often detect assumptions and other features that are so much second nature that the retread misses them. The retread may, however, see subtleties and nuances in the field that are missed by the straight liner. The approaches are complementary. Even the dabbler can contribute information useful in unraveling the complex history of the field.

I worked for twenty-five years or so as a comparative psychologist and began work in history as a dabbler. In about 1990 I realized that my interests were shifting and that my efforts were limited by the time demands of my other work. The only way to satisfy my growing enthusiasm for the history of psychology and to attempt the transition to retread was to make its study my primary focus. Taking advantage of the academic freedom afforded a tenured professor, I finished up one more research grant and my last comparative psychology graduate student and plunged headlong into a program of reading, attending meetings, teaching, and generally trying to get at least some sensitivity to the complexity of historical studies.

One of the advantages of this field is that one can follow interests in any of the wonderfully rich and diverse aspects of psychology. I have done that to some degree. However, as I examined my efforts of the last decade or so, in preparation for the writing of this chapter, I found that most of my work followed a consistent theme. Having gotten a late start in the field, I decided to work primarily on the approaches I knew best. Write about what you know. I have thus concentrated on the work and careers of a group of animal psychologists, most of whom trace their academic lineages through either Robert M. Yerkes or Karl S. Lashley. I would like to discuss some of that work, both published and unpublished, in relation to the importance of archival collections for such scholarly efforts.[2] Clearly, the Archives of the History of American Psychology at the University of Akron (AHAP), founded by John Popplestone and Marion White McPherson, are the most important repository for the field. We are all indebted to them for their efforts.

This chapter provides an overview of some of my own work in this field but is not intended as a broad overview of the entire field. Although tempted to tell the story chronologically, in relation to my experience, I think it is more meaningful, for the most part, to intermix work that I happened to do at different times using only an approximate chronology of the events about which I am writing.

My visit to Akron and my first effort at historical work were perhaps characteristic of the dabbler. Actively engaged in comparative psychological research, I was concerned about the misperceptions that many others had about the field. Comparative psychology has often been stereotyped as the study of rat learning in artificial laboratory situations.[3] I saw within the broader field of animal experimental psychology a continuous, though not always large, thread of a truly comparative approach concerning a broad range of species and behavioral patterns along with the evolution of naturally occurring behavior in the natural habitats of animals. I turned to historical study to illuminate the then-present stereotype of the field. I wanted to show not only that there were current psychologists doing this kind of work, but also that it had long been so. This has been called ceremonial, as opposed to critical, history. The result was my 1984 book, *Comparative Psychology in the Twentieth Century*,[4] a chronology written to demonstrate the breadth and nature of the work that was done. I believe it to be a generally honest and accurate presentation of the field as far as it goes. However, I addressed few really significant historical questions about the development of the field. I wrote the book as a part of academic politics and only secondarily as an historical study, rather than the reverse. It is still a useful reference source nevertheless.

I cannot recall who first told me of the importance of archival studies in general and of the Akron archives in particular. Nevertheless, it was on George Washington's birthday in 1982 that I first wrote to John Popplestone concerning the possibility of a visit,[5] and the following August I made my first pilgrimage to Akron. I was properly impressed with the richness of the collections, gathered what materials I could, and included a three-page section on the archive in the book. My conversion to a retread had begun. As part of that conversion, I began studies of a less sweeping nature, focusing on the work of Robert M. Yerkes.

The Yerkes Laboratories of Primate Biology were founded by Robert M. Yerkes in Orange Park, Florida, and remained there until reconstituted as the Yerkes Regional Primate Research Center in Atlanta, Georgia, in 1965. They held the largest research collection of great apes in the world. Because of their pivotal importance, the proximity of Orange Park to Gainesville, and the critical role of Robert M. Yerkes in the history of comparative psychology, I adopted a project of preparing a history of the laboratories as a long-term effort. It has taken years of work but is approaching completion. I hope to deal with some important questions, such as the role of changing patterns of research funding in the evolution of the facility. Although much of the research done at Orange Park was published, a full understanding of the laboratory and its organization must be based almost entirely on archival sources. My primary sources for this project come from the Rockefeller Archive Center in North Tarrytown, New York, the Yerkes Papers at Yale University, the Archives of the American Philosophical Society, and materials now in the Woodruff Library at Emory University. Here, I shall discuss just three aspects of the research: Yerkes' efforts to establish the facility, his running of the laboratory during the 1930s, and the selection of its second director.

Robert M. Yerkes was born in Breadysville, Pennsylvania, and received an A.B. degree from Ursinus College in 1897 and a Ph.D. in psychology from Harvard University in 1902. He then joined the Harvard faculty, left Harvard for service in Washington, D.C., during and after World War I in

1917, and joined the faculty of Yale University in 1924. He was the pro-
totypical comparative psychologist, studying a variety of species early in
his career but focusing on nonhuman primates after leaving Harvard.

Yerkes traced his goal of founding a facility for research in psychobiology to his graduate school days around 1900. His actual efforts to establish
a primate station began in 1913. In the intervening years prior to 1930,
he visited numerous facilities and sites and lobbied with many foundations
and potential benefactors. It is difficult in a short space to convey the
persistent determination with which Yerkes lobbied, and indeed pestered,
one potential benefactor after another. For example, Yerkes' diary of April
23, 1919, includes an entry that he had "had a good conference with Dr.
Merriam [John C. Merriam, president of the Carnegie Institution of Wash-
ington] about several matters—and among them my anthropoid station
plan." He explored with newspaper publisher E. W. Scripps, benefactor of
the Scripps Institution for Biological Research, the possibility of a facility
on Marco Island, Florida. On several occasions, Yerkes appealed to the well-
connected Flexner brothers. Yerkes explained his scheme in a letter seeking
the advice of Abraham Flexner, of the General Education Board of the
Rockefeller Foundation, in securing funding. Yerkes also sent his plan to
Simon Flexner, Abraham's brother and Director of the Rockefeller Institute
for Medical Research.[6]

During this period he purchased four chimpanzees with his own meager
funds and studied them in New Haven, at his summer home in Franklin,
New Hampshire, and elsewhere, and he spent a summer studying animals
kept in Havana, Cuba. While serving in Washington, D.C., Yerkes built
political connections that would later aid him in securing funding for the
facility.

Eventually, with the support of Yale University President James Rowland
Angell, Yerkes was able to secure Rockefeller funding first for a facility in
New Haven and later in Orange Park. The extensive correspondence
among Rockefeller Foundation officers leading up to the grant reveals their
great skepticism about the utility of the proposed facility. One almost gets
the impression that he was given the funds primarily as a way to stop his
lobbying. Foundation officers were less than enthusiastic. Edwin Embree,
who had left the Rockefeller Foundation, wrote to Max Mason expressing

delight that the little appropriation he had made to get the Yale facility started had blossomed into funding for a primate station. Mason replied, "We went into such measure only after a very careful study by everybody whose field was touched by this work. I think it was somewhat chancy, but large values may come."[7] Yerkes got his funding but had not earned great confidence from the Rockefeller Foundation officers, nor was he ever really able to do so.

The Orange Park facility, which opened in 1930, was conceived as the southern branch of what were then called the Yale Laboratories of Primate Biology. Yerkes established an advisory board and secured some funds from other sources. He built a staff that conducted and published some research during the 1930s. In his 1943 book, Yerkes summarized the work done at the facility during his tenure as director. Perhaps the major accomplishment, which was more ground-breaking than it seems today, was that he showed that chimpanzees could indeed be bred and maintained for study in such a captive situation. Yerkes and his associates studied the development of young animals, their reproductive behavior and processes, and their social behavior. An early study of morphine addiction is a classic. Although many cognitive psychologists have forgotten it, much attention was also given to cognitive processes; Yerkes' text is filled with reference to memory, foresight, insight, and symbolism in chimpanzees.[8]

Relations with the Rockefeller officers, never secure, continued to worsen. Visits by officer Warren Weaver and former officer Lawrence K. Frank did not help. In his diary entry, Frank raised what would become one of the central issues—the need for broad utilization of the Orange Park facility. Yerkes wanted to limit use of the animals to his own staff, whereas the foundation wanted broader usage. Yerkes never got along with Weaver, who visited a month after Frank. As the time for consideration of extending the original ten-year commitment approached, during 1936 and 1937, the foundation officials sought the opinions of some experts in the field regarding continued support. They were only marginally supportive. Sir Solly Zuckerman noted, "The chimpanzee cannot be handled and is therefore entirely unsuitable for the sort of work which Y[erkes] is doing." Karl Lashley concluded that "from the standpoint of the comparative neurologist and psychologist, the further development of the chimpanzee as a laboratory animal is not of sufficient importance to justify the cost." The evaluators criticized the level of productivity of the laboratories. As had Weaver earlier, Heinrich Klüver expressed a low opinion of Yerkes' staff. Lashley added, "I think it unlikely that the present staff will contribute anything of fundamental importance here." They were critical of Yerkes' handling of his junior staff. Edward Tolman summarized the majority view that had spread around the country that Yerkes was "adept in getting rid of his best young men, magnifying their minor faults and overlooking their real values." There was also much criticism of Yerkes as a scientist. Eventually, Yerkes saw the handwriting on the wall. In May, Yerkes wrote to Angell, "My only way to assist further, and perhaps even to save the Laboratories from wreckage, is to withdraw from the leadership."[9] Much negotiation among Yerkes, Rockefeller officials, and the Yale administration followed, but the final resolution was that funding would be continued as long as Yerkes retired as director. Yerkes, of course, was crushed, as the facility for which he had worked so many years was taken from him. Perhaps he was a better builder than administrator.

The process of selecting a new director was as complex as the process of negotiating Yerkes' departure. It is somewhat ironic that the man chosen as Yerkes' successor was Karl Lashley, one of the primary critics of Yerkes' administration. Lashley had been born in Davis, West Virginia, and attended West Virginia University and the University of Pittsburgh before completing his Ph.D. at the Johns Hopkins University in 1914. He then served in various positions, moving to Harvard in 1935. Lashley's political situation at Harvard was deteriorating as the Orange Park opening arose, and he was hired. Lashley was a very different director from Yerkes. He was non-directive where Yerkes sought to control closely nearly all aspects of the operations. Lashley wanted to increase the physiological research and add colonies of monkeys to the ape collections favored by Yerkes. Lashley was able to bring in some creative young scientists, including Donald Hebb, Roger Sperry, and Karl Pribram. He was also able to increase the funding base.

Lashley and his successors as director kept the facility going until 1965 when Emory University, which had bought the facility from Yale and Harvard for one dollar, moved it to their Atlanta campus as the Yerkes Regional

Primate Research Center, part of the federally funded Primate Research Center system being funded at the time.

I would like to note that nearly all of this story was pieced together solely from archival materials. Lacking such sources, the picture of the operation of the Yerkes Laboratories of Primate Biology would be a very sketchy one. This provides an excellent example of the importance of such collections.

While I have been working on this project, various ancillary projects have suggested themselves or been suggested by others. Some of this work has concerned the lives of the directors themselves and has generally been done in response to invitations to contribute to larger projects. Thus, I completed studies of the life of Robert M. Yerkes for the *Portraits of Pioneers in Psychology* series and for the *Encyclopedia of Psychology*. Henry W. Nissen worked in Orange Park during both the Yerkes and Lashley regimes, becoming the third director of the facility in 1955. I have published two studies of Nissen's life as well.[10]

Several other projects emerged from this work. As I read of Yerkes' work on dominance in chimpanzees, I became aware of considerable discrepancies between the data he collected and the interpretation of the research that he later presented and which has been cited in various sources. I conducted a thorough study of Yerkes' handling of the data and coined the term *data simplification* to refer to the progressive simplification and distortion of the results from the primary data to secondary and tertiary sources.[11]

Work in archival collections is usually greatly constrained by pressures of time. Often one barely has enough time to complete the collection of material for the project leading to the visit. On occasion, however, one allots more time than needed and this allows one to explore other aspects of the collection, *archival snooping*. On other occasions, ancillary folders just seem so interesting that one cannot resist the temptation to take time away from the primary project to explore them. Two projects related to Yerkes originated in this way. While working on another project, I became aware that the current journal editors and referees had assumed that the editorial process used by Yerkes and Knight Dunlap in editing the *Journal of Comparative Psychology* between 1921 and 1943 was as rigorous as the present refereeing system. Editorial correspondence in the Yerkes Papers at Yale revealed a quite different picture: responsibility for accepting or rejecting articles lay almost exclusively in the hands of the co-editors. I explored the process in another article. I had long been concerned about the variability of the manner in which different psychologists used the term "psychobiology." In the Yerkes Papers I found a folder of correspondence dealing with that issue. It provided the foundation for a much broader analysis of the uses of this term.[12]

One of my latest projects was stimulated by this then-upcoming festschrift in honor of John Popplestone and Marion White McPherson. In recent years, I have focused on the 1930s as a critical time in the history of comparative psychology. Pressures on newly trained comparative psychologists to pursue applied interests and from World War I had nearly depleted the field by the 1920s. During the 1930s the new generation of psychologists began to establish careers, five of whom had worked with Karl Lashley at the University of Chicago during the period from 1929 to 1935. I call them the Chicago Five, and I believe they constitute an academic *family*, a group with common origins and similar approaches who nevertheless pursue different career paths.[13] More broadly, I believe that more study is needed of the commonalities of approach among groups of psychologists who come together with one mentor at one place and time and then go on to independent careers, what I call psychological families.

Norman R. F. Maier, who received his Ph.D. from the University of Michigan, was in Chicago from 1929 to 1931 and went on to a career spread across comparative and industrial psychology, with an emphasis on reasoning and problem solving. Theodore C. Schneirla, another Michigan Ph.D., worked with Lashley during 1930–31 and went on to an important career in comparative psychology with an emphasis on the behavior of ants. Frank A. Beach did his Ph.D. work at Chicago and worked with Lashley there during 1933–34 and at Harvard during 1936–37; he became a leading comparative psychologist especially noted for studies of sexual behavior in animals. Yitzhok-Eizik Krechevsky, later David Krech, received a Ph.D. from the University of California, Berkeley, worked with Lashley at Chicago from 1933 to 1935, and had a prominent career in animal learning, applied social psychology, and physiological psychology. Donald O.

Hebb worked with Lashley at Chicago during 1934–35 and followed Lashley to Harvard, where he completed a Ph.D.; he became a prominent behavioral neuroscientist and pioneer of cognitive neuroscience.

Upon examining the work of the Chicago Five, I originally isolated thirteen characteristics that define the family and are expressed by most, but not all, of them; the number of characteristics was later reduced to nine. First, all were committed to *teaching* but, although some (for example, Krech and Hebb) were gifted lecturers, most stressed informal mentoring where graduate students work through their own research problems. Like Lashley, few got really close to their students, but all provided the guidance required for successful graduate study.

For the most part, they favored *basic science* aimed at discovery rather than application. Clearly, the best source for information on Maier, who would appear to be an exception, is an oral history completed with Popplestone in 1967. Maier told him that he entered the field to do basic research and continued in that line during the 1930s. He shifted to an applied focus later when his animal research, which ran counter to prevailing approaches, was under siege and he came to believe that the principles he formulated while studying problem solving in rats applied to humans in work situations as well.[14]

Although many psychologists get lost in trivia, the Chicago Five seemed able to focus on *big questions*. Beach, for example, believed that "simply because certain statistical operations are possible it does not follow automatically that they are worth carrying out." He noted further that "the philosopher Whitehead once observed that the last thing to be discovered in any science is what that science is all about."[15] Like the others, he tried to focus on the forest, not just the trees.

In a time when it was somewhat out of favor, most in the family favored the study of *mind*, were interested in cognition, and through that found the then-current behavioristic approaches of but limited value. In many respects, Lashley favored a more cognitive approach than the behaviorisms of his time; he argued in favor of central integration of motor action and against the reflexological interpretations of others. Maier conducted studies designed to show that reasoning was a separate process from simple learning. Hebb believed that Skinner's approach relied on an erroneous epistemology but that his ideas spread because of his personal influence. In 1960, at the dawn of the so-called cognitive revolution, Hebb wrote that "serious analytical study of the thought process cannot be postponed any longer."[16]

Members of the Chicago Five focused on *organization* as the key problem for psychologists. Key articles by Lashley included "Cerebral Organization and Behavior" and "The Problem of Serial Order and Behavior." Hebb's landmark book was *Organization of Behavior*.[17] Krech objected to the notion that when first placed in a situation, the animal's behavior is random. Rather, he wrote, "animals are already equipped to deal systematically with their environment because of their long evolutionary history."[18]

A common view among these men was that *physiological study* is critical for psychologists; all except Schneirla conducted important physiological analyses. However, they believed that such analysis should be focused on psychological, not physiological, questions. Lashley, of course, made a career in studies of brain and behavior and was arguably the leading physiological psychologist of his century. However, of material in textbooks that begin with chapters on neural structure and activity he wrote, "I have been impressed chiefly by its futility. The chapter on the nervous system seems to provide an excuse for pictures in an otherwise dry and monotonous text. That it has any other function is not clear." Krech suggested that "hypothetical constructs . . . are to be conceived as molar neurological events—that and nothing more." Typical of their view that physiological study should be focused on psychological questions, Hebb wrote that one should take physiological knowledge "seriously but not reverently."[19]

A key aspect of the study of mind and behavior for the Chicago Five was analysis of its *evolution*. These psychologists were better versed in evolutionary theory than biologists generally thought they were. In a classic critique of research in comparative psychology, William Hodos and C. B. A. Campbell chided psychologists for their belief in a *Scala Naturae*, the misguided notion from Aristotle that there is a linear arrangement of species along a single dimension from higher to lower. Beach made the same point in a letter to Hebb twenty years earlier. In part, he wrote, "There is no justification for any sort of straight line order and it should be obvious that the terms 'higher' and 'lower' or 'specialized' and 'generalized' are to be used with extreme caution, if at all."[20] Most of these men stressed the notion of emergent evolution; as a result of natural evolutionary forces, mechanisms can evolve that are fundamentally different in recently evolved species from those of older forms.

Research on *nonhuman animals* was focal for Lashley and the Chicago Five. Hebb and William Thompson stressed the importance of animal research for social psychology. At the same time, however, they were concerned about their research subjects. Beach, for example, noted, "I have sat up all night with more than one operated dog. You are a human being before you are a scientist, and human beings are empathic by nature."[21]

More specifically, *comparative psychology* was a family interest. Lashley's work in comparative psychology came to fruition with a summer with John B. Watson studying terns in the Dry Tortugas islands of Florida and continued throughout his life.

An interesting example of the value of archival research can be seen with regard to Beach's views on comparative psychology. Always an ardent supporter in public, in private correspondence he was concerned about the role of comparative study in psychology. In a fascinating letter to Hebb, Beach traced the history of the field from Darwin to the Watsonian revolution, to a more cognitive approach and an anthropocentric use of nonhuman animals with "little interest in animals *qua* animals." He hit Hebb with two proposals. First, "let's give Psychology to the psychologists who have been insisting for generations that psychology is a science of *human* behavior." Psychology could study the human mind, though one cannot study the animal mind. With that proposal, he also proposed "a comparative science of behavior which will treat the behavior of all species" and include ethology and material on behavior from diverse biological sciences. He added, "My students tell me that a responsible psychologist shouldn't say such things in public, and I'm considering doing just that."[22]

Hebb, another advocate for comparative psychology, disagreed, writing that he liked the proposal but wanted to keep it within psychology. For Hebb, the comparative science of behavior described by Beach "is exactly what I think psychology should be and now is." Hebb counseled Beach: "(A) follow the line of defining a new science, in order to put an end to such blind alleys as the subjective study, and equating rat and man (as at

Yale) [but] (B) keep on pounding away at the line you describe, but call it *psychology*." In his interview with John Popplestone, Maier, like Beach and Schneirla, lamented what he perceived as a decrease in truly comparative research directed at understanding the animal rather than at generalizing to humans. Maier was concerned about "questions which reflect an interest in the animal, not in learning more about human beings, but in exploring the potential of that animal."[23]

All family members except Schneirla had great respect for European *ethology*, as developed by Konrad Lorenz, Niko Tinbergen, and their colleagues, and believed that their influence could be an asset for psychology. Beach and Lashley were important in gaining recognition for ethology in the United States. For their part, the ethologists appreciated Beach's efforts. Nobel laureate Tinbergen wrote to Beach that "you and he [Daniel Lehrman] have done more than any other American psychologists to bring our fields so close together." Beach did, however, express some reservations about Lorenz in correspondence, writing that "he is an amazingly egotistical and charming person" and that his wife "came away with the feeling that she would never believe anything that he published, scientific or otherwise."[24]

Lehrman, a student of Schneirla, is an interesting case. He wrote the most thorough and devastating critique of Lorenz's theory. Paradoxically, this critique eventually facilitated the interaction, as issues were laid out clearly and men of good will discussed them amicably. It became one of the most important articles in the history of the field and thus its development is of some interest. Lehrman sent copies of his draft to both Beach and Hebb. Hebb wrote to Beach for advice before replying to Lehrman. Following Beach's advice, Hebb was forthright and critical. Hebb wrote to Lehrman that he erred as much in favor of environmental interpretations of ontogeny as did Lorenz on the other side. Hebb agreed with some of Lehrman's criticisms, but he advised Lehrman to present the positive aspects of ethology as well as the negative. He wrote that "your paper to me seems to reveal *a priori* bias, against 'instinct' ideas; I should say at once that I am biased the other way." Hebb added, "We can't just throw away 'instinct,' bad as the idea is, without putting something better in its place."[25]

European *Gestalt psychology* had an important influence on the work of Lashley, Maier, Krech, and Hebb. All had personal contact with the Gestalt psychologists and acknowledged their effect. In unpublished notes in the Akron archives, Hebb speculated, "It may be doubted whether he [Lashley] would have been as effective without the (unacknowledged) support of Köhler and Koffka." Maier relied mainly on "table problems" with rats. The animals were given several kinds of experience in a room with assorted spatial routes and then tested to see if they could combine these experiences when faced with a new problem requiring them to choose a new path to a goal. Maier concluded that the rats solve the problems "without 'trial and error,' but with intelligence and insight" and that "patterns or Gestalten" were involved.[26]

The family members viewed the *development of behavior* as a continuous, dynamic interaction of genes, environment, and the organism. Hebb and Beach stressed the impossibility of determining the relative importance of genes and environment in behavioral development.[27] At the same time, however, Lashley and the others had a great interest in the behavioral patterns usually labeled instinctive and in genetic influences on behavior.[28] More than the others, it was perhaps Krech who followed Lashley's interest in genetic influences. Early in his career, Krech investigated genetic influences on hypotheses in rats. He wrote, "I can still recapture my excitement when [Robert] Tryon first demonstrated to me his selectively bred Bright and Dull rats." Later at Berkeley, he followed Tryon and was supportive of such research.[29]

The family tended to view *individual differences* as important in understanding behavior, not as something to be ignored or minimized. Thus, Lashley was impressed by the individual differences in the motor patterns of rats with lesions of the spinal cord or cerebellum; Hebb studied individual differences in temperament in chimpanzees; Beach and Burney J. LeBoeuf demonstrated individual difference in the mating preferences in female dogs.[30]

I do not wish to minimize the differences among the family members. Not all accepted all thirteen premises. They disagreed about such issues as the role of theory in psychology and the role of the scientist in social action. However, many influences on the family members from both their time with Lashley at Chicago and from the many interactions among them continued for many years thereafter.

My interests in comparative psychology and the comparative psychologists trained during the 1930s have led me to a variety of related projects.

Beach was my mentor during a postdoctoral year at the University of California, Berkeley, in 1965–66. This, combined with my interest in history, has led to extensive work on his life and career. He had been a student of Lashley at both Chicago and Harvard and a colleague of Yerkes at Yale. Shortly after his death, I was asked to prepare an obituary for the *American Journal of Psychology*. I was also asked to write similar pieces for the *Biographical Memoirs of the National Academy of Sciences, USA*, the *American National Biography*, and the *Encyclopedia of Psychology*, as well as two other sources. By the time I was invited to write a chapter for *Portraits of Pioneers in Psychology*, I felt that I had said all that I could about Beach, more times than needed! However, by concentrating on his interesting career as a teacher, whereas the other work had been focused on his research, I hope that I was able to produce a chapter with some degree of freshness.[31]

Included in the Beach materials that I transferred to Akron was Beach's unfinished textbook in comparative psychology. During the 1950s, Beach, arguably the leading comparative psychologist of his generation, completed the manuscript for a textbook that would have pleased most authors. By contrast, Beach was unhappy with the result as he was becoming skeptical of the place for comparative studies of behavior within the discipline of psychology; he never published the book. I completed a summary and analysis of the work.[32]

Beach's most influential article in comparative psychology was his famous "The Snark was a Boojum." I had long believed that, though the message Beach delivered was appropriate and much needed, the analyses on which it was based were seriously flawed. I explored this in greater depth in a subsequent article.[33]

I have also done some work on the career of Maier, another member of the Chicago Five. On my second visit to Akron, I dined one night with John Popplestone who informed me of the materials in the archives concerning the controversy between Maier and Clifford T. Morgan over the genesis of seizures in rats. Maier's was an important study that won him the prestigious Thousand Dollar Prize of the American Association for the Advancement of Science, a major event in psychological science. Maier believed that the seizures suffered by rats faced with unsolvable discrimination problems originated in their conflict. Morgan, by contrast, interpreted the seizures as a response to the air puff used to stimulate the rat to jump in the Lashley Jumping Stand apparatus. The prevalent opinion of the controversy favored Morgan's interpretation. The criticism stemming from this project was one major factor leading Maier to abandon animal research entirely several years later. The unpublished materials in the Akron collection, including important editorial correspondence, revealed that Morgan had actually conceded error. Popplestone wanted someone to tell the story. I could not resist such a juicy opportunity handed to me on a silver platter, and I completed the project.[34]

In another Maier-related project, I completed a retrospective review of the classic 1935 textbook of Maier and Schneirla.[35]

The received view of animal psychology during the 1930s is that behaviorism was so dominant that studies of animal cognition were virtually non-existent. My work on the Yerkes laboratories and studies by Maier on reasoning showed that significant work on animal cognition was indeed being done during this period. I expanded the project to examine all of the studies in animal cognition during the 1930s that I could find. The corpus of research during this period was substantial.[36]

I do not wish to imply that all of my historical work has been limited to this group of comparative psychologists related to Yerkes and Lashley. I have tried to provide a coherent picture here by reviewing just those studies, but cannot review all the various other projects I have been able to conduct. One of the great things about work in the field is the ability to explore diverse aspects of the rich panorama of psychology, which suits my personality and proclivities. However, I do want to mention a few projects that reveal aspects of archival research.

The governing board of the Psychonomic Society, an organization of experimental psychologists formed in Chicago in 1959, wanted a history of the organization prepared for publication. Robert C. Bolles accepted the assignment. Tragically, he died after beginning work on the project. I was invited to complete the history. The Psychonomic Society provided funds so that I could travel to use the collections in Akron and at the Psychonomic Society publication office in Austin, Texas. I was also able to interview William S. Verplanck, the founding secretary-treasurer, at his home in Knoxville, Tennessee. As a result, I was able to use these materials to complete a four-part history of the society."[37]

Another organizational feature in which I became interested was the division structure of the American Psychological Association (APA). This structure was adopted during the 1940s as a way of unifying the fragmented organizations representing different interest groups within psychology. I wrote about the evolution of the divisions since World War II and edited a five-volume series of division histories. For the series I wrote a history of Division 6 (Behavioral Neuroscience and Comparative Psychology).[38] I found some materials in the APA collection at the Library of Congress and in other collections. Most of the story of Division 6, however, came from materials I and others collected from former officers and that have been in my possession ever since. I recently shipped six cartons of Division 6-related materials to the new APA archive at the central office in Washington, D.C., which is headed by my former doctoral student, Wade E. Pickren.

Clearly, archival collections are critical for sound historical research. However, those of us working in the field should not take the existence of such collections for granted. It is our responsibility to help ensure that such collections grow and are available not only for our own use but for future generations. I have tried to take this responsibility seriously and counseled various psychologists and their families about the importance of archival preservation. They have generally been quite cooperative and anxious to help in preserving the work of their loved one.

I would like to review just two experiences. After recovering from the initial shock of Frank Beach's death, I asked his widow and close colleagues about his papers and the possibility of preservation. They were enthusiastic and cooperative; the papers now reside at Akron. There were a couple of problems, however. First, like many senior scientists, he had previously discarded much old material. Historians ought to impress on such significant psychologists the importance of retaining significant material. Second, in many contexts Beach was a very private man who kept his personal and private lives separate. The family wanted to respect this and, over my protests, removed much material related to his health and other private matters. Unfortunately, then, the materials in Akron have been sanitized and do not represent the full range of Beach's correspondence. Some of this can be found in the collections of his correspondents, but one needs to be aware of this process when using a collection such as this.

My other experience began with an off-handed remark about Karl Lashley in a University of Florida lecture and a comment from one of our students that her family had purchased Lashley's house from his widow. Though skeptical, I checked it out, found it to be true, and discovered that Claire Lashley too had died. I was, however, able to locate Claire's daughter, Karl Lashley's stepdaughter, Christina Schlusemeyer. She now owns a beautiful and successful horse farm in the rich Ocala horse country not far from the University of Florida. She is the daughter of Claire and a prominent European psychologist, Paul Harkai Schiller. She invited me to visit and showed me cartons of material stored in her garage from both her father and her stepfather, or "Curley" as she called Lashley. I made several visits, each time borrowing a few cartons to use. She even had a bedroom suite and file cabinet handmade by Karl Lashley. In the file cabinet I found some wonderful materials, including a folder of his late correspondence with John B. Watson. Late in his life, Watson, to the chagrin of historians everywhere, burned almost all of his papers. Watson's secretary, however, had taken the Lashley folder from him and sent it to Claire. I explored the possibility of archival preservation with Christina, who preferred to have the materials remain in Florida where her daughter might have access to them, rather than sending them to Akron or elsewhere. The materials are now in the Special Collections Division of the Smathers Library of the University of Florida.

The materials have been useful. I became interested in the career of Paul Schiller and published several articles about him. Remarkably, Lashley had written an obituary for Schiller but it had been rejected for publication by several editors, including Edwin G. Boring, Karl M. Dallenbach, and Carroll C. Pratt. I was able to publish the piece more than thirty-five years after Lashley's death. I came into contact with scholars in California, Hungary, and Germany, all with an interest in Schiller who either visited or arranged for photocopies of material from the collection.

Also in the papers were Lashley's unpublished Vanuxem Lectures delivered at Princeton University in 1952. These have now been published by Jack Orbach.[39] Several scholars have visited Florida to use the collection and/or to talk with the always-gracious Ms. Shlusemeyer.

This has been a very rewarding experience and shows how the responsibility for aiding in the collecting process also can be of great benefit to the historian.

These diverse "adventures" illustrate many ways in which archival research can enrich historical study. Archival materials are essential to the retread and the straight liner, but can also be useful to the dabbler. As a dabbler, I used the Akron collections to fill in missing information for my history of comparative psychology. My biographical work, like most such endeavors, has made similar use of such sources, as only a small part of an individual's life can be garnered from published sources. For institutional histories, such as those of the Yerkes Laboratories, Psychonomic Society, and APA divisions, archival material has been virtually the only source. With "archival snooping" I was able to find unexpected material that led to interesting projects other than those that got me to the facility in the first place. In conversation with archivist John Popplestone, a whole new project, that on Maier, was opened. In this case, the archival information was used to correct the misperceptions prevalent in the field about the Maier-Morgan controversy. I have had numerous other conversations with researchers and archive staff as I worked or took breaks from work in collections; some of these helped to enrich my own work. An example of how archival materials provide perspective can be seen in the way in which the exchange between Beach and Hebb showed that Beach, the great promoter of the field, was much less confident of the place of comparative studies in the field of psychology at large than appeared in print. In the process of finding new materials for archival preservation, a new project, such as my work on Paul Schiller, can develop. There are, indeed, many ways in which archival work can be useful.

I hope that I have shown the value of archival collection for the research projects that have evolved through my career. We all owe a debt of gratitude to John Popplestone, Marion White McPherson, and the other archivists who preserve these materials.

CHAPTER 9

A Tale of Two Institutions: York University's History of Psychology Program and the Archives of the History of American Psychology

Raymond E. Fancher

THE UNIVERSITY OF AKRON AND my home institution of York University in Toronto both have long traditions of support for the study of the history of psychology—the former through its Archives of the History of American Psychology and the latter through its unique program for graduate study in the history of psychology. The virtues of the two institutions intersected a few years ago when three York students visited the archives while pursuing their Ph.D. research and profited enormously from doing so. This paper will tell their story, prefaced by some general background information about York's graduate program for study in the history and theory of psychology.

York University is a relatively young institution; it was chartered in 1960 and established in its main campus in the northern part of Toronto, Ontario, five years later. In that same year of 1965, just as John Popplestone and Marion McPherson were establishing the Akron archives, York's graduate program in psychology was established with a faculty of eight members. The program expanded extremely rapidly, and by the time I arrived in 1970 its graduate faculty in psychology already numbered among the largest in Canada with more than fifty members. By the mid-1970s it had grown to seventy-five and at present it has more than ninety members.

When I arrived in 1970, faculty could voluntarily affiliate themselves with one or more of the official specialty areas in which we offered advanced degrees: namely, clinical/counseling, developmental, social/personality, and general experimental psychology. I got the job largely on the strength of two "mainstream" experimental research projects I had going, on interpersonal perception and on the recollection of dreams, and my own original affiliations were with the clinical/counseling and social/personality areas. My real passion at that time, however, was for an historical analysis of Freudian theory—definitely *not* a subject calculated to win favor in traditional psychology departments.

But York's was not a traditional department, a fact of which I had had a small inkling before I came. Indeed a significant part of York's initial attractiveness to me had lain in the fact that David Bakan had just come there. I knew about Bakan's provocative speculations in *Sigmund Freud and the Jewish Mystical Tradition*, and his papers on the history of introspection, the "mystery-mastery complex" in psychology, and the fallacies of significance testing had been favorites of mine in graduate school. These and several others of his papers had just been published in a collection titled *On Method: Toward a Reconstruction of Psychological Investigation*.[1] In 1970–71 Bakan was also serving his term as the fifth president of Division 26 of the American Psychological Association. I thought that any psychology department capable of attracting this multifaceted and iconoclastic figure could not be all bad.

Sure enough, once I got to York I found a substantial number of other colleagues, both senior and junior, who also actively pursued interests that were out of the mainstream. At a senior level in the department, Kurt Danziger, whom I then knew by reputation as a distinguished social and developmental psychologist, was just about to begin his monumental historical reanalyses of Wilhelm Wundt. The department chair, Malcolm Westcott, was conducting qualitative investigations of intuition and freedom, and the clinic director, Neil Agnew had written incisively, with Sandra Pyke, on what they ironically called "The Science Game." Among my closer contemporaries, Peter Kaiser and Hiroshi Ono had strong interests in the historical background to their research on visual sensation and perception, Michael Cowles taught statistics from an historical perspective, and Fred Weizmann was nurturing interests in the history of developmental psychology. In general, here was a substantial group of colleagues who were open to historical, theoretical, and nonquantitative approaches to psychology. My historical interests in psychoanalysis were not only tolerated but actually encouraged. I gained a great deal of support and advice from this group as I completed my first book on the history of psychoanalysis and worked throughout the mid-1970s on the first edition of *Pioneers of Psychology*.[2]

One of the more surprising things to me about York was that the senior figures in this group occasionally supervised historical/theoretical master's theses and Ph.D. dissertations. Further, this did not turn out to be a kiss of death to the careers of these students, at least as long as they had received a good grounding in mainstream psychology in other aspects of their training. As broadly educated psychologists with a gift for the effective communication of their scholarship, they often made unusually good teachers.

When the Ontario Council on Graduate Education formally assessed York's graduate program in psychology in the late 1970s, its final report explicitly highlighted our unusual strength and productivity in historical and theoretical psychology. This "official" recognition provided the immediate stimulus that led a number of the faculty, under the leadership of Bakan, Danziger, and our then graduate director, Michael Cowles, to formalize the opportunity we offered by creating a distinct specialty area of "history and theory of psychology" to which prospective graduate students could apply. A curriculum was drawn up and approved, and in 1981 Danziger became the area's first coordinator. Bakan and I declared the history/theory area as our primary graduate affiliation, and a dozen others named it as secondary. Bakan and Danzinger have since retired, but York has maintained its commitment to the program by hiring three outstanding younger scholars—Christopher Green, Thomas Teo, and Alexandra Rutherford—as replacements.

The first class of history and theory students was accepted in 1981, and since then a small but regular stream of outstanding candidates from Europe and the United States as well as Canada have enrolled. Their research over the years has been diverse and of extremely high quality, as they have won competitive fellowships, teaching appointments, and thesis and dissertation awards out of all proportion to their relatively small numbers at York. They have regularly reported on their work at major conferences, with more than a dozen of their presentations winning best student paper awards. Their research topics have ranged widely, including studies of the evolutionary foundations of psychoanalysis, the origin and development of personality psychology, theories of body expression, the social history of community psychology, the development of cognitive psychotherapy, military psychology in Canada, the history of the ego concept, a cultural history of lie detection, the Anna Freud-Melanie Klein debate, and bio-graphically oriented investigations of Gordon Allport, William Blatz, Franz Brentano, Karl Bühler, Erasmus Darwin, Erich Fromm, Francis Galton, Ed-mund Husserl, William James, and Friedrich Nietzsche. Several graduates of our program have won highly competitive tenure stream academic po-sitions.

I now turn to three of our fine students in particular, and the memo-rable visit they made together to the Akron archives. Paul Ballantyne, Geoff Bunn, and Ian Nicholson had quite divergent research interests—about which more later—but discovered that the Akron archives held papers of potentially great interest to all of them. Thus in February of 1995 the three York *caballeros* left together from Toronto by car, for what turned out to be quite a grand adventure. Each of the trio privately sent me reminis-cences about their trip, from which I will freely quote in the following account.

The trip was almost aborted at the outset, when the group arrived at the United States/Canada border. The American immigration officer seemed unworried about the Canadians Ballantyne and Nicholson, but as the Englishman Bunn recalls, "He was mighty suspicious of me and kept pounding me with questions." In fairness to the officer it should be said that Bunn had only a student visa, and a British accent such that "when-ever I ordered coffee in a diner, they would only bring me tea." The officer was not initially impressed by Bunn's explanations of the purpose of his visit, apparently regarding "archival research in the history of psychology" as a potential cover for all sorts of subversive activity. Finally, as Bunn recalls, "I remembered why I was going to Akron in the first place, and asked him if he knew who Wonder Woman was." Of course the officer did know, and when Bunn explained that her creator was a psychologist whose papers he was hoping to study in Akron, he and his companions were promptly waved through.

Once in Akron the hospitality improved markedly; indeed Ballantyne recalls that the group was received at the archives as if they were "honored guests." They were given an office to work in and, as Bunn put it: "What was so great about the trip was the access we were granted to the archive. It is very well run, and we got anything we wanted very quickly. We must have drawn a lot of boxes in those three days. Sharon Ochsenhirt, the assistant, was brilliant and very generous with her time and patience. We noticed that there must have been four or five students helping out with the archival activities." Nicholson adds: "Everyone working in the archive was extraordinarily understanding and helpful. I remember saying to Bunn and Ballantyne that the friendly atmosphere of the Akron archive contrasted favourably with some of the larger university archives I had visited."

Although each had his own independent area of research, the three sometimes found items of common interest or amusement that they would read aloud to each other. Indeed Nicholson suspects that they "may have irritated some of the archival staff with our laughter," especially following their discovery of a "red tabbed" (confidential) file concerning an illustrious American psychologist whom I shall only refer to here as Professor X. The eminent professor had been asked by a graduate student to supervise a project on a topic that shall also go unnamed here, except to say that it would have anticipated by many years some of the work of the sex researchers Masters and Johnson. Discretion dictated that Professor X decline this request, and Bunn concludes the story as follows: "As if this wasn't enough, later on we discovered in a separate file that a student had once burst in to Professor X's dorm one night and beaten him up. To cap it off we then found a group photo and Professor X had a black eye! It didn't take much to historically reconstruct the events that happened. Laugh? I'm still laughing now!" Presiding benignly over all of this tumult were the founders of the archives, who, Bunn recalls, "endured the periodic shrieks of raucous hilarity as we shared anecdotes back and forth as we found them. They very good natured about it all, I must say."

It is perhaps needless to say that the students' trip was much more than just fun and games. Each of them came away with some major research benefits to which I turn now, taking up the three students in alphabetical order.

All three of the students came to York with outstanding training and master's degrees from other institutions. Ballantyne came from the University of Victoria, where he had studied with Charles Tolman and completed a master's thesis titled "The Task of Theoretical Unification in Psychology." He has continued to have a productive graduate career at York, with publications including an article titled "From Initial Abstractions to a Concrete Concept of Personality," which was significant for presenting and sympathetically analyzing the work of several Soviet/Russian figures little known in the west, including I. Scheffler, V. V. Davydov, and E. V. Ilyenkov.[3]

Ballantyne recently completed his Ph.D. dissertation as part of a larger project on "Psychology, Society, and American Ability Testing: Transformative Alternatives to Mental Darwinism and Interactionism." This dissertation is unusual in that it is intended to provide an interdisciplinary teaching resource, as well as an historical analysis of the ability testing technologies designed by twentieth-century American scientists to assess the variety and potential of both animal and human mentality. Along the way, it will evaluate past traditions of animal research, intelligence testing, and vocational assessment, while making concrete proposals for alternative, "transformative" ability testing technologies (for school testing, vocational guidance, and job training). In the draft introduction to his dissertation Ballantyne writes, "Stated briefly, a transformative approach to ability testing will have to do what the other two standard approaches (i.e., Mental Darwinism and Interactionism) have never been designed to do. It will have to deal specifically with the typical 'three-fold transformation' of human mentality—the transformation from a strictly individual, *biologically mediated*, mentality; into a group, *socially mediated* mentality; into a cultural, *societally mediated* mentality. In other words, contrary to the shared 'innate capacity' or 'social relations' assumption of the other two approaches, the very 'capacity for paying attention' is transformed phylogenetically, ontogenetically, and socio-historically."

Ballantyne's efforts to make the dissertation a teaching resource as well as an original scholarly contribution have led him to place special emphasis on obtaining illustrative pictorial material associated with various tests and testing trials. Indeed, he has long been very interested in developing the potential of pictorial materials to illuminate the teaching not only of history of psychology but also of psychology in general. One main purpose of his visit to Akron was to explore its rich photographic archives, and one result was his collaboration with Kurt Danziger on the illustrated article on "Psychological Experiments," published in *A Pictorial History of Psychology*.[4] Ballantyne will also make extensive use of pictures in his Ph.D. dissertation. Among the topics to receive pictorial treatment will be: Oskar Pfungst's appreciation of Clever Hans as a *social* animal; Leon Vygotsky's account of childhood language development; Alexander Luria's Usbekistan research; the Iowa group's field studies on rural (consolidated vs. one room school) children; Loren Baritz's account of the Hawthorne experiments; the Depression-era "Eight-Year Study" of college entrance exams; the New Deal youth oriented programs; the ongoing Head Start program; and the implications of the so-called Flynn effect.

Geoff Bunn came to York after earning a master's degree in the history of scientific thought from Leeds University in England, where he studied with the well-known historians of science Jon Hodge and Robert Olby. His thesis at Leeds involved archival research on the establishment of the aesthetics section of the British Psychological Society. At York, under the supervision of Kurt Danziger, Bunn started on an historical survey of the concept of emotion but soon became fascinated by that peculiarly North American phenomenon: the "lie detector." What particularly intrigued him was not so much the rather mundane technology itself, nor even the extravagantly exaggerated claims typically made by its practitioners about its accuracy. Instead, Bunn was struck by the degree to which lie detection was heavily involved with popular culture.

Part of Bunn's dissertation relates the fascinating stories of the two men who independently "invented" the technique of polygraphic lie detection. William Moulton Marston (1893–1947) had experimented with polygraphic techniques for measuring emotional reactivity while a Ph.D. student at Harvard, but was unable to secure a permanent academic post following his degree in 1921. In due course he wound up working as director of public service for Universal Pictures in Hollywood, where he used the polygraph to assess the emotional reactions of audience members as they watched movies. In one of his studies he used the "love detector" (as his machine was dubbed by the popular press) to compare the reactivity of blondes, brunettes, and redheads to various film clips. In 1928 the *New York Times* reported: "Blondes lose out in film love test; Brunettes far more emotional, Psychologist proves by Charts and Graphs; Theater a Laboratory."[5] Toward the end of his life Marston engaged popular culture in yet another way when he created and developed the *Wonder Woman* comic book character. As some of you may recall, this superheroine always carried her own sort of portable polygraph, a "golden lasso of truth," within the coils of which no evildoer was able to lie.

Marston's chief rival for polygraphic priority was Leonarde Keeler (1903–49), who also had Hollywood roots as the son of a successful scriptwriter. Keeler had little formal academic training, but as a young man came under the influence of August Vollmer, the enterprising and scientifically minded chief of the Berkeley, California police force. Under Vollmer's supervision, Keeler developed the polygraph as a form of "painless third degree," the now-classic technique of monitoring polygraphic responses while interrogating criminal suspects. Keeler soon moved on to Chicago, where he became a leader in the city's Scientific Crime Detection Laboratory and achieved great popular celebrity by subjecting Al Capone's gangsters to the technique. Hollywood remained in Keeler's blood, and in the 1947 film *Call Northside 777* he appeared with Jimmy Stewart, playing himself as the polygraphic expert who helped Stewart's character free a wrongfully convicted man from jail. Keeler also impacted the comic strips, although more indirectly than Marston did: the varied accomplishments of his Scientific Crime Detection Lab provided a direct inspiration for the creation of the ace detective *Dick Tracy*.

Bunn's 1998 Ph.D. dissertation, "The Hazards of the Will to Truth: A History of the Lie Detector," dealt with considerably more than just the biographies of Marston and Keeler. Its abstract reads as follows:

Although it remains one of the most famous psychological technologies in existence, no scholarly history of the lie detector has yet appeared. This dissertation corrects this oversight. It argues that the lie detector was created in and sustained by American popular culture. The instrument was not first developed in the scientific laboratory, only to later find its way into popular culture. Rather, the lie detector was initially created in the public domain and its claims were only scientifically scrutinized once it had become established.

This is not to say that the lie detector had no forerunners prior to 1921, the alleged date of its "invention." From the early years of the twentieth century, the American press became fascinated by a whole series of "soul machines" that promised to "detect criminals" and "cure liars." But because they functioned within a clinical experimental tradition that sought to analyze mental pathology, none of them can be regarded as lie detectors. The lie detector was unconcerned with those personological entities which had so preoccupied the "soul machine" and its brethren: the dementia praecox case, the feeble-minded child, the degenerate, the "criminal mind."

The lie detector was formed at the intersection of three forces: popular psychology, the drive to professionalize the American police, and a sensationalist press that depicted "the war against crime" as a simplistic opposition between heroes and villains. While the instrument was a product of negotiations between these groups, a discourse emerged during the early 1920s that exhibited a number of structural regularities. The semiotics of lie detection can be profitably divided into three overlapping clusters: the rhetoric of science, the rhetoric of magic, and the rhetoric of law and order. Regulating the discourse were the great pioneers Leonarde Keeler and William Moulton Marston.

The dissertation concludes that the lie detector can be understood in terms of Michel Foucault's notion of "semio-technique." Not only does the category communicate the importance of semiotics to the practice of lie detection, but it also expresses the interplay between the liberal and the illiberal that has characterized the instrument's history.[6]

During his stay at York, Bunn presented aspects of his research in sixteen conference papers or invited addresses, in a major article for the *History of the Human Sciences*, and in a piece for *Border/Lines* magazine titled "Constructing the Suspect: A Brief History of the Lie Detector." (The title, of course, is a clever play on that of his supervisor Kurt Danziger's 1990 book, *Constructing the Subject: Historical Origins of Psychological Research.*)[7] Following graduation Bunn held a research fellowship at the Science Museum in London where he oversaw the development of a major exhibition celebrating the centenary of the British Psychological Society. Currently he holds a full-time teaching position at Liverpool Hope University in the United Kingdom.

Ian Nicholson came to York after earning his B.A. with Henry Minton at the University of Windsor and an M.A. with Frances Cherry from Carleton University. Under these two distinguished mentors he had already done archival research at Akron and in Ottawa, and had begun to develop something of a specialty in biographically oriented studies emphasizing the role of religion and ethical concerns in the development of American psychology. Nicholson's master's thesis at Carleton focused on the role of the American social and personality psychologist Goodwin Watson (1899–1976) in the formation of the Society for the Psychological Study of Social Issues (SPSSI) and in the establishment of the "social engineering" movement. At York Nicholson continued along these lines, conducting further research on the role of the "Social Gospel" in the work of Goodwin Watson and Carl Rogers, and on the relationship between Protestant reconstruction and academic professionalization as exemplified in the work of the turn-of-the-century psychologist of religion George Albert Coe. His proposed dissertation subject was the role of religion and ethics in the life and career of the Harvard personality and social psychologist Gordon Allport, a subject that held particular interest for me because Allport had been my teacher and a major influence in my own development.

Nicholson's graduate career at York was markedly successful. While still a student he presented his research in numerous conference presentations and refereed historical publications.[8] One of these which made particular use of his Akron archival research was "The Politics of Scientific Social Reform, 1936–60: Goodwin Watson and the Society for the Psychological Study of Social Issues," which appeared in the *Journal of the History of the Behavioral Sciences*. This paper explored the development and subsequent transformation of a "radical" professional model in American psychology by focusing on Watson's role in SPSSI, an organization he had helped found in 1936. During the Depression, Watson and his SPSSI colleagues had called upon psychologists to abandon value neutrality and political disinterestedness in favor of an explicit set of social democratic goals and left-wing political alliances. Government service and political persecution during World War II led Watson to conclude that his Depression-era calls for sweeping change had neglected a number of significant political dimensions, particularly the problematic interface between psychological expertise and policy formation. In response to this concern, Watson encouraged the development of the now more familiar model of the psychologist as a disinterested purveyor of value-neutral expertise.

Nicholson's Ph.D. dissertation, "Moral Projects and Disciplinary Practices: Gordon Allport and the Development of American Personality Psychology," focused on ethical and religious influences on Allport's psychology.[9] As is well known, Allport helped establish "personality" as a subdiscipline in American psychology by undertaking one of the first dissertations in the field, writing the first literature review on the subject, teaching one of the first courses in the field in 1924, and publishing the field's first definitive textbook in 1937. Nicholson's dissertation charted the development of Allport's interest in personality from his childhood to his election to the presidency of American Psychological Association in 1939, and showed that this work was embedded in a complex network of intellectual, personal, and institutional contexts. Allport became a psychologist with a view to mobilizing the discipline's scientific techniques in the service of ethical concerns. His choice of psychology as a profession and of "personality" as a subject also reflected an important transformation in the American moral landscape. Between 1880 and 1920, industrialization and urbanization had shifted the dominant model of American selfhood from that of "character" to that of personality, and the emphasis on self-sacrifice and stability that had been so central in the language of character was gradually displaced by a concern with self-realization and self-presentation.

This shift provided the primary cultural impetus behind Allport's early work in personality psychology. As a young scholar, he embraced the up-to-date category of "personality" and eagerly pursued a career in one of the new professions devoted to its study. At the same time, however, he found many of the points of emphasis in the new language of selfhood highly unsettling. He was particularly troubled by the growing emphasis on sexuality, unconscious motivation, determinism, and a number of other cultural and scientific trends that seemed to diminish the essential dignity and uniqueness of each individual person. In his early work on personality, Allport attempted to stake out a middle ground between the newly developing personality ideal on the one hand, and the traditions and ideals of character on the other.

Nicholson's beautifully written work won high praise from his examining committee and was selected as York's best Ph.D. dissertation in psychology for 1996. He subsequently adapted part of it for an article which appeared in the inaugural issue of the Division 26 journal *History of Psychology*, which was selected by a divisional committee as the best contribution to appear in Volume 1 of the new journal.[10] Nicholson completed a book based on his dissertation research entitled *Inventing Personality: Gordon Allport and the Science of Selfhood* published by the American Psychological Association in 2003. He is currently on the faculty at St. Thomas University in Fredericton, New Brunswick, and has been elected chair of the Canadian Psychological Association's History and Philosophy Section.

I trust that these necessarily abbreviated and secondhand accounts have been sufficient to provide at least an idea of why I feel proud of these students and grateful for the assistance that they received from everyone at the Archives of the History of American Psychology. I will let the final word go to Geoff Bunn, who wrote to me just before the celebration: "I can tell that the tribute to John and Marion is going to be quite a considerable undertaking. This is quite appropriate, for the little band of scholars that set off in Nicholson's car that winter were only one of many groups who have benefited immensely from Akron's expertise and hospitality." Indeed, all of us who study the history of American psychology owe Marion White McPherson and John Popplestone an enormous debt of gratitude.

Contributors

David B. Baker is director of the Archives of the History of American Psychology and associate professor of psychology at the University of Akron. He received his Ph.D. in counseling psychology from Texas A & M University in 1988. His area of specialization is the rise of professional psychology in America. With Ludy T. Benjamin Jr., he is co-author of *From Séance to Science: A History of the Profession of Psychology in America* (2003).

Ludy T. Benjamin Jr. is professor of psychology and educational psychology at Texas A&M University and holder of the Murray and Celeste Fasken Professorship in Distinguished Teaching. He received his Ph.D. in experimental psychology from Texas Christian University in 1971, specializing in perception. From 1970 to 1978 he was a member of the faculty at Nebraska Wesleyan University. Following a two-year appointment as director of educational affairs for the American Psychological Association (APA) in Washington, DC, Benjamin joined the faculty at Texas A&M in 1980. His research specialty is in the history of psychology where he has focused on the development of the early American psychology laboratories and organizations, on the origins of applied psychology, and on the popularization of psychology, including a concern with the evolution of psychology's public image. Benjamin is a past president of two of the divisions of the American Psychological Association—the Division on the History of Psychology and the Division on the Teaching of Psychology—and is also past president of the Eastern Psychological Association. He

175

lives in College Station, TX with his wife Priscilla Benjamin, a former elementary school librarian.

John C. Burnham is research professor of history and (by courtesy) professor of psychiatry at Ohio State University, where he is scholar in residence at the Medical Heritage Center. He is the author of *Paths into American Culture: Psychology, Medicine, and Morals* (1988) and numerous other books and articles in the history of psychology and psychiatry. He has held visiting appointments at the University of Sydney, Bowdoin College, the University of Cambridge, and, as Fulbright Professor, at the University of Melbourne, the University of Tasmania, and the University of New England.

Donald A. Dewsbury was born in Brooklyn, New York, grew up on Long Island, and received an A.B. degree from Bucknell University. After completing his Ph.D. in psychology with Edward L. Walker, he spent a year as a postdoctoral fellow at the University of California, Berkeley with Frank A. Beach. Through much of his career he has been a comparative psychologist with a special interest in the evolution of reproductive and social behavior. In recent years, his interests have shifted so that he now works primarily in the area of the history of psychology, with a secondary interest in comparative psychology. He is the author or editor of 12 books, including *Comparative Animal Behavior* (1978) and *Comparative Psychology in the Twentieth Century* (1984). In addition, he has published more than 300 articles and book chapters. He is a fellow of the American Psychological Association's Divisions 1, 2, 6, and 26, the American Association for the Advancement of Science, the American Psychological Society, and the Animal Behavior Society. He has served as President of the Animal Behavior Society and the American Psychological Association's Divisions 6 and 26. He is the historian for Divisions 1, 6, and 26, the Psychonomic Society, and the Animal Behavior Society.

Raymond E. Fancher is professor of psychology and a founding member of the History and Theory of Psychology program at York University in Toronto. Author of *Pioneers of Psychology* and *The Intelligence Men: Makers* *of the IQ Controversy*, he has served as executive officer of Cheiron (The International Society for the History of the Behavioral and Social Sciences), and as president of the American Psychological Association's Division 26 (History of Psychology). He is currently the editor of the *Journal of the History of the Behavioral Sciences*.

C. James Goodwin earned his doctorate in cognitive psychology from Florida State University and is a professor of psychology at Wheeling Jesuit University in Wheeling, West Virginia. He is a Fellow of Divisions 2 (Society for the Teaching of Psychology) and 26 (History of Psychology) of the American Psychological Association. His areas of interest in history include the early history of experimental psychology, the origins and evolution of E. B. Titchener's Experimentalists, the history of laboratory equipment and apparatus (especially mazes), and the work of experimental psychologists Edmund Sanford, Raymond Dodge, and Walter Miles. He is the author of the undergraduate textbooks *A History of Modern Psychology* (Wiley) and *Research in Psychology: Methods and Design* (Wiley).

Marion White McPherson (Popplestone) (1919–2000) was the co-founder and associate director of the Archives of the History of American Psychology from their inception in 1965, until her formal retirement in 1990. She continued to be of service to the archives until her death in 2000. Through her efforts she helped to create the largest archival collection of material in the history of psychology in the world. Her knowledge of the archive's holdings was encyclopedic and she led many researchers to topics of considerable interest and importance in the history of psychology. She was co-author with John A. Popplestone of two books, *An Illustrated History of American Psychology*, and the *Dictionary of Concepts in General Psychology*. In addition, she authored numerous articles and made countless professional presentations. Among her many professional activities was a term as president of Division 26 (History of Psychology) of the American Psychological Association in 1990.

John A. Popplestone was the co-founder, and first director of the Archives of the History of American Psychology. He came to the University of Akron in 1961 as an assistant professor of psychology, and retired in 1999 as professor emeritus of psychology and director emeritus of the archives. After 1972, he was largely sustained by the challenge of the archive's growth. Along with Marion White McPherson he published *An Illustrated History of American Psychology* and *the Dictionary of Concepts in General Psychology*. Of service to the history of psychology community throughout his career, he served as president of the American Psychological Association's Division 26 (History of Psychology) in 1979.

Michael M. Sokal (Ph.D., History of Science & Technology, Case Western Reserve University, 1972) has been professor of history in the Department of Humanities & Arts of Worcester Polytechnic Institute (WPI) since 1970. At WPI he has received the President's Award for Outstanding Student Project Advising and the Trustees' Award for Outstanding Creative Scholarship and has held the Paris Fletcher Distinguished Professorship in the Humanities. He has also served as the executive secretary of the History of Science Society (1988–92) and as a visiting program officer at the National Endowment of the Humanities (1995) and the National Science Foundation (1998–2000). His scholarship focuses on (among other topics) the history of psychological testing in the United States and the history of American scientific institutions and has led to (among other publications) *Psychological Testing and American Society, 1890–1930* (editor; Rutgers University Press, 1987) and (with Sally Gregory Kohlstedt and Bruce V. Lewenstein) *The Establishment of Science in America: 150 Years of the American Association for the Advancement of Science* (Rutgers University Press, 1999). In 1997 he became the founding editor of *History of Psychology*, a scholarly journal published quarterly by the American Psychological Association for its Division of the History of Psychology. In 2001 he was elected vice-president of the History of Science Society. He will serve as HSS vice-president through 2003 and will begin a two-year term as President in 2004.

Ryan D. Tweney is a cognitive scientist and holds the position of professor of psychology at Bowling Green State University. His cognitive-historical interest in the processes of scientific thinking has long had a focus upon the life and works of the English physicist Michael Faraday, and on the understanding of the role of apparatus and statistics in the history of psychology. The editor of Michael Faraday's *Chemical Notes, Hints, Suggestions, and Objects of Pursuit, 1822*, (London: Peter Pergrinus, 1991), Tweney and his students are currently replicating some of Faraday's experimental work with thin gold films, in the hopes of uncovering the embodied processes of experimental research and discovery.

Hendrika Vande Kemp is a clinical psychologist and historian of psychology. From 1976–2001 she served on the faculty of the Graduate School of Psychology at Fuller Theological Seminary in Pasadena, CA, where her courses included seminars focusing on the integration of psychology and theology, in addition to regular courses in History & Systems of Psychology, Family Therapy, Interpersonal Psychology, Qualitative Research, and Dreams in Psychotherapy. She is a past president (1988–89) of the American Psychological Association's Division 36 (Psychology of Religion) and president (for 2002–3) of Division 26 (History of Psychology).

Leila Zenderland is professor of American Studies at California State University, Fullerton. She received her B.A. in American Studies from the University of Miami, and her Ph.D. in American Civilization from the University of Pennsylvania. Her research has focused on the production and dissemination of ideas from psychology, the social sciences, and American popular culture. Among her publications is an edited collection of essays entitled *Recycling the Past: Popular Uses of American History* (University of Pennsylvania Press, 1978). Her book, *Measuring Minds: Henry Herbert Goddard and the Origins of American Intelligence Testing* (Cambridge University Press, 1998), was begun with help from a Graduate Student Summer Research Grant from the Archives of the History of American Psychology, as well as with support from the National Endowment for the Humanities and the National Science Foundation. She has also conducted research at the Rockefeller Archive Center and the Wellcome Institute for the History of Medicine in London, and in 2002 she was a Fulbright Professor of American History at the University of Bremen in Germany.

Notes

Preface

1. The convening of the event was made possible through the generous support of Delmus Williams, dean of the university libraries at the University of Akron, and through the efforts of the archives staff, including Dorothy Gruich, Dianna Ford, and Sharon Ochsenhirt.

Chapter 1

1. Most notably, Michael M. Sokal, ed., *An Education in Psychology: James McKeen Cattell's Journal and Letters from Germany and England, 1880–1888* (Cambridge, Mass.: MIT Press, 1981), and Michael M. Sokal, "Life Span Developmental Psychology and the History of Science," in *Beyond History of Science: Essays in Honor of Robert E. Schofield*, ed. Elizabeth Garber (Bethlehem, Pa.: Lehigh University Press, 1990), 67–80.

2. Michael M. Sokal, "*Science* and James McKeen Cattell, 1894–1945," *Science* 209 (4 July 1980): 43–52.

3. Michael M. Sokal, "Graduate Study with Wundt: Two Eyewitness Accounts," in *Wundt Studies: A Centennial Collection*, ed. Wolfgang G. Bringmann and Ryan D. Tweney (Toronto: C. J. Hogrefe, 1980), 210–25.

4. Michael M. Sokal, "Psychology at Victorian Cambridge—The Unofficial Laboratory of 1887–1888," *Proceedings of the American Philosophical Society* 116 (1972): 145–147.

5. Michael M. Sokal, "James McKeen Cattell and the Failure of Anthropometric Mental Testing," in *The Problematic Science: Psychology in Nineteenth-Century Thought*, ed. William R. Woodward and Mitchell G. Ash (New York: Praeger, 1982), 322–345.

6. Leila Zenderland, *Measuring Minds: Henry Herbert Goddard and the Origins of American Intelligence Testing* (New York: Cambridge University Press, 1998).

7. Michael M. Sokal, "Baldwin, Cattell, and the *Psychological Review*: A Collaboration and Its Discontents," *History of the Human Sciences* 10 (1997): 57–89.

8. Michael M. Sokal, "Stargazing: James McKeen Cattell, *American Men*

of Science, and the Reward Structure of the American Scientific Community, 1906–1944," in *Psychology, Science, and Human Affairs: Essays in Honor of William Bevan*, ed. Frank Kessel (Boulder, Colo.: Westview Press, 1995), 64–86.

9. Nicholas Murray Butler to Cattell, March 4, 1907, James McKeen Cattell files, Columbia University, New York, N.Y.; Butler to Seth Low, March 29, 1909, Cattell files; Edwin B. Wilson to George Ellery Hale, January 22, 1917, California Institute of Technology Archives, Pasadena, Calif.; Philip J. Pauly, *Controlling Life: Jacques Loeb and the Engineering Ideal in Biology* (New York: Oxford University Press, 1987), 142–143, 227; Carol Singer Gruber, "Academic Freedom at Columbia University, 1917–1918: The Case of James McKeen Cattell," *AAUP Bulletin* 58 (1972): 297–305.

10. James McKeen Cattell, "Academic Slavery," *School and Society* 6 (1917): 421–26; Ernest R. A. Seligman to the University Trustees, June 18, 1917, Cattell files.

11. Michael M. Sokal, "The Origins of the Psychological Corporation," *Journal of the History of the Behavioral Sciences* 17 (1981): 54–67; and Michael M. Sokal, "James McKeen Cattell and American Psychology in the 1920s," in *Explorations in the History of Psychology in the United States,* ed. Josef Brozek (Lewisburg, Pa.: Bucknell University Press, 1984), 273–323; Sally Gregory Kohlstedt, Michael M. Sokal, and Bruce V. Lewenstein, *The Establishment of Science in America: 150 Years of the American Association for the Advancement of Science* (New Brunswick, N.J.: Rutgers University Press, 1999).

12. Sokal, "Life Span Developmental Psychology."

13. Francis G. Gosling, "Neurasthenia in Pennsylvania: A Perspective on the Origins of American Psychotherapy," *Journal of the History of Medicine* 40 (1985): 188–206.

14. Entry for August 20, 1869, Israel Platt Pardee, "A Boy's Trip to Europe, 1869–1870," typescript copy of diary, Skillman Library, Lafayette College, Easton, Pa.

15. James McKeen Cattell, "The School and the Family," *Popular Science Monthly* 74 (1909): 84–95.

16. Daniel J. Levinson (with Charlotte N. Darrow, Edward B. Klein, Maria H. Levinson, and Braxton McKee), *The Seasons of a Man's Life* (New York: Alfred A. Knopf, 1978); Richard Lebeaux, *Thoreau's Seasons* (Amherst: University of Massachusetts Press, 1984).

17. Gail Sheehy, *Passages: Predictable Crises of Adult Life* (New York: Dutton, 1976); Sokal, "Life Span Developmental Psychology."

18. Sokal, "*Science* and James McKeen Cattell," and Kohlstedt, Sokal, and Lewenstein, *The Establishment of Science in America;* Entry for April 13, 1883, James McKeen Cattell Student Journal, Manuscript Division, Library of Congress, Washington, D.C.

19. Sokal, "Baldwin, Cattell, and the *Psychological Review*"; Burton E. Livingston to Herman L. Fairchild, February 17, 1931, Fairchild Papers, University of Rochester Library, Rochester, N.Y.

20. F. Scott Fitzgerald, "The Rich Boy," *Redbook*, January and February 1926; Ernest Hemingway, "The Snows of Kilimanjaro," *Esquire*, August 1936.

21. C. P. Snow, *The Masters* (New York: Charles Scribner's Sons, 1951), 195.

22. George Stade, "A Romance for Highbrows," review of *Nuns and Soliders* by Iris Murdoch, *The New York Times*, January 4, 1981; Iris Murdoch, *Metaphysics as a Guide to Morals* (New York: Allen Lane, 1993).

23. Iris Murdoch, *The Message to the Planet* (New York: Penguin Books, 1989), 562; Iris Murdoch, *The Green Knight* (New York: Viking Press, 1993), 185.

24. Jill C. Gitten, "Reading Logs, PSY 6609, Spring 1997," University of Florida, Gainesville, Fla; Ludy T. Benjamin Jr., *A History of Psychology in Letters* (Dubuque, Iowa: Brown & Benchmark, 1993), 39–53; *Diagnostic and Statistical Manual of Mental Disorders: DSM-IV*, 4th ed. (Washington, D.C.: American Psychiatric Association, 1994).

25. Lorna Smith Benjamin, *Interpersonal Diagnosis and Treatment of Personality Disorders*, 2nd ed. (New York: The Guilford Press, 1996), esp. chapter 6, "Narcissistic Personality Disorder," 141–61. I am most grateful to Hendrika Vande Kemp, who referred me to this chapter at the Popplestone-McPherson Festschrift Conference.

26. Clifford Geertz, *A Life of Learning: Charles Homer Haskins Lecture for 1999*, ACLS Occasional Paper no. 45 (New York: American Council of Learned Societies, 1999) 14–15.

27. Michael M. Sokal, "History of Psychology and History of Science: Reflections on Two Subdisciplines, Their Relationship, and Their Convergence" in *Psychology in Its Historical Context: Essays in Honour of Prof. Josef Brozek* (Valencia: Monografias de la Revista de Historia de la Psicologia, 1985), 337–47; Michael M. Sokal, "On *History of Psychology*'s Launch," *History of Psychology* 1 (1998): 3–7.

28. Sokal, "*Science* and James McKeen Cattell"; Michael M. Sokal, "Companions in Zealous Research, 1886–1986," *American Scientist* 74 (1986): 486–508; Michael M. Sokal, "Origins and Early Years of the American Psychological Association," *American Psychologist* 47 (1992): 111–22; reprinted in *The American Psychological Association: A Historical Perspective*, ed. Rand B. Evans, Virginia S. Sexton, and Thomas C. Cadwallader (Washington, D. C.: American Psychological Association, 1992), 43–71; and Kohlstedt, Sokal, and Lewenstein, *The Establishment of Science in America*.

Chapter 2

1. I am not attempting here a full discussion of the use of oral histories but simply reporting my own experience. The evolution of oral history in the late twentieth century is described in such publications as John Murphy, "The Voice of Memory: History, Autobiography and Oral Memory," *Historical Studies* 22 (1986): 157–75.

2. The Boring and the Healy-Bronner oral histories are, by the request of the interviewees, deposited and available in the Harvard University libraries. A copy of the Ogburn tapes was presented to the University of Chicago archives for safekeeping.

3. John C. Burnham, "John B. Watson: Interviewee, Professional Figure, Symbol," in *Modern Perspectives on John B. Watson and Classical Behaviorism*, ed. James T. Todd and Edward K. Morris (Westport, Conn.: Greenwood Press, 1994), 65–73.

4. One generalization that I came to after many interviews of older people was that the more intellectually lively any one of them was at the height of his or her career, the more likely that reminiscences in old age would be insightful. In other words, quality carried through, even though memory might not.

5. Mitchell Ash has provided full biographical articles for the Bühlers in the *American National Biography*.

6. See, for example, the issues dedicated to her of the *Journal of Humanistic Psychology* 3 (Fall 1963) and 4 (Spring 1964).

7. There is an obituary in the *New York Times*, September 27, 1977, 42. He was also listed in *Contemporary Authors*. Unless otherwise noted, I have, here and below, added or checked biographical material from such standard sources as *The Psychological Record*, *Who's Who in America*, and other standard published directories.

8. My interview material is, of course, superseded by the later oral history in the Archives of the History of American Psychology.

9. Shepard was listed in standard sources such as *Who's Who in America*.

10. Details of the history of the Michigan department appear in Walter B. Pillsbury, "The Department of Psychology," in *The University of Michigan: An Encyclopedic Survey*, ed. Wilfred B. Shaw, 4 vols. (Ann Arbor: University of Michigan Press, 1951), 2: 708–14. Angell, Mead, and Dewey all had Michigan ties of one kind or another.

11. Fite went on to become, not a psychologist, but a philosopher—of considerable distinction—at Princeton.

12. Clark L. Hull, in *A History of Psychology in Autobiography, Volume 4*, ed. Edwin G. Boring et al. (Worcester Mass.: Clark University Press, 1952), 153: "Professor Shepard, who as a graduate student had come into contact with Watson at the University of Chicago, mentioned him in a rather sympathetic way."

13. See especially Karl M. Dallenbach, "Walter Bowers Pillsbury: 1872–1960," *American Journal of Psychology* 74 (1961): 165–73; "Walter B. Pillsbury," in *A History of Psychology in Autobiography, Volume II*, ed. Carl Murchison (Worcester Mass.: Clark University Press, 1932). Pillsbury, "The Department of Psychology." There is also an entry in the *American National Biography*, by Paul F. Ballantyne. My notes do have one entry that does not seem to be recorded elsewhere, but I have not determined the accuracy of it: Pillsbury apparently tried West Point, but he did not like it. How this squared with his petit mal that Dallenbach mentions is hard to surmise.

14. This was another story detailed in Pillsbury, "The Department of Psychology."

15. Pierce, according to his obituary in the *New York Times*, February 17, 1929, was a successful businessman who had retired ten years before his death. He was active in Harvard affairs and in 1924 published *The Philosophy of Character* (Cambridge: Harvard University Press, 1924).

16. W. B. Pillsbury, *Attention* (c.1908; London: George Allen & Unwin, 1921), mentioned Freud's views with great respect. There was an earlier French edition.

17. According to an obituary in the *Daily Local News*, West Chester, Pa, May 6, 1961, courtesy of the Paoli Library, Mateer from 1921 to 1945 operated a school for abnormal children, the Merryheart School, in Columbus, Ohio, and from 1947 to 1950 was psychologist for the Pomona California public school system before becoming, from 1950 to 1957, professor of psychology at Claremont Graduate School.

18. Full background is in Leila Zenderland, *Measuring Minds: Henry Herbert Goddard and the Origins of American Intelligence Testing* (New York: Cambridge University Press, 1998).

19. Leila Zenderland informs me that this cannot have been correct, that there was another worker there who knew French and, indeed, had a degree from the Sorbonne.

20. My notes are unclear here, and this assertion is not consistent with what she had just told me.

21. Florence Mateer, "The Vocabulary of a Four Year Old Boy," *Pedagogical Seminary* 15 (1908): 63–74. A note on the first page by H. H. Goddard stated, "This study was made under my direction, as a graduation thesis at the West Chester State Normal School." Goddard went from West Chester to Vineland, and so it was not surprising that Mateer worked with him at Vineland a few years later.

22. Henry H. Goddard, "The Form Board as a Measure of Intellectual Development in Children," *The Training School* 9 (1912): 49–52 (at that point the board was already available from the Stoelting company of Chicago); Reuel Hull Sylvester, "The Form Board Test," *Psychological Monographs*, 15 (1913): 1–4, provided his own historical account.

23. See, for example, Albert T. Poffenberger, "Robert Sessions Woodworth: 1869–1962," *American Journal of Psychology,* 75 (1962), 677–89; Gardner Murphy, "Robert Sessions Woodworth," *American Psychologist* 18 (1963), 131–33; and the entry by Andrew S. Winston in the *American National Biography*.

24. Actually it was pages 585 and 586, in George Trumbull Ladd and Robert Sessions Woodworth, *Elements of Physiological Psychology: A Treatise of the Activities and Nature of the Mind from the Physical and Experimental Points of View,* 2d ed. (New York: Charles Scribner's Sons, 1911).

25. See especially Laurance F. Shaffer, "Frederic Lyman Wells: 1884–1964," *American Journal of Psychology* 77 (1964): 679–82, and the entry in the *American National Biography* by Eugene Taylor.

26. Frederic Lyman Wells, "Critique of Impure Reason," *Journal of Abnormal Psychology* 7 (1912): 89–93.

27. Shaffer, "Frederic Lyman Wells."

28. My notes say "probably"—apparently Wells's memory was not clear on this.

29. John M. Reisman, *A History of Clinical Psychology,* 2nd ed. (New York: Hemisphere Publishing Corporation, 1991), 157–61.

30. Ibid.

Chapter 3

1. See Ludy T. Benjamin Jr., "Research at the Archives of the History of American Psychology: A Case History," in *Historiography of Modern Psychology*, ed. Josef Brozek and Ludwig J. Pongratz (Toronto: C. J. Hogrefe, 1980), 241–51; Ludy T. Benjamin Jr., "Remarks Honoring John A. Popplestone and Marion White McPherson for Contributions to the History of Psychology," *History of Psychology* 3(2000): 75–7.

2. See, for example, Ludy T. Benjamin Jr., "The Pioneering Work of Leta Hollingworth in the Psychology of Women," *Nebraska History* 56 (1975): 493–505; Ludy T. Benjamin Jr., "Harry Hollingworth: Portrait of a Generalist," in *Portraits of Pioneers in Psychology*, vol. 2, ed. Gregory A. Kimble, C. Alan Boneau, and Michael Wertheimer (Mahwah, NJ: Lawrence Erlbaum, 1996), 119–35.

3. Ludy T. Benjamin Jr., "The Psychological Round Table: Revolution of 1936," *American Psychologist* 32 (1977): 542–49; Ludy T. Benjamin Jr., "The Midwestern Psychological Association: A History of the Organization and Its Antecedents," *American*

Psychologist 34 (1979): 201–13; Ludy T. Benjamin Jr., "A History of the New York Branch of the American Psychological Association, 1903–1935," *American Psychologist* 46 (1991): 1003–11; Ludy T. Benjamin Jr., "A History of Division 14: The Society for Industrial and Organizational Psychology," in *Unification through Division: Histories of the Divisions of the American Psychological Association*, ed. Donald A. Dewsbury, vol. 2 (Washington, D.C.: American Psychological Association, 1997), 101–26; Ludy T. Benjamin Jr., "Organized Industrial Psychology before Division 14: The ACP and the AAAP," *Journal of Applied Psychology* 82 (1997): 459–66.

4. Ludy T. Benjamin Jr., "David Pablo Boder's Psychological Museum and the Exposition of 1938," *Psychological Record* 29 (1979): 559–65; Ludy T. Benjamin Jr. and Darryl Bruce, "From Bottle-fed Chimp to Bottlenose Dolphin: A Contemporary Appraisal of Winthrop Niles Kellogg," *Psychological Record* 32 (1982): 461–82; Ludy T. Benjamin Jr., "A History of Teaching Machines," *American Psychologist* 43 (1988): 703–12; Ludy T. Benjamin Jr. and Elizabeth Nielsen-Gammon, "B. F. Skinner and Psychotechnology: The Case of the Heir Conditioner," *Review of General Psychology* 3 (1999): 155–67; David B. Baker and Ludy T. Benjamin Jr., "The Affirmation of the Scientist-Practitioner: A Look Back at Boulder," *American Psychologist* 55 (2000): 241–47.

5. Some of these reports are in the Harry Hollingworth Papers in the Archives of the History of American Psychology, University of Akron, Akron, Ohio (hereafter Hollingworth Papers). Other reports are mentioned in Hollingworth's unpublished autobiography included in the Hollingworth Papers.

6. Harry L. Hollingworth, "The Influence of Caffein on Mental and Motor Efficiency," *Archives of Psychology* No. 22 (1912): 1–166; Harry L. Hollingworth, *Advertising and Selling: Principles of Appeal and Response* (New York: D. Appleton, 1913); Harry L. Hollingworth, *Vocational Psychology: Its Problems and Methods* (New York: D. Appleton, 1916); Harry L. Hollingworth and Albert T. Poffenberger, *Applied Psychology* (New York: D. Appleton, 1917).

7. Harry L. Hollingworth, *The Psychology of Functional Neuroses* (New York: D. Appleton, 1920); Harry L. Hollingworth, *Judging Human Character* (New York: D. Appleton, 1922); Harry L. Hollingworth, *Vocational Psychology and Character Analysis* (New York: D. Appleton, 1929); Harry L. Hollingworth, *Abnormal Psychology: Its Concepts and Theories* (New York: Ronald Press, 1930); Harry L. Hollingworth, *Educational Psychology* (New York: D. Appleton, 1933); Harry L. Hollingworth, *The Psychology of the Audience* (New York: American Book Company, 1935).

8. A typed and handwritten page in the Hollingworth Papers showed that Hollingworth's Barnard College salary reached a high of nine thousand dollars in 1929 and remained at that figure each year until his retirement in 1946. Documents concerning the Leta S. Hollingworth Fellowship at Columbia University are in the Hollingworth Papers.

9. Harry Hollingworth's unpublished autobiography is dated 1940 and organized in two volumes titled "Born in Nebraska" and "Years at Columbia." The original is housed in the Hollingworth Papers at Akron; a copy is in the collections of the Nebraska State Historical Society in Lincoln. Permission to quote from the autobiography was granted to the author by Benjamin H. Florence, executor of the Hollingworth estate.

10. Hollingworth, "Years at Columbia," 56.

11. Peter Novick, *That Noble Dream: The "Objectivity Question" and the American Historical Profession* (New York: Cambridge University Press, 1988); Hollingworth, "Years at Columbia," 56, 58.

12. Hollingworth, "Born in Nebraska," 79a.

13. Hollingworth, "Born in Nebraska," 90a.

14. Hollingworth, "Born in Nebraska," 232–34, from a chapter titled "The University of Montgomery Ward."

15. Thaddeus Bolton was exceptionally important to both Hollingworths, and probably Hollingworth's most significant mentor. It was also through Bolton that Hollingworth met Leta Stetter.

16. For information on Leta Hollingworth, see Harry Hollingworth, *Leta Stetter Hollingworth: A Biography* (Lincoln: University of Nebraska Press, 1943; rpt Bolton, Mass.: Anker Publishing, 1990); Stephanie A. Shields, "Ms. Pilgrim's Progress: The Contributions of Leta Stetter Hollingworth to the Psychology of Women," *American Psychologist* 30 (1975): 852–57; Ludy T. Benjamin Jr. and Stephanie A. Shields, "Leta Stetter Hollingworth" in *Women in Psychology: A Biobibliographic Sourcebook*, ed. Agnes N. O'Connell and Nancy F. Russo (New York: Greenwood Press, 1990) p 173–83; Ann G. Klein, *A Forgotten Voice: A Biography of Leta S. Hollingworth* (Scottsdale, AZ: Great Potential Press, 2003).

17. Hollingworth, "Born in Nebraska," 86.

18. Unpublished paper, "On the Accuracy of Some Acquired Habits," read before the Sigma Xi chapter at the University of Nebraska, 1906, Hollingworth Papers; Hollingworth, "Years at Columbia," 21; Harry L. Hollingworth, "The Inaccuracy of Movement," *Archives of Psychology* 13 (1909): 1–80.

19. See for example, Elizabeth Scarborough and Laurel Furumoto, *Untold Lives: The First Generation of American Women Psychologists* (New York: Columbia University Press, 1987).

20. Harry L. Hollingworth, "Memories of the Early Development of the Psychology of Advertising Suggested by Burtt's Psychology of Advertising," *Psychological Bulletin* 35 (1938): 307–11.

21. Walter D. Scott, *The Theory of Advertising* (Boston: Small, Maynard & Co., 1903); Walter D. Scott, *The Psychology of Advertising* (Boston: Small, Maynard & Co., 1908); Hollingworth, *Advertising and Selling*.

22. Ludy T. Benjamin Jr., Anne M. Rogers, and Angela Rosenbaum, "Coca-Cola, Caffeine, and Mental Deficiency: Harry Hollingworth and the Chattanooga Trial of 1911," *Journal of the History of the Behavioral Sciences* 27 (1991): 42–55.

23. Hollingworth, "Memories of the Early Development of the Psychology of Advertising," 308.

24. According to his autobiography and the preface to the published account of the caffeine studies, Hollingworth said that his contract with Coca-Cola called for the studies to be published regardless of their outcome. Further, Coca-Cola was barred from using the research in its advertising or from using Hollingworth's or Columbia University's names in advertising. No copies of this agreement were found in the Hollingworth Papers nor in the Coca-Cola Archives in Atlanta, Georgia.

25. Hollingworth, "Years at Columbia," 65.

26. A letter from Leta Hollingworth to Anna Stetter Fischer (Leta's cousin) dated

April 28, 1911, states, "We did a big experiment for the Coca-Cola Company and made quite a neat little 'wad' of money." A copy of the letter is in the author's possession; original is in family papers in Garland, Neb.

27. Hollingworth, "Years at Columbia," 111–12.

28. Hollingworth, "Years at Columbia," 79.

29. "Hollingworth Tests for Selection of Salesmen," no date, Hollingworth Papers.

30. Katherine Blackford was an American physician who developed a nonscientific characterological system for selecting employees. Her system was popular with American businesses from the publication of her books around 1915, into the 1930s. Katherine M. H. Blackford and Arthur Newcomb, *Analyzing Character: The New Science of Judging Men, Misfits in Business, the Home and Social Life* (New York: The Review of Reviews Co., 1913); Katherine M. H. Blackford and Arthur Newcomb, *The Job, the Man, the Boss* (New York: The Review of Reviews Co., 1914). The Blackford system was a frequent target of psychologists who lamented the common acceptance of such pseudopsychologies in business and industry.

31. Paul Fargis and Sheree Bykofsky (Eds.) *The New York Public Library Desk Reference* (New York: Simon & Schuster, 1989) 714.

32. Hollingworth, "Years at Columbia," 176–79.

33. Harry L. Hollingworth, "Psychological Influence of Alcohol," *Journal of Abnormal and Social Psychology* 18 (1923): 204–37; Harry L. Hollingworth, "Psychological Influence of Alcohol, Part 2," *Journal of Abnormal and Social Psychology* 18 (1924): 317–33; Harry L. Hollingworth, "When is a Man Intoxicated?" *Journal of Applied Psychology* 9 (1925): 122–30.

34. Hollingworth, "Years at Columbia," 82.

35. William Jennings Bryan, *The First Battle: A Story of the Campaign of 1896* (Chicago, 1897, 199–206); Hollingworth, "Years at Columbia," 83. Bryan was not born in Nebraska but in Salem, Ill. in 1860. He moved to Nebraska when he was twenty-three years old.

36. For the story of this book, see Ludy T. Benjamin Jr., "A Platform Disaster: Harry Hollingworth and the Psychology of Public Speaking," *Nebraska History* 81 (2000): 67–73.

37. Harry L. Hollingworth, "Psycho-Dynamics of Chewing," *Archives of Psychology* No. 239 (1939): 5–6.

38. Hollingworth, "Psycho-Dynamics of Chewing," 90.

39. Columbia University subscribed to a clipping service for its faculty. The Hollingworth Papers contain a large number of clippings on the alcohol and gum-chewing studies.

40. Hollingworth, "Years at Columbia," 56.

41. Harry L. Hollingworth, *Psychology: Its Facts and Principles* (New York: D. Appleton, 1928); Hollingworth, "Years at Columbia," 196.

42. Hollingworth, *Psychology: Its Facts and Principles*, vi.

43. Hollingworth, "Years at Columbia," 207–8.

44. Hollingworth, "Years at Columbia," 200.

45. Hollingworth, "Years at Columbia," 178.

Chapter 4

1. C. James Goodwin, "Maze Learning as Method: Origins and Early Development," paper presented at the American Psychological Association, August 1991, San Francisco, Calif.; Walter R. Miles, "On the History of Research with Rats and Mazes: A Collection of Notes," *Journal of General Psychology* 3 (1930): 324–37.

2. Ernest R. Hilgard, "Walter Richard Miles: 1885–1978," *American Journal of Psychology* 93 (1980): 565–68; Harry Helson to Neal Miller, March 3, 1953, Miles Papers, Archives of the History of American Psychology, University of Akron, Akron, Ohio.

3. William James, *Psychology: The Briefer Course* (New York: Henry Holt, 1892); Walter R. Miles, "Walter R. Miles," in *A History of Psychology in Autobiography,* Volume 5, ed. E. G. Boring and Gardner Lindzey (New York: Appleton-Century-Crofts, 1967), 221–52; George D. Stoddard, "Carl Emil Seashore," *American Journal of Psychology* 63 (1950): 456–62.

4. Walter R. Miles, "Accuracy of the Voice in Simple Pitch Singing," *Psychological Review Monographs* 16 (1914): 13–66; C. James Goodwin, "On the Origins of Titchener's Experimentalists," *Journal of the History of the Behavioral Sciences* 21 (1985): 383–89; Laurel Furumoto, "Shared Knowledge: The Experimentalists, 1904–1929," in *The Rise of Experimentation in American Psychology*, ed. Jill G. Morawski (New Haven: Yale University Press, 1988), 94–113.

5. Robert M. Yerkes, "Raymond Dodge 1871–1942," *American Journal of Psychology* 55 (1942): 584–600; Hilgard, "Walter R. Miles," 566.

6. Walter R. Miles, "Some Psycho-physiological Processes as Affected by Alcohol," *Proceedings of the National Academy of Sciences* 2 (1916): 703–9; Walter R. Miles, "The Effect of a Prolonged Reduced Diet on Twenty-five College Men," *Proceedings of the National Academy of Sciences* 4 (1918): 152–56.

7. Henry L. Minton, *Lewis M. Terman: Pioneer in Psychological Testing* (New York: New York University Press, 1988), 131–36; Hilgard, "Walter R. Miles," 566.

8. Walter R. Miles, "Horizontal Eye Movements at the Onset of Sleep," *Psychological Review* 36 (1929): 122–41; Walter R. Miles, "The Narrow-Path Elevated Maze for Studying Rats," *Proceedings for the Society of Experimental Biology and Medicine* 24 (1927): 454–56; Walter R. Miles, "Change of Dexterity with Age," *Proceedings for the Society of Experimental Biology and Medicine* 29 (1931): 136–38; Miles, "Walter R. Miles," 235.

9. Miles to Raymond Dodge, September 7, 1927, Miles Papers; Walter R. Miles, "Studies in Physical Exertion I: A Multiple Chronograph for Measuring Groups of Men," *American Physical Education Review* 33 (1928): 379–87; "Studies in Physical Exertion II: Individual and Group Reaction Time in Football Charging," *Research Quarterly* 2, no. 3 (1931): 5–13; "Studies in Physical Exertion III: Effect of Signal Variation in Football Charging," *Research Quarterly* 2, no. 3 (1931): 14–31; Daniel Gould and Sean Pick, "Sport Psychology: The Griffith Era, 1920–1940," *The Sport Psychologist* 9 (1995): 391–405; Miles to B. C. Graves, February 19, 1932, Miles Papers.

10. Walter R. Miles, "A Pursuit Pendulum," *Psychological Review* 27 (1920): 361–76; Walter R. Miles "Pursuitmeter," *Journal of Experimental Psychology* 4 (1921): 77–105.

11. Walter R. Miles, "The Narrow-Path Elevated Maze for Studying Rats," *Proceedings for the Society of Experimental Biology and Medicine* 24 (1927): 454–56; Walter R. Miles, "On the History of Research With Rats and Mazes: A Collection of Notes," *Journal of General Psychology* 3 (1930): 324–37; Josephine R. Knotts and Walter R. Miles, "Notes on the History and Construction of the Stylus Maze," *Journal of General Psychology* 35 (1928): 415–25; Walter R. Miles, "The Two-Story Duplicate Maze," *Journal of Experimental Psychology* 10 (1927): 365–77; Walter R. Miles, "The High relief Finger Maze for Human Learning," *Journal of General Psychology* 1 (1928): 3–14; John A. Popplestone and Ryan D. Tweney, eds., *The Great Catalog of the C. H. Stoelting Company, 1930–1937* (Delmar, N.Y.: Scholars Facsimiles & Reprints, 1997), originally published as *Psychological and Physiological Apparatus.* (Delmar, N.Y.: Scholars Facsimiles & Reprints, 1930).

12. With Terman, Miles initially requested between ten and twenty-five thousand dollars, to be spread over a ten-year period. The Carnegie granted ten thousand dollars in 1928 and gave another twelve thousand dollars in 1932. Miles and Terman also applied for funds, without success, to the National Research Council and to the Social Science Research Council. For further details, see Walter R. Miles, "The Stanford University Studies of Later Maturity," unpublished and undated manuscript of a talk delivered by Miles, Miles Papers, Box 1102.

13. Walter R. Miles, "Age and Human Ability," *Psychological Review* 40 (1933): 99–123; Nancy Bayley, "Development of Mental Abilities," in *Carmichael's Manual of Child Psychology*, vol. 1, 3rd ed., ed. Paul H. Mussen (New York: Wiley, 1970), 1163–1209; Catherine M. Cox, *Genetic Studies of Genius, Volume 2: The Early Mental Traits of Three Hundred Geniuses* (Stanford, Calif.: Stanford University Press, 1926); Lewis M. Terman and Catherine Cox Miles, *Sex and Personality: Studies in Masculinity and Femininity* (New York: McGraw-Hill, 1936).

14. Hilgard, "Walter R. Miles," 567; Robert R. Sears, "Catherine Cox Miles: 1890–1984," *American Journal of Psychology* 99 (1986): 431–33.

15. Walter R. Miles, "Red Goggles for Producing Dark Adaptation," *Federal Proceedings of American Societies for Experimental Biology* 2 (1943): 109–15. The award citation referred specifically to Miles's "researches on the use of red filters for adapting the eyes to vision at low levels of illumination. This work, conducted with theoretical insight, has led to many practical outcomes and was of inestimable value in our war-time experiences"; William A. Hunt to Miles, January 17, 1949, Miles Papers.

16. Edwin G. Boring, "The Society of Experimental Psychologists: 1904–1938," *American Journal of Psychology* 51 (1938): 410–23; Edwin G. Boring, "Titchener's Experimentalists," *Journal of the History of the Behavioral Sciences* 3 (1967): 315–25.

17. Miles, Diary, April 20–22, 1916, April 7, 1917, Miles Papers.

18. Miles, Diary, April 7, 1917, Miles Papers.

19. Miles to Raymond Dodge, March 14, 1929, Dodge Papers, Archives of the History of American Psychology, University of Akron, Akron, Ohio.

20. National Research Council, "Annual Meeting of the Division of Anthropology and Psychology, April 20 and 21, 1928," NRC Papers, Archives of the National Academy of Sciences, Washington, D.C.; Knight Dunlap to E. G. Boring, January 30, 1928, E. G. Boring Papers, Harvard University Archives, Boston, Mass. For more on

the origins of the NRC and psychology's place in the organization, see Robert M. Yerkes, "Report of the Psychology Committee of the National Research Council," *Psychological Review* 26 (1919): 83–149; Albert T. Poffenberger, "A History of the National Research Council, 1919–1933. VIII. Division of Anthropology and Psychology," *Science* 78 (August 25 1933): 158–61; Ronald C. Tobey, *The American Ideology of National Science, 1919–1930* (Pittsburgh, Pa.: University of Pittsburgh Press, 1971), chapter 2.

21. Boring to Miles, February 21, 1928, Miles Papers; Boring to Miles, March 10, 1928, Miles Papers. There were to have been thirty-three psychologists at the meeting, but Harvey Carr cancelled at the last minute due to illness; Miles, Diary, March 28, 1928, Miles Papers.

22. Miles, Diary, March 29, 1928, Miles Papers.

23. Miles, Diary, March 30, 1928, Miles Papers.

24. Ibid.

25. James H. Capshew and Ernest R. Hilgard, "The Power of Service: World War II and Professional Reform in the American Psychological Association," in *100 Years: The American Psychological Association, A Historical Perspective*, ed. Rand B. Evans, Virginia S. Sexton, and Thomas C. Cadwallader (Washington, D.C.: American Psychological Association), 149–75.

26. National Research Council, "Annual Meeting of the Division of Anthropology and Psychology, April 12 and 13, 1929," NRC Papers, Archives of the National Academy of Sciences, Washington, D.C.

27. Boring, "The Society of Experimental Psychologists: 1904–1938," 416–19.

28. Miles, Diary, September 3, 1929, Miles Papers.

29. Miles, Diary, March 28, 1928, Miles Papers.

30. Miles, Diary, September 3, 1929, Miles Papers.

31. Franz Samelson, "Organizing for the Kingdom of Behavior: Academic Battles and Organizing Policies in the Twenties," *Journal of the History of the Behavioral Science* 21 (1985): 33–47.

32. Miles, Diary, April 28, 1916, Miles Papers.

33. Miles, Diary, April 1, 1931, Miles Papers.

34. Laurel Ulrich, *A Midwife's Tale: The Life of Martha Ballard, Based on Her Diary, 1785–1812* (New York: Vintage Books, 1990).

Chapter 5

1. Leon Kamin, *The Science and Politics of I.Q.* (Potomac, Md.: Erlbaum, 1974). For some of the controversies surrounding intelligence testing, see Lee J. Cronbach, "Five Decades of Public Controversy over Mental Testing," *American Psychologist* 30 (January 1975): 1–14; Raymond Fancher, *The Intelligence Men: Makers of the IQ Controversy* (New York: Norton, 1985); N.J. Block and Gerald Dworkin, eds., *The IQ Controversy: Critical Readings* (New York: Pantheon, 1976); and Russell Jacoby and Naomi Glauberman, eds., *The Bell Curve Debate: History, Documents, Opinions* (New York: Times Books, 1995).

2. Some of the most sophisticated work that emerged at this time concerned the army testing program of World War I. See, for example, Franz Samelson, "Putting

Psychology on the Map: Ideology and Intelligence Testing," in *Psychology in Social Context,* ed. Allan R. Buss (New York: Irvington, 1979), 103–68; and Daniel Kevles, "Testing the Army's Intelligence: Psychologists and the Military in World War I," *Journal of American History* 55 (1968): 565–81.

3. Stephen Jay Gould, *The Mismeasure of Man* (New York: Norton, 1981), 160; Knight Dunlap, "Antidotes for Superstitions Concerning Human Heredity," *Scientific Monthly* 51 (September 1940): 221.

4. Robert Fischer to Henry Herbert Goddard, February 10, 1948, Fischer Papers, Archives of the History of American Psychology, University of Akron, Akron, Ohio.

5. Goddard to Robert Fischer, February 15, 1948, Fischer Papers.

6. The phrase "history from the bottom up" is most closely associated with the work of historian Jesse Lemisch in the 1960s. On changes in historiography, see Peter Novick, *That Noble Dream: The "Objectivity Question" and the American Historical Profession* (New York: Cambridge University Press, 1988), esp. 415–521.

7. There are currently some Web sites that effectively chronicle the career of Lowell Thomas. See for example, "Cinerama Pioneers' Bios." and "High Adventure: A Way of Life for Lowell Thomas" at the Cinerama Adventure Web site, http://www.cineramaadventure.com/thomas.htm

8. Lowell Thomas to Goddard, January 10, 1933, File M32, Goddard Papers, Archives of the History of American Psychology, University of Akron, Akron, Ohio.

9. Goddard to Lowell Thomas, January 23, 1933, File M32, Goddard Papers.

10. Lowell Thomas to Goddard, February 9, 1933, File M32, Goddard Papers.

11. "Copy for Dr. Goddard" of letter from "SCK" to Edwin J. Schanfarber, September 28, 1938, File M31, Goddard Papers.

12. For my brief summary of Goddard's efforts to help Selina Krenberger, see *Measuring Minds,* 333–34.

13. Dr. Krenberger to Goddard (written in German), September 7, 1926, January 29, 1928, both in File M35, and February 10, 1929, File M36, Goddard Papers.

14. The letter from "SCK" [Samuel C. Kohs] to Edwin J. Schanfarber includes retyped paragraphs from Goddard's original letter (which is missing). In these, Goddard states that Krenberger had been a friend of Freud's and had introduced Goddard to him.

15. Krenberger to Goddard (in German), 1925, File M33.1, Goddard Papers.

16. For an analysis of the rapid nazification of Austria, see Saul Friedlander's discussions of Vienna and the "Austrian model" in *Nazi Germany and the Jews, Vol. I: The Years of Persecution, 1933–1939* (New York: HarperCollins, 1997), 239–68.

17. Much of my description of Selina comes from her father's letters. Apparently, in 1938 Selina sent Goddard a curriculum vitae that included her publications. Goddard mentioned some of her work (such as stories published in an American newspaper) in his letter to Kohs, which Kohs reproduced in his letter to Schanfarber. See "Copy for Dr. Goddard" of letter from "SCK" to Edwin J. Schanfarber, September 28, 1938. While Goddard estimated Selina to be "approximately 35 years old," material I later received (see below) showed that she was forty-three.

18. Samuel S. Fels to Goddard, August 10, 1938, File M37, Goddard Papers.

19. Ibid.

20. Ibid. Fels may have been referring to the International Conference convened

by Roosevelt to deal with the refugee issue in 1938, in which representatives from thirty-two countries met from July 6 to 14 in the French town of Evian (not London). This conference established an Intergovernmental Committee for Refugees, but this committee ultimately proved worthless. In fact, the Evian conference was considered a disaster, for instead of presenting solutions, it aided Nazi propaganda in showing that none of these countries really wanted Jewish refugees. See, for example, Friedlander, *Nazi Germany and the Jews*, Vol. I, 248–49.

21. Samuel Kohs to Goddard, January 8, 1946, File M42, Goddard Papers. On Kohs's work as an intelligence tester, see Zenderland, *Measuring Minds*, 246–47.

22. While Goddard's original letter is missing, parts are recopied in Kohs's letter to Schanfarber. See "Copy for Dr. Goddard" of letter from "SCK" to Edwin J. Schanfarber, September 28, 1938.

23. Ibid.

24. Samuel D. Luchs to Goddard, October 3, 1938, File M37, Goddard Papers.

25. Many secondary sources document the efforts of the United States government in general and the State Department in particular to thwart immigration from Jewish refugees. See for example, Richard Breitman and Alan M. Kraut, *American Refugee Policy and European Jewry, 1933–1945* (Bloomington: Indiana University Press, 1987). Even Varian Fry, the head of the Emergency Rescue Committee that tried to arrange emigration for prominent artists and writers in France in 1940, considered the actions of the United States consulate as seriously impeding immigration; he too describes problems with delays, currency exchanges, and bureaucratic requirements that hampered even legal efforts to emigrate. See Andy Marino, *A Quiet American: The Secret War of Varian Fry* (New York: St. Martin's Griffith, 1999).

26. Selina Krenberger to Goddard, July 7, 1938? [date very unclear], October 11, 1938, October 19, 1938, [month omitted] 17, 1938, December 23, 1938, File M37, Goddard Papers.

27. Samuel D. Luchs to Goddard, December 19, 1938, File M37, Goddard Papers. Selina Krenberger to Goddard, January 12, 1939, February 21, 1939, March 10, 1939, March 15, 1939, April 30, 1939, File M37, Goddard Papers. She may have contacted Goddard about this as early as July of 1938, but the date can't be deciphered clearly on the earliest letter, and this letter doesn't specifically mention emigrating, although it does ask for advice.

28. Selina Krenberger to Goddard, March 15, 1939, File M37, Goddard Papers.

29. Although Goddard's letters are missing, he sometimes noted on her letters the dates of his answers. (Perhaps he was trying to keep track, since letters may not have been getting through.) Goddard noted that he answered the letter dated March 15, which discusses the "sham-marriage," on April 9. Shortly thereafter, in her letter dated April 30, Selina describes her meeting with a Quaker woman named "Mrs. Haughton." With Goddard's strong Quaker connections, and with his friends such as Rufus M. Jones deeply involved with relief work in Europe, it is likely that Goddard arranged this contact.

30. Selina Krenberger to Goddard, July 17, 1939, File M37, Goddard Papers. Selina has somewhat difficult handwriting, and on occasion she uses a German word or a combination of both languages in her letters. In the fifth line, I am assuming she means "mixes," which she spells "misces."

31. Selina Krenberger to Luchs, October 8, [1939] (copy sent to Goddard), File M37, Goddard Papers.

32. Fels to Luchs, October 16, 1939; Luchs to Fels, October 17, 1939 (copies sent to Goddard), File M37, Goddard Papers.

33. Based on surviving letters and what they say about who received what, it seems that Luchs, Fels, and Goddard exchanged at least seven letters in the nine-day period from October 9 to 17. Existing letters include Fels to Goddard, October 11, 1939, and October 16, 1939; Fels to Luchs, October 16, 1939; Luchs to Goddard, October 17, 1939; Luchs to Fels, October 17, 1939, File M37, Goddard Papers. Several of these letters cite correspondence received from Goddard during this period.

34. "At the request of Miss Krenberger I am sending you herewith a copy of the letter which I received from her this morning," Luchs wrote Goddard on October 24, 1939. The letter that follows is apparently a retyped version of Selina's letter. It is dated October 26, 1939, so this date is probably typed incorrectly. File M37, Goddard Papers.

35. Leila Zenderland to International Tracing Service, Arolsen, Germany, April 15, 1996; Zenderland to Israelitische Kultusgemeinde Wien, Vienna, Austria, April 23, 1996.

36. M. Schlenke, Archives of the International Tracing Service, Arolsen, Germany, to Leila Zenderland, February 18, 1997.

37. Mrs. H. Weiss, Department of Records, Israelitische Kultusgemeinde Wien, Vienna, Austria, to Leila Zenderland, May 21, 1996.

38. On Goddard's views about the war and on the connections that contemporaries made between his ideas and the war, see *Measuring Minds,* 326–35.

39. Draft of letter from Goddard to Mr. Pastore, April 3, 1948, File M32, Goddard Papers.

40. Nicholas Pastore, *The Nature-Nurture Controversy* (New York: King's Crown Press, 1949), 1; Goodwin Watson, Foreword to *Nature-Nurture Controversy,* vii–ix.

41. Nicholas Pastore to Lewis Terman, February 28, 1948, Lewis M. Terman Papers, Stanford University Archives, Stanford, Calif.

42. Ibid.

43. Terman to Pastore, March 4, 1948, Terman Papers. Relevant portions of Terman's response are reproduced in Pastore, *Nature-Nurture Controversy,* 94–5. Pastore only noted two exceptions to his argument: Terman, whom he reclassified as a liberal hereditarian, and John B. Watson, whom he called a conservative environmentalist. See *Nature-Nurture Controversy,* 176. For an analysis of Terman's political views and his response to Pastore, see Henry Minton, "Lewis Terman and Mental Testing: In Search of the Democratic Ideal" in *Psychological Testing and American Society, 1890–1930,* ed. Michael M. Sokal (New Brunswick, N.J.: Rutgers University Press, 1987), 95–112; and Henry Minton, *Lewis M. Terman: Pioneer in Psychological Testing* (New York: New York University Press, 1988), 234–42.

44. Draft of letter from Goddard to Pastore, April 3, 1948, File M32, Goddard Papers. For further analysis of both Goddard's and Terman's reactions to Pastore's thesis, see Zenderland, *Measuring Minds,* 4–6, 343–46.

45. For a listing of more than seven hundred articles on Binet testing published in this decade, see Samuel C. Kohs, "The Binet-Simon Measuring Scale for Intelli-

gence; An Annotated Bibliography," *Journal of Educational Psychology*, Part I, 5, no. 4 (April 1914): 215–24; Part II, 5, no. 5 (May 1914): 279–90; and Part III, 5, no. 6 (June 1914): 335–46; and Samuel C. Kohs, "An Annotated Bibliography of Recent Literature on the Binet-Simon Scale (1913–1917)," *Journal of Educational Psychology*, Part I, 8, no.7 (September 1917): 425–38; Part II, 8, no. 8 (October 1917): 488–502; Part III, 8, no. 9 (November 1917): 559–65; and Part IV, 8, no. 10 (December 1917): 609–18. For an analysis of some of the issues found within this early testing literature, see Zenderland, *Measuring Minds*, 235–50.

46. Binet's earliest articles on developing his intelligence scale are collected in Alfred Binet and Theodore Simon, *The Development of Intelligence in Children*, trans. Elizabeth Kite (Baltimore: Williams and Wilkins, 1916). On medical responses, see Leila Zenderland, "Henry Herbert Goddard and the Medical Acceptance of Intelligence Testing," in *Psychological Testing and American Society*, ed. Sokal, 46–74. See also *Measuring Minds*, 71–104.

47. Martin Barr, "Moral Paranoia," *Proceedings of the Association of Medical Officers of Institutions for Idiotic and Feeble-Minded Persons* (1895): 530–31.

48. E. H. Mullan, *Mental Deficiency: Some of Its Public Health Aspects, With Special Reference to Diagnosis*, Public Health Reports Reprint 236 (November 27, 1914; rpt. Washington, D.C.: Government Printing Office, 1919), 4. For some of the conflicts between psychologists and physicians about the use of testing, see Zenderland, *Measuring Minds*, 250–60.

49. On early educational responses to testing, see Zenderland, *Measuring Minds*, 105–42, 237–50.

50. Isabel Lawrence, "A Study of the Binet Definition Tests," *Psychological Clinic* 5 (1911): 207–16. Lawrence recorded these answers to compare Binet-Simon scale evaluations with teachers' evaluations of students' abilities. See also Zenderland, *Measuring Minds*, 237–50.

51. Julia C. Lathrop, "Memorandum: Address before Washington Alliance of Jewish Women," February 11, 1913, Box 69 (1914–20), Records of the Children's Bureau, Department of Labor, National Archives. For a discussion of the complexities involved in defining progressivism, see Daniel T. Rodgers, "In Search of Progressivism," *Reviews in American History* 10 (December 1982): 113–32.

52. William James, *Varieties of Religious Experience . . .* (1901–2; rpt. New York: Modern Library, 1939); G. Stanley Hall, *Jesus, the Christ, in the Light of Psychology* (Garden City, N.Y: Doubleday, Page, 1917).

53. "Review of *The Kallikak Family*," *Independent* 73 (October 3, 1912): 794. On religious themes within this literature, see Zenderland, *Measuring Minds*, 143–85, and Leila Zenderland, "Biblical Biology: American Protestant Social Reformers and the Early Eugenics Movement," *Science in Context*, 11, no. 3–4 (Fall and Winter 1998): 511–25.

54. Henry Herbert Goddard, "Psychological Work Among the Feeble-Minded," *Journal of Psycho-Asthenics* 12 (September 1907): 18.

55. Mary Agnes Best, *Rebel Saints* (New York: Harcourt, Brace, 1925), 25.

56. Thomas Carlyle, *Sartor Resartus* (1831); reprinted as vol. 1 in *The Works of Thomas Carlyle in Thirty Volumes* (London: Chapman and Hall, 1986), 166–68. Carlyle puts these words into the mouth of this book's main character, "Herr Teufels-

drockh," a German professor who is supposed to be an authority on the "Philosophy of Clothes," although various commentators have seen these comments as reflecting Carlyle's own views. In Best, *Rebel Saints,* these words are attributed directly to Carlyle and are explained as a response to attacks on Fox made by British historian Lord Macauley.

57. Goddard, "Psychological Work," 18.

Chapter 6

1. The International Society for the History of the Behavioral and Social Sciences.

2. See Hendrika Vande Kemp, "A Faculty Genealogy for the Travis Years," in *Psychology and the Cross: The Early History of Fuller Seminary's School of Psychology,* by H. Newton Malony (with Hendrika Vande Kemp) (Pasadena, Calif.: Fuller Seminary Press, 1996), 228–59.

3. David Baker to Hendrika Vande Kemp, September 15, 1999, Archives of the History of American Psychology, University of Akron, Akron, Ohio; John C. Burnham, "Assessing Historical Research in the Behavioral and Social Sciences: A Symposium. Editor's Introduction," *Journal of the History of the Behavioral Sciences* 35 (1999): 225–26; Henrika Kulick, "Assessing Research in the History of Sociology and Anthropology," *Journal of the History of the Behavioral Sciences* 35 (1999): 227–37; Franz Samelson, "Assessing Research in the History of Psychology: Past, Present, and Future," *Journal of the History of the Behavioral Sciences* 35 (1999): 247–55; Andrew Scull, "A Quarter Century of the History of Psychiatry," *Journal of the History of the Behavioral Sciences* 35 (1999): 239–46; William D. G. Balance, "Frustrations and Joys of Archival Research," *Journal of the History of the Behavioral Sciences* 11 (1975): 37–40; Wolfgang G. Bringmann, "Design Questions in Archival Research," *Journal of the History of the Behavioral Sciences* 11 (1975): 23–26; Josef Brožek, "Irons in the Fire: Introduction to a Symposium on Archival Research," *Journal of the History of the Behavioral Sciences* 11 (1975): 15–19; Thomas C. Cadwallader, "Unique Values of Archival Research," *Journal of the History of the Behavioral Sciences* 11 (1975): 27–33; Ludy T. Benjamin, "Archival Adventures: From Secret Societies to the Supreme Court" (the Wallace Russell Memorial Lecture presented to Division 26, The History of Psychology, at the convention of the American Psychological Association, Boston, Mass., August 20–24, 1999).

4. Milton Rokeach, "The Nature and Meaning of Dogmatism," *Psychological Review* 61 (1954): 194–204; Milton Rokeach., *The Open and Closed Mind* (New York: Basic Books, 1960);, "Political and Religious Dogmatism: An Alternative to the Authoritarian Personality," *Psychological Monographs 70* 18, no. 425 (1956); Milton Rokeach, Warren C. McGovney, and M. Ray Denny, "A Distinction between Dogmatic and Rigid Thinking," *Journal of Abnormal and Social Psychology* 51 (1955): 87–93; Hendrika Vande Kemp, "The Rokeach Dogmatism Scale" (Hope College, Holland, Mich., 1970).

5. For some of the earliest treatises on religion and psychopathology, see Amariah Brigham, *Observations on the Influence of Religion upon the Health and Physical Welfare of Mankind* (Boston: Marsh, Capen & Lyon, 1835); William Cooke, *A Commentary of Medical and Moral Life; or Mind and the Emotions, Considered in Relation to*

Health, Disease, and Religion (Philadelphia: C. J. Price, 1853); Henry Maudsley, *Natural Causes and Supernatural Seemings* (London: Kegan Paul, Trench, 1886).

6. Paul Everett Meehl, Richard Klann, Alfred Schmieding, Kenneth H. Breimeier, and Sophie Schroeder-Slomann, *What, Then, is Man? A Symposium of Theology, Psychology, and Psychiatry* (Saint Louis, Mo.: Concordia, 1958); Hendrika Vande Kemp, "The Psychology of Paul Meehl" (Hope College, Holland, Mich., 1969); Hendrika Vande Kemp, "Great Psychologists as 'Unknown' Psychologists of Religion" (paper presented at the annual meeting of the American Psychological Association, Los Angeles, Calif., August 1983). For a bibliography of Meehl's contributions, see "American Psychological Association Distinguished Scientific Contribution Awards," *American Psychologist* 13 (1958): 733–35. Meehl wrote little on theology and religion, but he played a minor role in the founding of the Graduate School of Psychology at Fuller Theological Seminary. Meehl's brief term as a member of the National Steering Committee is examined in Malony, *Psychology and the Cross.*

7. Paul Tillich, *The Courage to Be* (New Haven, Conn.: Yale University Press, 1952). The Dwight Harrington Terry Lectures on Religion in the Light of Science and Philosophy were established in 1924. Psychologists who contributed to the series in its early years include William Brown, John Dewey, Carl G. Jung, Erich Fromm, and Gordon W. Allport. For a detailed examination of the lectureship and a list of published Terry Lectures, see Ronald Joseph Burwell, "Religion and the Social Sciences: A Study of Their Relationships as Set Forth in the Terry Lectures, 1924–1971" (Ph.D. diss., New York University, 1976), abstract in *Dissertation Abstracts International* 37 (1976): 1037A. The lectures are also listed on the Yale web site at http://www.yale.edu/terrylecture/

8. My picks for this list are Anton Boisen, *The Exploration of the Inner World: A Study of Mental Disorder and Religious Experience* (Chicago: Willet Clark, 1936); Anton Boisen, *Out of the Depths: An Autobiographical Study of Mental Disorder and Religious Experience* (New York: Harper, 1960); Igor Caruso, *Existential Psychology: From Analysis to Synthesis*, trans. Eva Krapf (New York: Herder & Herder, 1964), originally published as *Psychoanalyse und Synthese der Existenz: Beziehungen zwischen psychologischer Analyse und Daseinswerten* (Vienna: Herder, 1952); Wilfried Daim, *Depth Psychology and Salvation*, trans. Kurt F. Reinhardt (New York: Frederick Ungar, 1963), originally published as *Tiefenpsychologie und Erlösung* (Vienna: Herold, 1954); Harry Guntrip, *Psychotherapy and Religion: The Constructive Use of Inner Conflict* (New York: Harper, 1957), also published as *Mental Pain and the Cure of Souls* (London: Independent Press, 1956); Seward Hiltner, *Theological Dynamics* (Nashville, Abingdon, 1972); Paul E. Johnson, *Personality and Religion* (New York: Abingdon, 1957); Frank Lake, *Clinical Theology: A Theological and Psychological Basis to Clinical Pastoral Care* (London: Darton, Longman, & Todd, 1966); John MacMurray, *The Form of the Personal. Vol. 1, The Self as Agent* and *Vol 2, Persons in Relation* (London: Faber & Faber, 1957–61); Paul W. Pruyser, *A Dynamic Psychology of Religion* (New York: Harper & Row, 1968).

9. R. Timothy Kearney, "Psychology and the Soul: An Historical Investigation" (Ph.D. diss., Fuller Theological Seminary, 1985), abstract in *Dissertation Abstracts International* 47 (1985): 3526B; Hendrika Vande Kemp, "From Soul to Self" (Hope College, Holland, Mich., 1969);, "The Tension between Psychology and Theology: I. The Etymological Roots," *Journal of Psychology and Theology* 10 (1982): 105–12; Hen-

drika Vande Kemp, "The Tension between Psychology and Theology. II. An Anthro-
pological Solution," *Journal of Psychology and Theology* 10 (1982): 205–11; Hendrika
Vande Kemp, "Spirit and Soul in No-Man's Land: Reflections on Haule's 'Care of
Souls,' " *Journal of Psychology and Theology* 11 (1983): 117–22; Hendrika Vande Kemp,
"Psyche and Soul," in *Encyclopedia of Psychology*, ed. Allen E. Kazdin (Washington,
D.C.: American Psychological Association, 2000): 334–37; Hendrika Vande Kemp,
"Pastoral Counseling and Some Thoughts on the Psychology of Religion" (Hope
College, Holland, Mich., 1970). This movement is explored in depth by E. Brooks
Holifield, *A History of Pastoral Care in America: From Salvation to Self-Realization* (Nash-
ville: Abingdon Press, 1983).

10. William G. Perry, *Forms of Intellectual and Ethical Development in the College
Years: A Scheme* (New York: Holt, Rinehart & Winston, 1970); Hendrika Vande Kemp,
"Dimensions of Religious Growth and Development in the College Years" (master's
thesis, the University of Massachusetts/Amherst, 1973). This work was completed
under the direction of Harold Jarmon, James I. Chumbley, and David M. Todd.

11. James W. Fowler, *The Stages of Faith: The Psychology of Human Development
and the Quest for Meaning* (New York: Harper & Row, 1981); John J. Gleason Jr.,
Growing up to God: Eight Steps in Religious Development (Nashville: Abingdon Press,
1975); Benedict J. Groeschel, *Spiritual Passages: The Psychology of Spiritual Development*
(New York: Crossroad, 1984); John McDargh, *Psychoanalytic Object Relations Theory
and the Study of Religion* (Lanham, Md.: University Press of America, 1983); Hendrika
Vande Kemp, "G. Stanley Hall and the Clark School of Religious Psychology," *American Psychologist* 47 (1992): 290–98.

12. Hendrika Vande Kemp, "Teaching Psychology/Religion in the Seventies: Monopoly or Cooperation?" *Teaching of Psychology* 3 no. 1 (1976): 15. This article stimulated a commentary: Carl Wagner and Anthony Struzynski, "On the Autonomy of
Psychology in Psychology/Religion Courses: An Optimistic View," *Teaching of Psychology* 6 (1979): 140–43. The journal also published my response: Hendrika Vande
Kemp, "On Seeing Yourself Through Another's Eyes: Response to Wagner and Struzynski," *Teaching of Psychology,* 6 (1979): 143–45. For a recently-completed follow-
up to this study, see Maureen P. Hester & Martin D. Lampert, "Psychology of Religion
in Academic Programs: Current Status," poster session presented at the annual meeting of the Western Psychological Association, Portland, Oregon, April 13–15, 2000.

13. Hendrika Vande Kemp, "Lectures in Psychology and Religion" (comprehensives paper, University of Massachusetts/Amherst, 1974). This work was completed
under the direction of Howard Gadlin, James I. Chumbley, and Dee G. Appley. See
Gordon W. Allport, *The Individual and His Religion* (New York: Collier-McMillan,
1950); William James, *The Varieties of Religious Experience* (New York: Longmans,
Green, 1902); Charles C. Tart, ed., *Altered States of Consciousness: A Book of Readings*
(New York: John Wiley, 1969); Paul W. Pruyser, *A Dynamic Psychology of Religion;* Paul
W. Pruyser, *Between Belief and Unbelief* (New York: Harper & Row, 1974); Paul W.
Pruyser, *The Play of the Imagination: Toward a Psychoanalysis of Culture* (New York:
International Universities Press, 1983).

14. Hendrika Vande Kemp, "The Dream in Periodical Literature: 1860–1910.
From *Oneirocriticon* to *Die Traumdeutung* via the Questionnaire" (Ph.D. diss., University of Massachusetts/Amherst, 1976), abstract in *Dissertation Abstracts International*

38 (1977): 342B; Hendrika Vande Kemp, "The Dream in Periodical Literature: 1860–1910," *The Journal of the History of the Behavioral Sciences* 17 (1981): 88–113; Hendrika Vande Kemp, "Psycho-Spiritual Dreams in the Nineteenth Century: I. Dreams of Death," *Journal of Psychology and Theology* 22 (1994): 97–108; Hendrika Vande Kemp, "Psycho-Spiritual Dreams in the Nineteenth Century: II. Metaphysics and Immortality," *Journal of Psychology and Theology* 22 (1994): 109–19. The dissertation committee consisted of Howard Gadlin, James R. Averill, Barry F. O'Connell, David M. Todd, and Marcia Westkott.

15. Hendrika Vande Kemp, "Teaching Psychology Through the Case Study Method," *Teaching of Psychology* 7 (1980): 38–41.; Hendrika Vande Kemp, "Teaching Psychology of the Family: Bibliography and an Experiential Approach," *Teaching of Psychology* 8 (1981): 152–56; Hendrika Vande Kemp, "Mate Selection and Marriage: A Psychodynamic Family Oriented Course," *Teaching of Psychology* 12 (1985): 161–64.

16. For a delightful treatise on this, see Carlo Ginzburg, "Morelli, Freud and Sherlock Holmes: Clues and Scientific Method," trans. Anna Davin, *History Workshop Journal* 9 (1980): 5–36. I am grateful to Wade Pickren for bringing this article to my attention.

17. Franz Julius Delitzsch, *A System of Biblical Psychology,* trans. Robert Ernest Wallis (1867; rpt, Grand Rapids, Mich.: Baker Book House, 1966), originally published as *System der biblischen Psychologie* (Leipzig: Dorffling und Franke, 1855); François H. Lapointe, "Origin and Evolution of the Term 'Psychology,' " *American Psychologist* 25 (1970): 640–46; François H. Lapointe, "The Origin and Evolution of the Term 'Psychology,' " *Psychologia: An International Journal of Psychology in the Orient* 16 (1972): 1–16; François H. Lapointe, "Who Originated the Term 'Psychology'?" *Journal of the History of the Behavioral Sciences* 8 (1972): 328–35; Hendrika Vande Kemp, "The Origin and Evolution of the Term 'Psychology': Addenda," *American Psychologist* 35 (1980): 774;, "A Note on the Term Psychology in English Titles: Predecessors of Rauch," *Journal of the History of the Behavioral Sciences* 19 (1983): 185; "Notes and News: Psychology/Theology Integration," in *The Newsletter of the Division of the History of Psychology* 11, no. 4 (August 1979): 15.

18. These issues are discussed in Vande Kemp, "The Tension" (parts I & II), "Psyche and Soul," and "Spirit and Soul."

19. Hendrika Vande Kemp (with H. Newton Malony), *Psychology and Theology in Western Thought, 1672–1965: A Historical and Annotated Bibliography* (Millwood, N.Y.: Kraus International, 1984).

20. Robert Brodie MacLeod, *Religious Perspectives of College Teaching in Experimental Psychology* (New Haven, Conn.: The Edward W. Hazen Foundation, n.d.); Vande Kemp, "Great Psychologists"; Hendrika Vande Kemp, "From Preacher's Kid to Phenomenologist: Robert B. MacLeod and the Religious 'Doctrine of Man' " (invited address presented to The History of Psychology division at the meeting of the American Psychological Association, New Orleans, La., August 1989).

21. Vande Kemp, "G. Stanley Hall." For this article and a still unpublished follow-up project, I relied on Clark University Archives lists of "master's theses signed by Hall" and "Ph.D. dissertations approved by G. Stanley Hall," a list of "Dr. Hall's courses," financial records related to the library and laboratory, and correspondence between Hall and contributors to *The Journal of Religious Psychology.*

22. Hendrika Vande Kemp, "Religion in College Textbooks: Allport's Historic 1948 Report," *The International Journal for the Psychology of Religion* 5 (1995): 197–209; Hendrika Vande Kemp, "Gordon Allport's Pre-1950 Writings on Religion: The Archival Record," in *Aspects and Contexts: Studies in the History of Psychology of Religion*, ed. by Jacob Belzen (Atlanta: Rodopi, 2000): 129–72; Hendrika Vande Kemp, "In Memoriam: Virginia Staudt Sexton (1916–1997)," *The International Journal for the Psychology of Religion* 8 (1998): 27–32; Hendrika Vande Kemp, "Wholeness, Holiness, and the Care of Souls: The Adler-Jahn Debate in Historical Perspective," *Journal of Individual Psychology*, 56, (2000): 242–56; Hendrika Vande Kemp, "Adler's Place in the Psychology and Religion Literature: An Empirical Investigation" (Graduate School of Psychology, Fuller Theological Seminary, Pasadena, Calif.).

23. Anne Coughlin, "A Unique Heathen: The Sexual Dogmatics of Theodore Schroeder" (Ph.D. diss., Fuller Theological Seminary, 1986), abstract in *Dissertation Abstracts International* 47 (1986): 2154B. Coughlin completed much of her research at the New York Public Library, which holds a complete collection of *The Truth Seeker*. She also relied on materials provided by the New York Academy of Medicine Library, the Los Angeles Public Library, the Library of the Los Angeles County Medical Association, and the South Pasadena (California) Public Library. For other aspects of Schroeder's legacy, see David Barry Brudnoy, "Liberty's Bugler: The Seven Ages of Theodore Schroeder" (Ph.D. diss., Brandeis University, 1971), abstract in *Dissertation Abstracts International* 32 (1971): 6329A.

24. J. John Steigenga, "The Contribution of Henry Burton Sharman to the Development of a Christocentric Psychology" (Ph.D. diss., Fuller Theological Seminary, 1990), abstract in *Dissertation Abstracts International* 51 (1991): 5593B. Steigenga completed much of the research at the National Archives of Canada, in Ottawa. The Henry Burton Sharman and Abbie Lyon Sharman collection consists of forty indexed volumes containing seventy-five linear feet of papers.

25. David Paul Johnson, "The Contributions of Fritz Künkel to the Development of a Religious Psychology" (Ph.D. diss., Fuller Theological Seminary, 1990), abstract in *Dissertation Abstracts International* 51 (1990): 2624B. For his research, Johnson relied on Künkel's published works and on archival materials available at the First Congregational Church in Los Angeles, at the Guild for Psychological Studies in San Francisco, and at the Graduate Theological Union Library in Berkeley, California. He did not explore the twenty-seven-volume sets of Künkel's notes and lectures which are available at the Graduate Theological Union Library and at the Dorothy Honnold Library at the Claremont Colleges.

26. Gordon W. Allport, "Psychology," in Edward W. Hazen Foundation, American Council on Education, Committee on Religion and Education, *College Reading and Religion: A Survey of Reading Materials* (New Haven, Conn.: Yale University Press, 1948): 80–114; Robert Brodie MacLeod, "Experimental Psychology," in *Religious Perspectives in College Teaching*, ed. Roy Fairchild et al. (New York: Ronald Press, 1952), 262–85; Vande Kemp, "Religion in College Textbooks"; Vande Kemp, "From Preacher's Kid to Phenomenologist"; Henry Burton Sharman, *The Records of the Life of Jesus* (New York: Association Press, 1917); Henry Burton Sharman, *Jesus in the Records* (New York: Association Press, 1918). For details on the seminars at Camp

Minnesing and MacLeod's teaching of *The Records* see Steigenga, "The Contribution of Henry Burton Sharman," n. 100, and Vande Kemp, "From Preacher's Kid to Phenomenologist."

27. Johnson, "The Contributions of Fritz Künkel"; Steigenga, "The Contribution of Henry Burton Sharman"; Vande Kemp, "From Preacher's Kid to Phenomenologist." The Guild for Psychological Studies continues to offer Sharman seminars and distributes its own reprint version of *Records of the Life of Jesus* (1917; rpt., Palo Alto, Calif.: Sequoia Seminar Foundation, n.d.).

28. James Mark Baldwin, "Psychotherapeutics or Psychotherapy," in *Dictionary of Philosophy and Psychology, Vol. II*, new ed., ed. James Mark Baldwin (1925; rpt. New York: Peter Smith, 1940), 394; Allen Bruce Fleming, "Psychology, Medicine, and Religion: Early Twentieth-Century American Psychotherapy (1905–9)" (Ph.D. diss., Fuller Theological Seminary, 1989), abstract in *Dissertation Abstracts International*, 50 (1990): 5313B. Fleming relied extensively on the archival collections of *The Boston Globe*, The Hispanic Society of America, *The Churchman*, Baker and Taylor Company, The New York Public Library, Seton Hall University, The Huntington Library, the South Orange (New Jersey) Public Library, the Library of Congress, the Harvard University Archives, the *Harvard Dental Alumni Bulletin*, and the Francis A. Countway Library of Medicine.

29. Fritz Künkel, "The Integration of Psychology and Religion," *Journal of Psychotherapy as a Religious Process* 1 (1954): 5–6. Earlier, Künkel described his work after 1943 as "the Integration of Christianity and Psychology" (letter to William Rickel, October 19, 1953, in the personal collection of Hendrika Vande Kemp).

30. Hendrika Vande Kemp, "Historical Perspective: Religion and Clinical Psychology in America," in *Religion and the Clinical Practice of Psychology*, ed. Edward Shafranske (Washington, D.C.: American Psychological Association, 1996), 71–112. See also Henryk Misiak and Virginia Staudt, *Catholics in Psychology: A Historical Survey* (New York: McGraw–Hill, 1954), who extensively employed this language as they stressed that Catholic psychologists "will always endeavor to integrate psychology, philosophy, and theology" (14).

31. Hendrika Vande Kemp, "Christian Psychologies for the 21st Century: Lessons from History," *Journal of Psychology and Christianity* 17 (1998): 197–209. Here I examine the nineteenth-century Christian phrenologies as a model for the application of psychological research to practice and the assimilation of standard secular practices by religious professionals. My original research on Fowler and Beecher at the Amherst College archives was done under the direction of Howard Gadlin at the University of Massachusetts/Amherst.

32. Rickel's collection amounts to a true archive, in that the "original context of documents is preserved" (Bringmann, "Design Questions," 23).

33. Hendrika Vande Kemp, "Psychotheological Integration in the 1950s: *The Journal of Psychotherapy as a Religious Process*" (paper presented at the meeting of the American Psychological Association, Los Angeles, Calif., August 1985 and at the meeting of the American Academy of Religion, Anaheim, Calif., November 1985); Hendrika Vande Kemp and Beth Houskamp, "An Early Attempt at Integration: *The Journal of Psychotherapy as a Religious Process*," *Journal of Psychology and Theology* 14 (1986): 3–14.

34. For an overview of related psychology and religion journals in historical context, see Vande Kemp, "Historical Perspective."

35. Harry Bone to Doris Mode, November 21, 1948, in the personal collection of Hendrika Vande Kemp. There is no further evidence that Rank's heirs or other Rankian therapists objected to the work of the institute.

36. William A. S. Rickel, 15th Anniversary Report, Harvard Class of 1934; William A. S. Rickel, 20th Anniversary Report. Harvard College—Class of 1934; William A. S. Rickel, 25th Anniversary Report, Harvard Class of 1934; William A. S. Rickel, 35th Anniversary Report, Harvard College—Class of 1934.

37. The third member of the staff was Prescott Vernon, who was also a clinical social worker.

38. William Rickel to Ohio Bell Telephone Company, October 20, 1948; N. E. Robinson, L. M. Berry & Company, Telephone Directory Advertising, to Rickel, November 9, 1948; H. I. McHenry, Ohio Bell, to Robinson, December 7, 1948; Künkel to Rickel, April 28, 1953. All letters are in the personal collection of Hendrika Vande Kemp.

39. Rudolf Ekstein to Doris Mode, July 31, 1953; Karl A. Menninger to Rickel, July 2, 1954. Letters are in the personal collection of Hendrika Vande Kemp. According to Paul W. Pruyser (Letter to Hendrika Vande Kemp, 14 November 1985), the reading notes were not published in the in-house *Library Journal* that circulated among Menninger staff, and most likely the notes were distributed only in a class.

40. The "New Viennese School" is discussed in some detail in Dieter Wyss, *Depth Psychology: A Critical History, Development, Problems, Crises,* trans. Gerald Onn (1961; London: George Allen & Unwin, 1966). The same book was also published under the title *Psychoanalytic Schools from the Beginning to the Present,* trans. G. Onn (1961; New York: Jason Aronson, 1973). Unfortunately, this text is not overall a reliable source.

41. Wilfried Daim, "Depth-Psychology and Grace," trans. C. Ernst, *Journal of Psychotherapy as a Religious Process* 1 (1954): 31–40; Igor A. Caruso, "Personalistic Psychoanalysis as Symbolic Knowledge," trans. William Rickel and Doris Mode, *Journal of Psychotherapy as a Religious Process* 2 (1955): 2–23; Igor Caruso to William Rickel, May 28, 1956, in the personal collection of Hendrika Vande Kemp.

42. Caruso, *Existential Psychology,* 124; I have a brief account of Frankl's version of the Frankl/Caruso relationship in a November 25, 1997 letter from Haddon Klingberg Jr., who has been working on a Frankl biography. Frankl told Klingberg that Caruso "was always socially cordial towards [the Frankls], even animatedly friendly," but that Caruso had been disappointed when Frankl declined the opportunity to co-edit a new psychotherapy journal with him. I suspect that Caruso envied Frankl's success—despite his own achievements as a leading Catholic integrator—but that the two were also separated by a genuine religious/theological difference: Caruso was a devout Roman Catholic, Frankl a Jew who understood religion and spirituality primarily in psychological terms. Frankl was amused by the notion that psychoanalysis might be replaced by "psychosynthesis." Caruso made synthesis an important element of the psychotherapeutic process, as did Roberto Assagioli, in *Psychosynthesis: A Manual of Principles and Techniques* (New York: Hobbs, Dorman, 1965).

43. "Information Market," *History of Psychology* 16 no. 1 (1984): 23; Beatrice MacLeod to Hendrika Vande Kemp, May 18, 1984.

44. Personal interview with John Nixon at Fuller Theological Seminary in Pasadena, March 10, 1988.

45. Shideler took extensive shorthand notes, and provided typed transcripts that clearly identified the participants in the discussion.

46. See Hendrika Vande Kemp, "Relational Ethics in the Novels of Charles Williams," *Family Process* 26 (1987): 283–94; Hendrika Vande Kemp, "Lord Peter Wimsey in the Novel/Comedy of Manners: Courtesy, Intimacy, and the Courage to Be," *The Lamp-Post (of the Southern California C. S. Lewis Society)* 23 no. 3 (1999): 11–23; Mary McDermott Shideler, *A Creed for a Christian Skeptic* (Grand Rapids, MI: William B. Eerdmans, 1968); Mary McDermott Shideler, *Consciousness of Battle: An Interim Report on a Theological Journey* (Grand Rapids, MI: William B. Eerdmans, 1970); Mary McDermott Shideler, *In Search of the Spirit: A Primer* (New York: Ballantine/Epiphany, 1985); Mary McDermott Shideler, *Starting Out. Stage 1 in the Series Visions and Nightmares, Ends and Beginnings. A Woman's Lifelong Journey* (Boulder, Colo.: Scribendi Press, 1996). Shideler died June 28, 2000 at the age of 83.

47. Robert Brodie MacLeod to Henry Burton Sharman, February 28, 1941, in the personal collection of Hendrika Vande Kemp; Vande Kemp, "G. Stanley Hall."

48. MacLeod to Sharman, March 14, 1941, in the personal collection of Hendrika Vande Kemp; Henry Burton Sharman, *Jesus as Teacher: Student Edition* (New York: Harper & Brothers, 1935); Henry Burton Sharman, *Studies in the Records of the Life of Jesus* (New York: Harper & Brothers, 1938). Sharman's 1938 volume contains a chapter on processes of group thinking, with suggestions for both members and leaders; a short statement about the records and their sources (an introduction to the M, L, Q [P & G], and R sources familiar to biblical scholars); a series of questions relating to the synoptic gospels; and a series of questions relating to the gospel of John. Readers familiar with biblical criticism will recognize in Sharman the nineteenth-century tradition of source criticism, which addresses the "problem of the synoptic gospels." The 1935 volume included all the material in *Studies* along with topical summaries of the synoptic and Johannine materials. Nixon's notes indicate that MacLeod relied on source documents he labeled Z, G, M, J, and A. Shideler's notes from the years 1935–38 indicate primarily the use of Q (comprised of G, P, and J). Ernest Hilgard, in a letter to Hendrika Vande Kemp, May 24, 1995, stated that he "was very critical of Sharman's work because I knew the international critical commentaries that give a much more scholarly interpretation of the Bible . . . [which] differed so much from those of Sharman's that I was not at all impressed by his effort to reconstruct the life of Jesus." Readers interested in the complex synoptic problem can find information on the web site created by Stephen C. Carlson, located at www.mindspring.com/~scarlson/synopt.

49. William H. Matchett to Hendrika Vande Kemp, October 25, 1988; Mary Morrison to Hendrika Vande Kemp, April 3, 1988; Clarkson T. Palmer to Hendrika Vande Kemp, June 16, 1988.

50. Hendrika Vande Kemp, "Personal Reflections on Trauma and Head Injury," *American Family Therapy Academy Newsletter,* no. 67 (1997): 38–42; Hendrika Vande Kemp, "The Patient-Philosopher Evaluates the Scientist-Practitioner," in *Critical Is-*

sues in Psychotherapy: Translating New Ideas into Practice, ed. by Brent D. Slife, Richard N. Williams, and Sally H. Barlow (Thousand Oaks, Calif.: Sage, 2001): 171–85.

51. Bruce J. Anderson, President, Danforth Foundation to Hendrika Vande Kemp, May 26, 1995; Dorwin Cartwright to Hendrika Vande Kemp, August 17, 1990; Patrick Murphy Malin, "The National Council on Religion in Higher Education," in *Liberal Learning and Religion*, ed. by Amos Niven Wilder (New York: Harper & Brothers, 1951), 326; John W. Nason to Hendrika Vande Kemp, June 14, 1996; Michael Wertheimer, "Robert Brodie MacLeod (1907–1972)," *Journal of the History of the Behavioral Sciences* 9 (1973): 287–99; Ernest R. Hilgard, "From the Social Gospel to the Psychology of Social Issues: A Reminiscence," *Journal of Social Issues* 42 (1986): 109. Hilgard was a Kent Fellow in 1925, Likert in 1927, and Cartwright in 1937.

52. Nason to Vande Kemp, June 14, 1996; "Curriculum Vitae," in *The MacLeod Symposium*, ed. David Krech, (Ithaca, N.Y.: Department of Psychology, Cornell University, 1973): 16–17; Jane Siegel, Curator, Graphic Arts, Columbia University, to Hendrika Vande Kemp, May 30, 1995; Robert Brodie MacLeod, *An Experimental Investigation of Brightness Constancy* (Ph.D. diss., Columbia University, 1932), reprinted in *Archives of Psychology* 135 (1932): 1, 102; Letter from Elaine Engst, Curator of Manuscripts, Cornell University Archives, to Hendrika Vande Kemp, July 6, 1995; "SVHE Begins Year-Long 70th Anniversary Observance," *Society for Values in Higher Education Newsletter* 30 no. 1 (1993): 1; *Selected Publications and National Projects: Society for Values in Higher Education 1923–1996* (Washington, D.C.: Society for Values in Higher Education, 1996); Cartwright to Vande Kemp. MacLeod's regular attendance at meetings, at least during the early years, was also documented in letters from Ernest Hilgard to Hendrika Vande Kemp, May 11, 1995 and from Teresina Havens to Hendrika Vande Kemp, May 6, 1989.

53. Alison MacLeod to Hendrika Vande Kemp, e-mail, December 8, 1999. I am grateful to David M. Wulff for introducing me to Ms. MacLeod.

54. I am grateful to William Brundage for performing these services and to Mike Raines, curatorial assistant at the Harvard University Archives, for providing access to the Allport materials.

55. Allport, "Psychology"; Gordon W. Allport, *Waiting for the Lord: 33 Meditations on God & Man,* ed. Peter Anthony Bertocci (New York: Macmillan, 1978); Vande Kemp, "Religion in College Textbooks"; Vande Kemp, "Gordon Allport's Pre-1950 Writings"; The archives contain two manuscripts with the same title, one dated 1933, the second undated. An examination of the contents indicates that they probably were used as one manuscript. For the published essay, see Gordon Willard Allport, "The Roots of Religion," *The Advent Papers. 1* (Mt. Vernon Street, Boston 8, Massachusetts, 1944), reprinted in *Pastoral Psychology* 5 no. 43 (1954): 13–24.

56. Gordon W. Allport, "The Clergyman as Mind Raid Warden" (address presented at the Massachusetts Clerical Association Cathedral of St. Paul, Boston, Mass., March 1, 1943), 12, 13.

57. Robert P. Parker, "The Psychological Function of the Hymn Tune in a Service of Worship," *Religious Education* 38 (1943): 216–22; James Stone, "War Music and War Psychology in the Civil War," *Journal of Abnormal and Social Psychology* 36 (1941): 543–60; Roland L. Warren, "German *Parteilieder* and Christian Hymns as

Instruments of Social Control," *Journal of Abnormal and Social Psychology* 38 (1943): 96–100; Kimball Young, "The Psychology of Hymns," *Journal of Abnormal and Social Psychology* 20 (1926):-391–406.

Chapter 7

1. This research could not have been conducted without the support and assistance of the Archives of the History of American Psychology. In particular, the friendship and personal help of John Popplestone and Marion White McPherson were essential in inspiring and furthering this project. Thanks are due to Sean Duncan, Yanlong Sun, John Leach, and Elke Kurz for early discussions on the topic, and to Laurence D. Smith for insightful critique of an early version of the paper. Michael Sokal, David Baker, Mike Doherty, and James Goodwin, among others, provided helpful comments on this research.

2. John A. Popplestone and Ryan D. Tweney, eds., *The Great Catalog of the C. H. Stoelting Company, 1930–1937. A Facsimile Reproduction, With An Introduction* (Delmar, N. Y.: Scholars' Facsimiles & Reprints, 1997); "Student" [William Sealey Gosset], "The Probable Error of A Mean," *Biometrika* 6 (1908) : 1–25; Ronald A. Fisher, *Statistical Methods for Research Workers* (London: Oliver & Boyd, 1925); Ronald A. Fisher, *The Design of Experiments* (London: Oliver & Boyd, 1935); A. D. Lovie, "The Analysis of Variance in Experimental Psychology: 1934–1945," *British Journal of Mathematical and Statistical Psychology* 32 (1979): 151–78.

3. Anthony J. Rucci and Ryan D. Tweney, "Analysis of Variance and the 'Second Discipline' of Scientific Psychology: A Historical Account," *Psychological Bulletin* 87 (1980): 166–84.

4. John A. Popplestone and Marion White McPherson, *An Illustrated History of American Psychology* (Akron, Ohio: The University of Akron Press, 1994).

5. Rucci and Tweney, "Analysis of Variance"; James H. Capshew, "Psychologists On Site: A Reconnaissance of the Historiography of the Laboratory," *American Psychologist* 47 (1992): 132–42.

6. Hans-Jörg Rheinberger, *Toward a History of Epistemic Things: Synthesizing Proteins in the Test Tube* (Stanford, Calif.: Stanford University Press, 1997).

7. Frank A. J. L. James, ed., *The Development of the Laboratory: Essays on the Place of Experiment in Industrial Civilization* (New York: American Institute of Physics, 1989); David Gooding, Trevor Pinch, and Simon Schaffer, eds., *The Uses of Experiment: Studies in the Natural Sciences* (Cambridge, U.K.: Cambridge University Press, 1989); John A. Popplestone and Marion White McPherson, "The Vitality of the Leipzig Model of 1880–1910 in the United States in 1950–1980," in *Wundt Studies: A Centennial Collection*, ed. Wolfgang G. Bringmann and Ryan D. Tweney (Toronto: C. J. Hogrefe, 1980), 226–57; John A. Popplestone and Marion White McPherson, "Pioneer Psychology Laboratories in Clinical Settings," in *Explorations in the History of Psychology in the United States*, ed. Josef Brozek (Lewisburg, Penn.: Bucknell University Press, 1984), 196–272; Ryan D. Tweney and Cheri A. Budzynski, "The Scientific Status of American Psychology in 1900," *American Psychologist* 55 (2000): 1014–17.

8. See, for a splendid example, Gerard L. E. Turner, *The Great Age of the Microscope: The Collection of the Royal Microscopical Society Through 150 Years* (Bristol, U. K.: Adam Hilger, 1989).

9. One exception is the catalog of the Florence collection, *Misura d'uomo: Strumenti, teorie e pratiche dell'antropometria e della psicologia sperimentale tra '800 e '900* (Firenze: Instituto e Museo di Storia della Scienza di Firenze, 1986). Catalogs of instrument dealers, e.g., the Stoelting Catalog noted in note 1, and the 1903 catalog of the Leipzig firm of E. Zimmermann are also useful; E. Zimmermann, *Preis-Liste über psycholgische und physiologische Apparate* (XVIII) (Leipzig: E. Zimmermann, 1903; rpt. Passau: Institut für Geschichte der Neueren Psychologie, Universität Passau, 1983). Further, some contemporary sources are helpful for specific descriptions and illustrations of apparatus, e.g., Robert Sommer, *Die Ausstellung von experimentalpsychologischen Apparaten und Methoden, bei dem Kongress für experimentelle Psychologie, Giessen 18.-21. April 1904* (Leipzig: Johann Ambrosius Barth, 1904; rpt. with an introduction by Horst Gundlach, *Passauer Schriften zur Psychologiegeschichte, Nr. 2.* (Passau: Passavia Universitätsverlag, 1984).

10. The distinction between *representing* and *intervening* is due, of course, to Ian Hacking, *Representing and Intervening: Introductory Topics in the Philosophy of Natural Science* (Cambridge, U.K.: Cambridge University Press, 1983).

11. Jeff Shrager, "High Throughput Discovery: Search and Interpretation on the Path to New Drugs," in *Designing for Science: Implications from Everyday, Classroom, and Professional Settings*, ed. Kevin Crowley, Christian Schunn, and Takeshi Okada (Mahwah, N.J.: Lawrence Erlbaum Associates, 2001), 325–50; Rheinberger, *Epistemic Things*; Bruno Latour, *Science in Action: How to Follow Engineers and Scientists Through Society* (Cambridge, Mass.: Harvard University Press, 1987).

12. Educational Testing Service, *Nomograph for Computing Multiple Correlation Coefficients* (Princeton, N.J.: Educational Testing Service, n.d., c. 1955); Jack W. Dunlap and Albert K. Kurtz, *Handbook of Statistical Nomographs, Tables, and Formulas* (Yonkers-on-Hudson, N.Y.: World Book Co., 1932). See also Thomas L. Hankins, "Blood, Dirt, and Nomograms: A Particular History of Graphs," *Isis* 90 (1999): 50–80.

13. Edward R. Tufte, *The Visual Display of Quantitative Information* (Cheshire, Conn.: The Graphics Press, 1983); Stephen M. Kosslyn, *Elements of Graph Design* (New York: W. H. Freeman and Co., 1994); Jiajie Zhang, "A Representational Analysis of Relational Information Displays," *International Journal of Human-Computer Studies* 45 (1996): 59–74.

14. Herbert A. Simon, *The Sciences of the Artificial* (Cambridge: MIT Press, 1996); David Marr, *Vision: A Computational Investigation into the Human Representation and Processing of Visual Information* (San Francisco: W. H. Freeman and Co., 1982).

15. Donald A. Norman, *Things That Make Us Smart: Defending Human Attributes in the Age of the Machine* (Reading, Mass.: Addison-Wesley, 1993); Jiajie Zhang and Donald A. Norman, "Representations in Distributed Cognitive Tasks," *Cognitive Science* 18 (1994) : 87–122; Jiajie Zhang and Donald A. Norman, "A Representational Analysis of Numeration Systems," *Cognition* 57 (1995): 271–95; Jiajie Zhang, "The Nature of External Representations in Problem Solving," *Cognitive Science* 21 (1997):

179–217; see also Zhang, "A Representational Analysis of Relevant Information Displays."

16. Zhang, "The Nature of External Representations"; Ryan D. Tweney, "Stopping Time: Faraday and the Scientific Creation of Perceptual Order," *Physis: Revista Internazionale di Storia Della Scienza* 29 (1992) : 149–64; Michael Faraday, "On A Peculiar Class of Optical Deceptions," *Journal of the Royal Institution* 1831 (1831a) : 205–23; Michael Faraday, "On A Peculiar Class of Acoustical Figures, and on Certain Forms Assumed by Groups of Particles Upon Vibrating Elastic Surfaces," *Philosophical Transactions* 1831 (1831b) : 299–340; Maria F. Ippolito and Ryan D. Tweney, "The Inception of Insight," in *The Nature of Insight*, ed. Robert J. Sternberg and Janet E. Davidson (Cambridge, MA: The MIT Press, 1995) 433–62; Sean C. Duncan and Ryan D. Tweney, "The Problem-Behavior Map as Cognitive-Historical Analysis: The Example of Michael Faraday," *Proceedings of the Nineteenth Annual Conference of the Cognitive Science Society* (Hillsdale, N.J.: Lawrence Erlbaum Associates, 1997), 901. Recently, I have been examining a collection of microscope slides made by Faraday in connection with his 1856 research on the optical properties of thin gold films; Ryan D. Tweney, "Epistemic Artifacts: Michael Faraday's Search for the Optical Effects of Gold" in *Model-Based Reasoning: Science, Technology, Values*, ed. Lorenzo Magnani and Nancy J. Nersessian (New York: Kluwer Academic/Plenum, 2002), 287–303.

17. Étienne Jules Marey, *La Méthode Graphique Dans Les Sciences Expérimentales, Et Principalement En Physiologie Et En Médecine*, 2d ed. (Paris: G. Masson, 1885); Merriley Borell, "Instruments and Independent Physiology: The Harvard Physiological Laboratory, 1871–1906," in *Physiology in the American Context, 1850–1940*, ed. Gerald L. Gieson (Bethesda, Md.: American Physiological Society, 1983), 293–322; Merriley Borell, "Instrumentation and the Rise of Modern Physiology," *Science and Technology Studies* 5 (1987): 53–62; Gerald L. Gieson, ed., *Physiology in the American Context, 1850–1940* (Bethesda, Md.: American Physiological Society, 1987).

18. Ludy T. Benjamin, Maureen Durkin, Michelle Link, Marilyn Vestal, and Jill Acord, "Wundt's American Doctoral Students," *American Psychologist* 47 (1992): 123–31; John M. O'Donnell, *The Origins of Behaviorism: American Psychology, 1870–1920* (New York: New York University Press, 1985); Michael M. Sokal, *An Education in Psychology: James McKeen Cattell's Journal and Letters from Germany and England, 1880–1888* (Cambridge, Mass.: MIT Press, 1981); Michael Lynch and Steve Woolgar, eds., *Representation in Scientific Practice* (Cambridge, Mass.: MIT Press, 1990).

19. Ruth Benschop and Douwe Draaisma, "In Pursuit of Precision: The Calibration of Minds and Machines in Late Nineteenth-Century Psychology," *Annals of Science* 57 (2000): 1–25; Wolfgang G. Bringmann, Norma J. Bringmann and William D.G. Balance, "Wilhelm Maximilian Wundt 1832–1874: The Formative Years," in *Wundt Studies*, ed. Bringmann and Tweney, 13–32; Wilhelm Wundt, *Lehrbuch der Physiologie des Menschen* (Erlangen: Verlag von Ferdinand Enke, 1865).

20. See Sokal, *An Education in Psychology*, where Cattell's "Journal" (1884) is transcribed on 99–105. Details about the problem and its resolution and a history of the instrument are given in Beatrice Edgell and W. Legge Symes, "The Wheatstone-Hipp Chronoscope. Its Adjustments, Accuracy, and Control," *British Journal of Psychology* 2 (1906): 58–88.

21. Michael M. Sokal, Audrey B. Davis, and Uta C. Merzbach, "Laboratory Instruments in the History of Psychology," *Journal of the History of the Behavioral Sciences* 12 (1976): 59–64; Wilhelm Wundt, *Handbuch der Medicinischen Physik* (Erlangen: Verlag von Ferdinand Enke, 1867); Popplestone and McPherson, *An Illustrated History of American Psychology.*

22. Ernest R. Hilgard, "Foreword," in *Wundt Studies*, ed. Bringmann and Tweney, 1–4. Hugo Münsterberg, "The Place of Experimental Psychology" (dedication remarks at the opening of Emerson Hall, December 1905), in Hugo Münsterberg, ed., *Harvard Psychological Studies, Vol. 2* (Boston: Houghton Mifflin, 1905), 31–39.

23. Charles H. Judd, *Laboratory Equipment for Psychological Experiments* (New York: Charles Scribner's Sons, 1907); Edmund C. Sanford, "A Laboratory Course in Physiological Psychology," *American Journal of Psychology* 4 (1891–92): 141–55; Edmund C. Sanford, *A Course in Experimental Psychology* (Boston: D. C. Heath & Co, 1898); Edward Bradford Titchener, *Experimental Psychology: A Manual of Laboratory Practice. Vol. I: Qualitative Experiments; Vol. II: Quantitative Experiments*, 2 vol. in 4 parts (New York: Macmillan, 1901–5).

24. Ryan D. Tweney, "Programmatic Research in Experimental Psychology: E. B. Titchener's Laboratory Investigations, 1887–1927," in *Psychology in Twentieth-Century Thought and Society*, ed. Mitchell G. Ash and William R. Woodward (Cambridge, U. K.: Cambridge University Press, 1987), 35–58.

25. See Popplestone and Tweney, *The Great Catalog*; emphasis added.

26. John B. Watson, "Kinaesthetic and Organic Sensations: Their Role in the Reactions of the White Rat to the Maze," *Psychological Review, Monograph Supplements* 8, no. 2 (1907): whole No. 33; Anna Wyczoikowska, "Theoretical and Experimental Studies in the Mechanism of Speech," *Psychological Review* 20 (1913) : 448–59; Judd, *Laboratory Equipment for Psychological Experiments*; John B. Watson, *Behavior: An Introduction to Comparative Psychology* (New York: Henry Holt and Co, 1914); John B. Watson, "The Place of Kinaesthetic, Visceral, and Laryngeal Organization in Thinking," *Psychological Review* 31 (1924): 339–47.

27. Robert M. Yerkes, ed., *Psychological Examining in the United States Army* (Washington, D. C.: Government Printing Office, 1921); Guy Montrose Whipple, *Manual of Mental and Physical Tests, A Book of Directions Compiled with Special Reference to the Experimental Study of School Children in the Laboratory or Classroom* (Baltimore, Md.: Warwick & York, 1910); Guy Montrose Whipple, *Manual of Mental and Physical Tests, In Two Parts. Part II: Complex Processes* (Baltimore, Md.: Warwick & York, 1915); Popplestone and McPherson, *An Illustrated History of American Psychology*, Chapter 6; David F. Noble, *America by Design: Science, Technology, and the Rise of Corporate Capitalism* (Oxford: Oxford University Press, 1977).

28. Kurt Danziger, *Constructing the Subject: Historical Origins of Psychological Research* (Cambridge: Cambridge University Press, 1990); Edward L. Thorndike, *An Introduction to the Theory of Mental and Social Measurements* (New York: Science Press, 1904). See also Steven Ward, *Modernizing the Mind: Psychological Knowledge and the Remaking of Society* (Westport, Conn.: Greenwood Publishing Group, Praeger, 2002).

29. Gustav Theodor Fechner, *Elemente der Psychophysik* (Leipzig: Breitkopf und Haertel, 1860); Charles Saunders Peirce and Joseph Jastrow, "On Small Differences

of Sensation," *Memoirs of the National Academy of Sciences* 3, no.1 (1884): 75–83; Stephen M. Stigler, "Statistical Concepts in Psychology," in *Statistics on the Table: The History of Statistical Concepts and Methods,* ed. Stephen M. Stigler (Cambridge, Mass.: Harvard University Press, 1999) 189–202; Franz Boas, *The Measurement of Variable Quantities: Archives of Philosophy, Psychology and Scientific Methods* (New York: The Science Press, 1906); Zeno G. Swijtink, "The Objectification of Observation: Measurement and Statistical Methods in the Nineteenth Century," in *The Probabilistic Revolution, Vol. 1: Ideas in History,* ed. Lorenz Krüger, Lorraine J. Daston and Michael Heidelberger (Cambridge, MA: MIT Press, 1987) 261–86.

30. George Stuart Fullerton and James McKeen Cattell, *On the Perception of Small Differences, With Special Reference to the Extent, Force and Time of Movement* (Philadelphia, Pa.: University of Pennsylvania Press, 1892).

31. Danziger, *Constructing the Subject.*

32. For example, Thorndike, *An Introduction to the Theory of Mental and Social Measurements.*

33. Laurence D. Smith, Lisa A. Best, Virginia A. Cylke, and D. Alan Stubbs, "Psychology Without *p* Values: Data Analysis at the Turn of the 19th Century," *American Psychologist* 55 (2000): 260–63; Arthur L. Bowley, *Elements of statistics,* 2d ed. (London: P. S. King & Son, 1902); George Chandler Whipple, *Vital Statistics: An Introduction to the Science of Demography* (New York: John Wiley & Sons, 1919).

34. Michael Cowles, *Statistics in Psychology: An Historical Perspective,* 2d ed. (Mahwah, N. J.: Lawrence Erlbaum Associates, 2001); see also Rucci and Tweney, "Analysis of Variance." Compare also the treatment of this issue given by Lovie, "The Analysis of Variance."

35. Note that the critical ratio has reappeared in psychology as a measure of *effect size*! Such use of the critical ratio is now known as "Cohen's d"; Robert Rosenthal and Ralph H. Rosnow, *Essentials of Behavioral Research: Methods and Data Analysis,* 2d ed. (New York: McGraw-Hill, 1991). An excellent early account of the critical ratio, one that anticipated the later discussion by Fisher of statistical tests, was given by Charles S. Myers, *A Text-Book of Experimental Psychology* (London: Edward Arnold, 1909).

36. Yerkes, *Psychological Examining*; James McKeen Cattell and Livingston Farrand, "Physical and Mental Measurements of the Students of Columbia University," *Psychological Review* 3 (1896): 618–48; Michael M. Sokal, "James McKeen Cattell and Mental Anthropometry: Nineteenth-Century Science and Reform and the Origins of Psychological Testing," in *Psychological Testing and American Psychology, 1890–1930,* ed. Michael M. Sokal (New Brunswick, N. J.: Rutgers University Press, 1987), 21–45; Clark Wissler, "The Correlation of Mental and Physical Tests," *Psychological Review Monograph Supplement* 3, no. 6 (1901).

37. Vannevar Bush and James B. Conant, "National Defense Research Committee Foreword," in *Transmission and Reception of Sounds Under Combat Conditions,* ed. S.S. Stevens (Washington D. C.: Office of Scientific Research and Development, 1946), v; James H. Capshew, *Psychologists on the March: Science, Practice, and Professional Identity in America, 1929–1969* (Cambridge, Mass.: Cambridge University Press, 1999); Stephen E. Fienberg, "Statistical Developments in World War II: An International Perspective," in *A Celebration of Statistics: The ISI Centenary Volume,* ed. An-

thony C. Atkinson and Stephen E. Fienberg (New York: Springer, 1985), 25–30; Lovie, "The Analysis of Variance."

38. See Capshew, *Psychologists on the March*; James P. Guilford, *Printed Classification Tests*, Army Air Forces Aviation Psychology Program, Research Report No. 5 (Washington, D. C.: Government Printing Office, 1947).

39. Arthur W. Melton, ed., *Apparatus Tests*, Army Air Forces Aviation Psychology Program, Research Report No. 4 (Washington, D. C.: Government Printing Office, 1947).

40. Lovie, "The Analysis of Variance." Ironically, Melton later embraced null hypothesis testing without reservation; as editor of an important journal, he privileged such tests, indicating that p values greater than .05 were "not publishable," while those that were between .05 and .01 were "marginally publishable." Potential authors were encouraged to seek results that were significant at the .01 level only! See Arthur W. Melton, "Editorial," *Journal of Experimental Psychology* 64 (1962): 553–57.

41. Neal E. Miller, ed., *Psychological Research on Pilot Training*, Army Air Forces Aviation Psychology Program, Research Report No. 8 (Washington, D.C.: Government Printing Office, 1947).

42. Paul M. Fitts, *Psychological Research on Equipment Design*, Army Air Forces Aviation Psychology Program, Research Report No. 19 (Washington, D.C.: Government Printing Office, 1947), 16–17; Laurence D. Smith, Lisa A. Best, D. Alan Stubbs, J. Johnston, and A.B. Archibald, "Scientific Graphs and the Hierarchy of the Sciences: A Latourian Survey of Inscription Practices," *Social Studies of Science* 30 (2000): 73–94.

43. John C. Flanagan, *The Aviation Psychology Program in the Army Air Forces*, Army Air Forces Aviation Psychology Program, Research Report No. 1 (Washington, D.C.: Government Printing Office, 1948). The relevant section is on pp. 281–92 and the quote is on p. 292. Flanagan's program contrasts sharply with the other large World War II assessment program conducted under "Wild Bill" Donovan at the Office of Strategic Services (OSS). Headed by Henry Murray, the focus of OSS research was on holistic personality assessment. Traditional mental testing (and its attendant statistical procedures) was not used. See Capshew, *Psychologists on the March*, 111–15, and Louise E. Hoffman, "American Psychologists and Wartime Research on Germany, 1941–1945," *American Psychologist* 47 (1992): 264–73.

44. My use of the term "hybrid model" follows Gerd Gigerenzer and David J. Murray, *Cognition as Intuitive Statistics* (Hillsdale, N. J.: Lawrence Erlbaum Associates, 1987), and refers to the combination of Fisherian and Neyman-Pearson approaches to statistical inference, common in psychology after World War II.

45. Donald W. Hastings, David G. Wright, and Bernard C. Glueck, *Psychiatric Experiences of the Eighth Air Force: First Year of Combat (July 4, 1942–July 4, 1943)*, report prepared for The Air Surgeon, Army Air Forces (New York: Josiah Macy, Jr. Foundation, 1944).

46. [Anon.], *Progress Report, 31 December 1946*, Office of Naval Research, U.S. Navy, Contract N5ori-76, unpublished manuscript (Cambridge, Mass.: Harvard University, Psycho-Acoustic Laboratory, 1946); S. S. Stevens, ed., *Transmission and Reception of Sounds Under Combat Conditions.*

47. Bernard J. Baars, *The Cognitive Revolution in Psychology* (New York: Guilford,

1986); Hunter Crowther-Heyck, "George A. Miller, Language, and the Computer Metaphor of Mind," *History of Psychology* 2 (1999): 37–64; William Hirst, ed., *The Making of Cognitive Science: Essays in Honor of George A. Miller* (Cambridge, U. K.: Cambridge University Press, 1988); George A. Miller and Walter G. Taylor, "The Perception of Repeated Bursts of Noise," *Journal of the Acoustical Society of America*, 20 (1949): 171–82; George A. Miller and Frederick C. Frick, "Statistical Behavioristics and Sequences of Responses," *Psychological Review* 56 (1949): 311–24; George A. Miller, "The Magical Number Seven, Plus or Minus Two; Some Limits on our Capacity for Processing Information," *Psychological Review* 63 (1956): 81–97.

48. Rucci and Tweney, "Analysis of Variance."

49. Peter Galison, *Image and Logic: A Material Culture of Microphysics* (Chicago: University of Chicago Press, 1997).

50. Ellen Herman, *The Romance of American Psychology: Political Culture in the Age of Experts* (Berkeley: University of California Press, 1995); Lee Cronbach, "The Two Disciplines of Scientific Psychology," *American Psychologist* 12 (1957): 671–84.

51. By "most popular," I mean most requested for viewing, according to David Baker, director of the archives. This machine was also featured on a television broadcast about the archives.

52. Raymond Hubbard, Rahul A. Parsa, and Michael R. Luthy, "The Spread of Statistical Significance Testing in Psychology: The Case of the *Journal of Applied Psychology*, 1917–1994," *Theory & Psychology* 7 (1997): 545–54; David Bakan, "The Test of Significance in Psychological Research," *Psychological Bulletin* 66 (1966): 423–37; Geoffrey R. Loftus, "A Picture is Worth a Thousand *p* Values: On the Irrelevance of Hypothesis Testing in the Microcomputer Age," *Behavior Research Methods, Instruments, & Computers* 25 (1993): 250–56.

Chapter 8

1. For example, Stephen Toulmin, "From Form to Function: Philosophy and History of Science in the 1950s and Now," *Daedalus* 106 (1977): 143–62.

2. See Thomas C. Cadwallader, "Unique Values of Archival Research," *Journal of the History of the Behavioral Sciences* 11 (1975): 27–33.

3. For example, Robert B. Lockard, "Reflections on the Fall of Comparative Psychology: Is There a Message for Us All?" *American Psychologist* 26 (1971): 168–79.

4. Benjamin Harris, "Ceremonial Versus Critical History of Psychology," *American Psychologist* 35 (1980): 218–19; Donald A. Dewsbury, *Comparative Psychology in the Twentieth Century* (Stroudsburg, Pa.: Hutchinson Ross, 1984).

5. Donald A. Dewsbury to John A. Popplestone, February 22, 1982, in possession of the writer.

6. Robert M. Yerkes, *Chimpanzees: A Laboratory Colony* (New Haven: Yale University Press, 1943); Robert M. Yerkes, Diary, 1919, Robert M. Yerkes Papers, Yale University Library, New Haven, Conn.; Yerkes to Abraham Flexner, February 25, 1914, Yerkes Papers; Yerkes to Simon Flexner, January 11, 1916, Yerkes Papers.

7. Edwin R. Embree to Max Mason, November 6, 1929, Rockefeller Archive Center, North Tarrytown, N.Y.; Max Mason to Edwin R. Embree, November 8, 1929, Rockefeller Archive Center.

8. Yerkes, *Chimpanzees*; Donald A. Dewsbury, "Comparative Cognition in the 1930s," *Psychonomic Bulletin and Review* 7 (2000): 267–83.

9. Lawrence K. Frank, Diary, February 9–16, 1935, Group 1.1, series 200D, Box 165, Folder 2024, Rockefeller Archive Center; H. M. Miller, Jr., Diary, February 20, 1936, Group 1.1, series 200D, Box 165, Folder 2024, Rockefeller Archive Center; Karl S. Lashley, 1937, to Frank B. Hanson, January 8, 1937, Group 1.1, series 200D, Box 165, Folder 2025, Rockefeller Archive Center; Warren Weaver, Diary, January 14, 1937, Group 1.1, series 200D, Box 165, Folder 2025, Rockefeller Archive Center: Frank B. Hanson, Diary, October 29–30, 1936, Group 1.1, series 200D, Box 165, Folder 2024, Rockefeller Archive Center; Robert M. Yerkes to James R. Angell, May 7, 1937, Yerkes Papers.

10. Donald A. Dewsbury, "Robert M. Yerkes: Man with a Plan," in *Portraits of Pioneers in Psychology*, Vol.1, ed. Gregory A. Kimble, C. Alan Boneau, and Michael Wertheimer (Washington, D.C.: American Psychological Association, 1996), 87–105; Donald A. Dewsbury, "Robert Yerkes," in *Encyclopedia of Psychology*, Vol. 8, ed. Alan E. Kazdin (Washington, D.C.: American Psychological Association and Oxford University Press, 2000), 295–96; Donald A. Dewsbury, "Henry W. Nissen: Quiet Comparative Psychologist," in *Portraits of Pioneers in Psychology* Vol. 3, ed. Gregory A. Kimble and Michael Wertheimer (Washington, D.C.: American Psychological Association, 1998); Donald A. Dewsbury, "Henry Nissen," in *Encyclopedia of Psychology*, Vol. 5, ed. Kazdin, 317.

11. Donald A. Dewsbury, "Robert Yerkes, Sex Research, and the Problem of Data Simplification," *History of Psychology* 1 (1998): 116–29.

12. Donald A. Dewsbury, "A Note on the Early Editorial Policies of the *Journal of Comparative Psychology*," *Journal of Comparative Psychology* 112 (1998): 406–7; Donald A. Dewsbury "Psychobiology," *American Psychologist* 46 (1991): 198–205.

13. Donald A. Dewsbury, "The Chicago Five: A Family of Integrative Psychobiologists," *History of Psychology* 5 (2002): 16–37.

14. John A. Popplestone, oral history of Norman R. F. Maier, 1967, Maier Papers, Archives of the History of American Psychology, The University of Akron, Akron, Ohio.

15. Frank A. Beach, "Frank A. Beach," in *A History of Psychology in Autobiography*, Vol. 4, ed. Gardner Lindzey (New York: Appleton-Century-Crofts, 1974), 39; Frank A. Beach, "Historical Origins of Modern Research on Hormones and Behavior," *Hormones and Behavior* 15 (1981): 327.

16. Karl S. Lashley, "The Problem of Serial Order in Behavior," in *Cerebral Mechanisms in Behavior*, ed. L. A. Jefress (New York: Wiley, 1951), 112–36; Donald O. Hebb, "The Role of Neurological Ideas in Psychology," *Journal of Personality* 20 (1951): 39–55; Donald O. Hebb, "The American Revolution," *American Psychologist* 15 (1960): 743.

17. Jack Orbach, *The Neuropsychological Theories of Lashley and Hebb: Contemporary Perspectives Fifty Years After Hebb's The Organization of Behavior* (Lanham, Md.: University Press of America, 1998).

18. Karl S. Lashley, "Cerebral Organization and Behavior," *Proceedings of the Association for Research on Nervous and Mental Diseases* 36 (1958): 1–18; Lashley, 1951; Donald O. Hebb, *Organization of Behavior* (New York: Wiley, 1949); John Garcia, "I.

Krechevsky and I," in *Knowing, Thinking, and Believing: Festschrift for Professor David Krech*, ed. Lewis Petrinovich and James L. McGaugh (New York: Plenum, 1976), 72.

19. Karl S. Lashley, "Basic Neural Mechanisms in Behavior," *Psychological Review* 37 (1930), 1; David Krech, "Dynamic Systems, Psychological Fields, and Hypothetical Constructs," *Psychological Review* 57 (1950), 288; Donald O. Hebb, "Alice in Wonderland or Psychology Among the Biological Sciences," in *Biological and Biochemical Bases of Behavior*, ed. H. F. Harlow and C. N. Woolsey (Madison: University of Wisconsin Press, 1958), 466.

20. William Hodos and C. B. G. Campbell, *"Scala Naturae*: Why There is No Theory in Comparative Psychology," *Psychological Review* 76 (1969): 337–50; Frank A. Beach to Donald O. Hebb, July 16, 1947, D. O. Hebb Papers, Archives, McGill University, Montreal, Quebec, Canada.

21. Donald O. Hebb and William R. Thompson, "The Social Significance of Animal Studies," in *Handbook of Social Psychology,* vol. 1, by Gardner Lindzey (Cambridge, Mass: Addison-Wesley, 1954), 532–61; Frank A. Beach, "Pursuit of Intellectual Orgasm (Interview with Joyce D. Fleming and David Maxey)," *Psychology Today* 8 no.10 (1975): 68–77.

22. Frank A. Beach to D. O. Hebb, July 25, 1959, Hebb Papers.

23. Donald O. Hebb to Frank A. Beach, August 18, 1959, Hebb Papers; Popplestone, oral history of Maier.

24. Niko Tinbergen to Frank A. Beach, October 17, 1973, Beach Papers, Archives of the History of American Psychology, The University of Akron, Akron, Ohio; Frank A. Beach to William S. Verplanck, January 24, 1955, Verplanck papers, Archives of the History of American Psychology, Archives of the History of American Psychology Akron, Ohio.

25. Daniel S. Lehrman, "A Critique of Konrad Lorenz's Theory of Instinctive Behavior," *Quarterly Review of Biology* 28: (1953), 337–63; Donald O. Hebb to Daniel S. Lehrman, September 30, 1949, Hebb Papers.

26. Donald O. Hebb, Notes on the position of Lashley in the schools of psychology, undated, Hebb Papers, Archives of the History of American Psychology, Archives of the History of American Psychology, Akron, Ohio; Norman R. F. Maier, "Reasoning in White Rats," *Comparative Psychology Monographs* 6 (1929): 88, 92.

27. Donald O. Hebb, "Heredity and Environment in Mammalian Behaviour," *British Journal of Animal Behaviour* 1 (1953): 243–54; Frank A. Beach, "The Descent of Instinct," *Psychological Review* 62 (1955): 401–10.

28. See, for example, Karl S. Lashley, "Experimental Analysis of Instinctive Behavior," *Psychological Review* 45(1938): 445–71.

29. Isadore Krechevsky, "Hereditary Nature of "Hypotheses" in Rats," *Journal of Comparative Psychology* 16 (1933): 99–116; David Krech, "David Krech," in *A History of Psychology in Autobiography* vol. 6, ed. Lindzey (Englewood Cliffs, N.J.: Prentice Hall, 1974), 221–50; Thomas H. Roderick, Richard E. Wimer, and Cynthia C. Wimer, "Genetic Manipulation of Neuroanatomical Traits," in *Knowing, Thinking, and Believing,* ed. Petrinovich and McGaugh, 143–78.

30. Karl S. Lashley, *Brain Mechanisms and Intelligence* (Chicago: University of Chicago Press, 1929); Donald O. Hebb, "Emotion in Man and Animal: An Analysis of the Intuitive Processes of Recognition," *Psychological Review* 53, (1954): 88–106;

Frank A. Beach and Burney J. LeBoeuf, "Coital Behaviour in Dogs. I. Preferential Mating in the Bitch," *Animal Behaviour* 15 (1967): 546–58.

31. Donald A. Dewsbury, "Frank Ambrose Beach: 1911–1988," *American Journal of Psychology* 102 (1989): 414–20; Donald A. Dewsbury, "Frank Ambrose Beach 1911–1988," *Biographical Memoirs of the National Academy of Sciences, USA* 73 (1997): 3–22; Donald A. Dewsbury, "Frank Ambrose Beach, Jr.," in *American National Biography,* vol. 2 (Oxford: Oxford University Press, 1999), 384–85; Donald A. Dewsbury, "Frank A. Beach," in *Encyclopedia,* vol. 1, ed. Kazdin, 374–75; Donald A. Dewsbury, "Reminiscences of Frank Ambrose Beach," *Hormones and Behavior* 22 (1988): 431–33; Donald A. Dewsbury, "Four Giants: Frank Beach, Curt Richter, Niko Tinbergen, and Konrad Lorenz," *Newsletter of the Animal Behavior Society* 34, no. 2 (1989): 2–3; Donald A. Dewsbury, "Frank A. Beach: Master teacher," in *Portraits of Pioneers in Psychology,* vol. 4, ed. Gregory Kimble and Michael Wertheimer (Washington, D.C.: American Psychological Association, 2000), 268–83.

32. Donald A. Dewsbury, "Frank Beach's Unpublished Textbook on Comparative Psychology," *Journal of Comparative Psychology* 104 (1990): 219–26.

33. Frank A. Beach, "The Snark was a Boojum," *American Psychologist* 5 (1950): 115–24; Dewsbury, *Comparative Psychology in the Twentieth Century;* Donald A. Dewsbury, "Animal Psychology in Journals, 1911–1927," *Journal of Comparative Psychology* 112 (1998): 400–403.

34. Donald A. Dewsbury, "On Publishing Controversy: Norman R. F. Maier and the Genesis of Seizures," *American Psychologist* 48 (1993): 869–77.

35. Norman R. F. Maier and Theodore C. Schneirla, *Principles of Animal Psychology* (New York: McGraw-Hill, 1935); Donald A. Dewsbury, "A Classic in Comparative Psychology," *Contemporary Psychology* 39 (1994): 797–99.

36. Dewsbury, Comparative Cognition.

37. Donald A. Dewsbury and Robert C. Bolles, "The Founding of the Psychonomic Society," *Psychonomic Bulletin and Review* 2 (1995): 1216–33; Donald A. Dewsbury, "History of the Psychonomic Society II: The Journal Publishing Program," *Psychonomic Bulletin and Review* 3 (1996): 322–38; Donald A. Dewsbury, "History of the Psychonomic Society III: The Meetings of the Psychonomic Society," *Psychonomic Bulletin and Review* 4 (1997): 350–58; Donald A. Dewsbury, "History of the Psychonomic Society IV: The Development of the Psychonomic Society," *Psychonomic Bulletin and Review* 4 (1997): 492–500.

38. Donald A. Dewsbury, "On the Evolution of Divisions," *American Psychologist* 52 (1997): 733–41; Donald A. Dewsbury, ed., *Unification Through Division: Histories of the American Psychological Association* vol. 1–5 (Washington, D.C.: American Psychological Association, 1996, 1997, 1998, 1999, 2000); Donald A. Dewsbury, "A History of Division 6: (Behavioral Neuroscience and Comparative Psychology): Now You See It, Now You Don't, Now You See It," in *Unification through Division* vol.1, ed. Dewsbury, 41–65.

39. Donald A. Dewsbury, "Paul Harkai Schiller," *Psychological Record* 44 (1994): 307–9; Donald A. Dewsbury, "A Supplement to Karl Lashley's Biographical Sketch of Paul Harkai Schiller," *Psychological Record* 44 (1994): 320–25; Donald A. Dewsbury, "The Comparative Psychology of Paul Schiller," *Psychological Record* 44 (1994): 326–50; Donald A. Dewsbury, "Paul Harkai Schiller: The Influence of His Brief Career,"

in *Portraits of Pioneers in Psychology,* vol.1, ed. Kimble et al., 281–93; Karl S. Lashley, "Paul Harkai Schiller: 1908–1949," *Psychological Record* 44 (1994): 309–19.

Chapter 9

1. David Bakan, *Sigmund Freud and the Jewish Mystical Tradition* (New York: Schocken Books, 1965), and *On Method: Toward a Reconstruction of Psychological Investigation* (San Francisco: Jossey-Bass, 1967).

2. Neil Agnew and Sandra Pyke, *The Science Game: An Introduction to Research in the Behavioral Sciences* (Englewood Cliffs, N.J.: Prentice Hall, 1969); Raymond E. Fancher, *Psychoanalytic Psychology: The Development of Freud's Thought* (New York: Norton, 1973); and *Pioneers of Psychology* (New York: Norton, 1979).

3. Paul Ballantyne, "From Initial Abstractions to a Concrete Concept of Personality," in *Recent Trends in Theoretical Psychology*, vol. 4, ed. I. Lubek et al. (New York: Springer, 1995) 150–60.

4. Kurt Danziger and Paul Ballantyne, "Psychological experiments," in *A Pictorial History of Psychology*, ed. W. Bringmann, H. Lück, R. Miller, and C. Early (Chicago: Quintessence Publishing Co., 1997), 233–39.

5. Quoted in Geoffrey Bunn, "Constructing the Suspect: A Brief History of the Lie Detector," *Border/Lines* 40 (1996): 8.

6. Geoffrey. Bunn, *"The Hazards of the Will to Truth: A History of the Lie Detector"* (Ph.D. dissertation, York University, Toronto 1998), iv-v.

7. Geoffrey Bunn, "The Lie Detector, Wonder Woman, and Liberty: The Life and Work of William Moulton Marston," *History of the Human Sciences* 10 (1997): 91–120; Bunn, "Constructing the suspect;" Kurt Danziger, *Constructing the Subject: Historical Origins of Psychological Research* (Cambridge, Mass.: Cambridge University Press, 1990).

8. See, for example, Ian Nicholson, "Academic Professionalization and Protestant Reconstruction, 1890–1901: George Albert Coe's Psychology of Religion," *Journal of the History of the Behavioral Sciences* 30 (1994): 348–68; Ian Nicholson, "From the Kingdom of God to the Beloved Community, 1920–1930: Psychology and the Social Gospel in the Work of Goodwin Watson and Carl Rogers," *Journal of Psychology and Theology* 22 (1994): 196–206; Ian Nicholson, "Humanistic Psychology and Intellectual Identity: The 'Open' System of Gordon Allport," *Journal of Humanistic Psychology* 37 (1997): 60–78; Ian Nicholson, "The Politics of Scientific Social Reform, 1936–1960: Goodwin Watson and the Society for the Psychological Study of Social Issues," *Journal of the History of the Behavioral Sciences* 33 (1997): 39–60.

9. Ian Nicholson, "Moral Projects and Disciplinary Practices: Gordon Allport and the Development of American Personality Psychology" (Ph.D. dissertation, York University, 1996).

10. Ian Nicholson, "Gordon Allport, Character, and the 'Culture of Personality,' " *History of Psychology* 1 (1998): 52–68.

Bibliography

Agnew, Neil, and Sandra Pyke. *The Science Game: An Introduction to Research in the Behavioral Sciences*. Englewood Cliffs, N.J.: Prentice Hall, 1969.

Allport, Gordon W. "The Clergyman as Mind Raid Warden." Address presented at the Massachusetts Clerical Association Cathedral of St. Paul, Boston, Mass., March 1, 1943.

————. *The Individual and His Religion*. New York: Collier-McMillan, 1950.

————. "Psychology." In *College Reading and Religion*. New Haven, Conn.: Yale University Press, 1948.

————. "The Roots of Religion," The Advent Papers. 1 (Mt. Vernon Street, Boston 8, Massachusetts, 1944); Reprinted in Pastoral Psychology 5(43) (1954): 13–24.

————. *Waiting for the Lord: 33 Meditations on God & Man*. Edited by Peter Anthony Bertocci. New York: Macmillan, 1978.

[Anon.]. "*Progress Report, 31 December 1946*." Prepared by the Office of Naval Research, U.S. Navy, Contract N5ori-76. Unpublished Manuscript. Cambridge, Mass.: Harvard University, Psycho-Acoustic Laboratory, 1946.

Assagioli, Roberto. *Psychosynthesis: A Manual of Principles and Techniques*. New York: Hobbs, Dorman, 1965.

Baars, Bernard J. *The Cognitive Revolution in Psychology*. New York: Guilford, 1986.

Bakan, David. *One Method: Toward a Reconstruction of Psychological Investigation*. San Francisco: Jossey-Bass, 1967.

————. *Sigmund Freud and the Jewish Mystical Tradition*. New York: Schocken Books, 1965.

————. "The Test of Significance in Psychological Research." *Psychological Bulletin* 66 (1966): 423–37.

Baker, David B., and Ludy T. Benjamin Jr. "The Affirmation of the Scientist-Practitioner: A Look Back at Boulder." *American Psychologist* 55 (2000): 241–47.

Balance, William D. G. "Frustrations and Joys of Archival Research." *Journal of the History of the Behavioral Sciences* 11 (1975): 37–40.

Baldwin, James Mark. "Psychotherapeutics or Psychotherapy." In *Dictionary of Philosophy and Psychology, Vol. II*. Edited by James Mark Baldwin. 1925. Reprint, New York: Peter Smith, 1940.

Ballantyne, Paul. "From Initial Abstractions to a Concrete Concept of Personality." In *Recent Trends in Theoretical Psychology*. Vol. 4. Edited by I. Lubek et al. New York: Springer, 1995.

Barr, Martin. "Moral Paranoia." *Proceedings of the Association of Medical Officers of Institutions for Idiotic and Feeble-Minded Persons* (1895): 530–31.

Bayley, Nancy. "Development of Mental Abilities." In *Carmichael's Manual of Child Psychology, Volume I, Third Edition*. Edited by Paul H. Mussen. New York: Wiley, 1970.

Beach, Frank A. "The Descent of Instinct." *Psychological Review* 62 (1955): 401–10.

———. "Frank A. Beach." In *A History of Psychology in Autobiography* Vol. 4. Edited by G. Lindzey. New York: Appleton-Century-Crofts, 1974.

———. "Historical Origins of Modern Research on Hormones and Behavior." *Hormones and Behavior* 15: 325–76.

———. "Pursuit of Intellectual Orgasm (Interview with Joyce D. Fleming and David Maxey)." *Psychology Today* 8, no. 10 (1975): 68–77.

———. "The Snark was a Boojum." *American Psychologist* 5 (1950): 115–24.

Beach, Frank A., and Burney J. LeBoeuf. "Coital Behaviour in Dogs. I. Preferential Mating in the Bitch." *Animal Behaviour* 15 (1967): 546–58.

Benjamin, Lorna Smith. *Interpersonal Diagnosis and Treatment of Personality Disorders*. 2d ed. New York: The Guilford Press, 1996.

Benjamin, Ludy T. Jr. "Archival Adventures: From Secret Societies to the Supreme Court." The Wallace Russell Memorial Lecture presented to Division 26, The History of Psychology, at the convention of the American Psychological Association, Boston, Mass., August 20–24, 1999.

———. "David Pablo Boder's Psychological Museum and the Exposition of 1938." *Psychological Record* 29 (1979): 559–65.

———. "Harry Hollingworth: Portrait of a Generalist." In *Portraits of Pioneers in Psychology*. Vol. 2. Edited by Gregory A. Kimble, C. Alan Boneau, and Michael Wertheimer. Mahwah, NJ: Lawrence Erlbaum, 1996.

———. "A History of Division 14: The Society for Industrial and Organizational Psychology." In *Unification through Division: Histories of the Divisions of the American Psychological Association*. Vol. 2. Edited by Donald A. Dewsbury. Washington, D.C.: American Psychological Association, 1997.

———. "A History of the New York Branch of the American Psychological Association, 1903–1935." *American Psychologist* 46 (1991): 1003–11.

———. *History of Psychology in Letters*. Dubuque, Iowa: Brown & Benchmark, 1993.

———. "A History of Teaching Machines." *American Psychologist* 43 (1988): 703–12.

———. "The Midwestern Psychological Association: A History of the Organization and Its Antecedents." *American Psychologist* 34 (1979): 201–13.

———. "Organized Industrial Psychology before Division 14: The ACP and the AAAP." *Journal of Applied Psychology* 82 (1997): 459–66.

———. "The Pioneering Work of Leta Hollingworth in the Psychology of Women." *Nebraska History* 56 (1975): 493–505.

———. "A Platform Disaster: Harry Hollingworth and the Psychology of Public Speaking." *Nebraska History* 81 (2000): 67–73.

————. "The Psychological Round Table: Revolution of 1936." *American Psychologist* 32 (1977): 542–49.

————. "Remarks Honoring John A. Popplestone and Marion White McPherson for Contributions to the History of Psychology." *History of Psychology* 3 (2000): 75–77.

————. "Research at the Archives of the History of American Psychology: A Case History." In *Historiography of Modern Psychology*. Edited by Josef Brozek and Ludwig J. Pongratz. Toronto: C. J. Hogrefe, 1980.

Benjamin, Ludy T. Jr., Anne M. Rogers, and Angela Rosenbaum. "Coca-Cola, Caffeine, and Mental Deficiency: Harry Hollingworth and the Chattanooga Trial of 1911." *Journal of the History of the Behavioral Sciences* 27 (1991): 42–55.

Benjamin, Ludy T. Jr. and Darryl Bruce. "From Bottle-fed Chimp to Bottlenose Dolphin: A Contemporary Appraisal of Winthrop Kellogg." *Psychological Record* 32 (1982): 461–82.

Benjamin, Ludy T. Jr. and Elizabeth Nielsen-Gammon. "B. F. Skinner and Psychotechnology: The Case of the Heir Conditioner." *Review of General Psychology* 3 (1999): 155–67.

Benjamin, Ludy T., Jr., Maureen Durkin, Michelle Link, Marilyn Vestal, and Jill Acord. "Wundt's American Doctoral Students." *American Psychologist* 47 (1992): 123–31.

Benjamin, Ludy T. Jr., and Stephanie A. Shields. "Leta Stetter Hollingworth." In *Women in Psychology: A Biobibliographic Sourcebook*. Edited by Agnes N. O'Connell and Nancy F. Russo. New York: Greenwood Press, 1990.

Benschop, Ruth, and Douwe Draaisma. "In Pursuit of Precision: The Calibration of Minds and Machines in Late Nineteenth-Century Psychology." *Annals of Science* 57 (2000): 1–25.

Best, Mary Agnes. *Rebel Saints*. New York: Harcourt, Brace, 1925.

Binet, Alfred, and Theodore Simon. *The Development of Intelligence in Children*. Translated by Elizabeth Kite. Baltimore: Williams and Wilkins, 1916.

Blackford, Katherine M. H., and Arthur Newcomb. *Analyzing Character: The New Science of Judging Men, Misfits in Business, the Home and Social Life*. New York: The Review of Reviews Co., 1913.

————. *The Job, the Man, the Boss*. New York: The Review of Reviews, 1914.

Block, N. J. and Gerald Dworkin, eds. *The IQ Controversy: Critical Readings*. New York: Pantheon, 1976.

Boas, Franz. *The Measurement of Variable Quantities: Archives of Philosophy, Psychology and Scientific Methods*. New York: The Science Press, 1906.

Boisen, Anton. *The Exploration of the Inner World: A Study of Mental Disorder and Religious Experience*. Chicago: Willet Clark, 1936.

————. *Out of the Depths: An Autobiographical Study of Mental Disorder and Religious Experience*. New York: Harper, 1960.

Borell, Merriley. "Instrumentation and the Rise of Modern Physiology." *Science and Technology Studies* 5 (1987): 53–62.

————. "Instruments and Independent Physiology: The Harvard Physiological Laboratory, 1871–1906." In *Physiology in the American Context, 1850–1940*. Edited by Gerald L. Gieson. Bethesda, Md.: American Physiological Society, 1983.

Boring, Edwin G. "The Society of Experimental Psychologists: 1904–1938." *American Journal of Psychology* 51 (1938): 410–23.

———. "Titchener's Experimentalists." *Journal of the History of the Behavioral Sciences* 3 (1967): 315–25.

Bowley, Arthur L. *Elements of Statistics.* Second Edition. London: P.S. King and Son, 1902.

Breitman, Richard, and Alan M. Kraut. *American Refugee Policy and European Jewry, 1933–1945.* Bloomington: Indiana University Press, 1987.

Brigham, Amariah. *Observations on the Influence of Religion upon the Health and Physical Welfare of Mankind.* Boston: Marsh, Capen & Lyon, 1835.

Bringmann, Wolfgang G. "Design Questions in Archival Research." *Journal of the History of the Behavioral Sciences* 11 (1975): 23–26.

Bringmann, Wolfgang G., Norma J. Bringmann, and William D. G. Balance. "Wilhelm Maximilian Wundt 1832–1874: The Formative Years." In *Wundt Studies: A Centennial Collection.* Edited by Wolfgang G. Bringmann and Ryan D. Tweney. Toronto: C. J. Hogrefe, 1980.

Brozek, Josef. "Irons in the Fire: Introduction to a Symposium on Archival Research." *Journal of the History of the Behavioral Sciences* 11 (1975): 15–19.

Brudnoy, David Barry. "Liberty's Bugler: The Seven Ages of Theodore Schroeder." Ph.D. diss., Brandeis University, 1971. Abstract in *Dissertation Abstracts International* 32 (1971): 6329A.

Bryan, William Jennings. *The First Battle: A Story of the Campaign of 1896.* Chicago, 1897.

Bunn, Geoffrey. "Constructing the Suspect: A Brief History of the Lie Detector." *Border/Lines* 40 (1996): 5–9.

———. "The Hazards of the Will to Truth: A History of the Lie Detector." Ph.D. dissertation, York University, Toronto, 1998.

———. "The Lie Detector, Wonder Woman, and Liberty: The Life and Work of William Moulton Marston." *History of the Human Sciences* 10 (1997): 91–120.

Burnham, John C. "Assessing Historical Research in the Behavioral and Social Sciences: A Symposium. Editor's Introduction." *Journal of the History of the Behavioral Sciences* 35 (1999): 225–26.

———. "John B. Watson: Interviewee, Professional Figure, Symbol." In *Modern Perspectives on John B. Watson and Classical Behaviorism.* Edited by James T. Todd and Edward K. Morris. Westport Conn.: Greenwood Press, 1994.

Burwell, Ronald Joseph. "Religion and the Social Sciences: A Study of Their Relationships as Set Forth in the Terry Lectures, 1924–1971." Ph.D. diss., New York University, 1976. Abstract in *Dissertation Abstracts International* 37 (1976): 1037A.

Bush, Vannevar, and James B. Conant. NDRC Foreword. In *Transmission and Reception of Sounds Under Combat Conditions.* Edited by S. S. Stevens. Washington D.C.: Office of Scientific Research and Development, 1946.

Cadwallader, Thomas C. "Unique Values of Archival Research." *Journal of the History of the Behavioral Sciences* 11 (1975): 27–33.

Capshew, James H. "Psychologists On Site: A Reconnaissance of the Historiography of the Laboratory." *American Psychologist* 47 (1992): 132–42.

———. *Psychologists on the March: Science, Practice, and Professional Identity in America, 1929–1969.* Cambridge, Mass.: Cambridge University Press, 1999.

Capshew, James H., and Ernest R. Hilgard. "The Power of Service: World War II and Professional Reform in the American Psychological Association." In *100 Years: The American Psychological Association, A Historical Perspective.* Edited by Rand B. Evans, Virginia S. Sexton, and Thomas C. Cadwallader. Washington, D.C.: American Psychological Association, 1992.

Carlyle, Thomas. *Sartor Resartus.* 1831. Reprinted as *Vol. 1 in The Works of Thomas Carlyle in Thirty volumes.* London: Chapman and Hall, 1986.

Caruso, Igor. *Existential Psychology: From Analysis to Synthesis.* Translated by Eva Krapf. New York: Herder & Herder, 1964. Originally published as *Psychoanalyse und Synthese der Existenz: Beziehungen zwischen psychologischer Analyse und Daseinswerten.* Vienna: Herder, 1952.

———. "Personalistic Psychoanalysis as Symbolic Knowledge." Translated by William Rickel and Doris Mode. *Journal of Psychotherapy as a Religious Process* 2 (1955): 2–23.

Cattell, James M. "The School and the Family." *Popular Science Monthly* 74 (1909): 84–95.

Cattell, James McKeen, and Livingston Farrand. "Physical and Mental Measurements of the Students of Columbia University." *Psychological Review* 3 (1896): 618–48.

C. H. Stoelting Co. *The Great Catalog of the C. H. Stoelting Company, 1930–1937.* Delmar, N.Y.: Scholars Facsimiles & Reprints, 1997. Originally published as *Psychological and Physiological Apparatus.* Delmar, N.Y.: Scholars Facsimiles & Reprints, 1930.

Cooke, William. *A Commentary of Medical and Moral Life; or Mind and the Emotions, Considered in Relation to Health, Disease, and Religion.* Philadelphia: C. J. Price, 1853.

Coughlin, Anne. "A Unique Heathen: The Sexual Dogmatics of Theodore Schroeder." Ph.D. diss., Fuller Theological Seminary, 1986. Abstract in *Dissertation Abstracts International* 47 (1986): 2154B.

Cowles, Michael. *Statistics in Psychology: An Historical Perspective.* 2d ed. Mahwah, N.J.: Lawrence Erlbaum Associates, 2001.

Cox, Catherine M. *Genetic Studies of Genius, Volume 2: The Early Mental Traits of Three Hundred Geniuses.* Stanford, CA: Stanford University Press, 1926.

Cronback, Lee. "Five Decades of Public Controversy over Mental Testing." *American Psychologist* (1975): 1–14.

———. "The Two Disciplines of Scientific Psychology." *American Psychologist* 12 (1957): 671–84.

Crowther-Heyck, Hunter. "George A. Miller, Language, and the Computer Metaphor of Mind." *History of Psychology* 2 (1999): 37–64.

Daim, Wilfried. "Depth-Psychology and Grace." Translated by C. Ernst. *Journal of Psychotherapy as a Religious Process* 1 (1954): 31–40.

———. *Depth Psychology and Salvation.* Translated by Kurt F. Reinhardt. New York: Frederick Ungar, 1963. Originally published as *Tiefenpsychologie und Erlösung.* Vienna: Herold, 1954.

Dallenbach, Karl M. "Walter Bowers Pillsbury: 1872–1960." *American Journal of Psychology* 74 (1961): 165–73.

Danziger, Kurt. *Constructing the Subject: Historical Origins of Psychological Research.* Cambridge, Mass.: Cambridge University Press, 1990.

Danziger, Kurt, and Paul Ballantyne. "Psychological Experiments." In *A Pictorial History of Psychology.* Edited by W. Bringmann, H. Lück, R. Miller, and C. Early. Chicago: Quintessence Publishing Co., 1997.

Delitzsch, Franz Julius. *A System of Biblical Psychology.* Translated by Robert Ernest Wallis. 1867. Reprint, Grand Rapids, Mich.: Baker Book House, 1966. Originally published as *System der biblischen Psychologie.* Leipzig: Dorffling und Franke, 1855.

Dewsbury, Donald A. "Animal Psychology in Journals, 1911–1927." *Journal of Comparative Psychology* 112(1998): 400–403.

———. "A Classic in Comparative Psychology." *Contemporary Psychology* 39 (1994): 797–99.

———. "Comparative Cognition in the 1930s." *Psychonomic Bulletin and Review* 7 (2000): 267–83.

———. *Comparative Psychology in the Twentieth Century.* Stroudsburg, Pa.: Hutchinson Ross, 1984.

———. "The Comparative Psychology of Paul Schiller." *Psychological Record* 44 (1994): 326–50.

———. "Four Giants: Frank Beach, Curt Richter, Niko Tinbergen, and Konrad Lorenz." *Newsletter of the Animal Behavior Society* 34 no. 2 (1989): 2–3.

———. "Frank A. Beach: Master Teacher." In *Portraits of Pioneers in Psychology* Vol. 4. Edited by Gregory Kimble and Michael Wertheimer. Washington, D.C.: American Psychological Association, 2000.

———. "Frank Ambrose Beach, Jr." In *American National Biography.* Vol. 2. Oxford: Oxford University Press, 1999.

———. "Frank Ambrose Beach: 1911–1988." *American Journal of Psychology* 102 (1989): 414–20.

———. "Frank Ambrose Beach: 1911–1988." *Biographical Memoirs of the National Academy of Sciences, USA* 73 (1997): 3–22.

———. "Frank Beach's Unpublished Textbook on Comparative Psychology." *Journal of Comparative Psychology* 104 (1990): 219–26.

———. "Henry Nissen." In *Encyclopedia of Psychology* v. 5, ed. Allen E. Kazdin. (Washington, D.C.: American Psychological Association, 2000).

———. "Henry W. Nissen: Quiet Comparative Psychologist." In *Portraits of Pioneers in Psychology* Vol. 3. Edited by Gregory A. Kimble and Michael Wertheimer. Washington, D.C.: American Psychological Association, 1998.

———. "History of the Psychonomic Society II: The Journal Publishing Program." *Psychonomic Bulletin and Review* 3 (1996): 322–38.

———. "History of the Psychonomic Society III: The Meetings of the Psychonomic Society." *Psychonomic Bulletin and Review* 4 (1997): 350–58.

———. "History of the Psychonomic Society IV: The Development of the Psychonomic Society." *Psychonomic Bulletin and Review* 4 (1997): 492–500.

———. "A Note on the Early Editorial Policies of the *Journal of Comparative Psychology.*" *Journal of Comparative Psychology* 112 (1998): 406–7.

———. "On Publishing Controversy: Norman R. F. Maier and the Genesis of Seizures." *American Psychologist* 48 (1993): 869–77.

———. "On the Evolution of Divisions." *American Psychologist* 52 (1997): 733–41.

———. "Paul Harkai Schiller." *Psychological Record* 44 (1994): 307–9.

———. "Paul Harkai Schiller: The Influence of His Brief Career." In *Portraits of Pioneers in Psychology* Vol. 1. Edited by Gregory A. Kimble, et al., pp. 281–93.

———. "Psychobiology." *American Psychologist* 46 (1991): 198–205.

———. "Reminiscences of Frank Ambrose Beach." *Hormones and Behavior* 22(1988): 431–33.

———. "Robert M. Yerkes: Man with a Plan." In *Portraits of Pioneers in Psychology.* Vol. 1. Edited by Gregory A. Kimble, C. Alan Boneau, and Michael Wertheimer. Washington, D.C.: American Psychological Association, 1996.

———. "Robert Yerkes." In *Encyclopedia of Psychology* v. 8. Edited by Alan E. Kazdin. Washington, DC: American Psychological Association and Oxford University Press, 2000.

———. "Robert Yerkes, Sex Research, and the Problem of Data Simplification." *History of Psychology,* 1 (1998): 116–29.

———. "A Supplement to Karl Lashley's Biographical Sketch of Paul Harkai Schiller." *Psychological Record* 44 (1994): 320–25.

———, ed. *Unification Through Division: Histories of the American Psychological Association.* Vols. 1–5. Washington, D.C.: American Psychological Association, 1996, 1997, 1998, 1999, 2000.

Dewsbury, Donald A., and Robert C. Bolles. "The Founding of the Psychonomic Society." *Psychonomic Bulletin and Review* 2 (1995): 1216–33.

Diagnostic and Statistical Manual of Mental Disorders: DSM-IV, Fourth Edition. Washington, D.C.: American Psychiatric Association, 1994.

Duncan, Sean C., and Ryan D. Tweney. "The Problem-Behavior Map as Cognitive-Historical Analysis: The Example of Michael Faraday." *Proceedings of the Nineteenth Annual Conference of the Cognitive Science Society.* Hillsdale, N.J.: Lawrence Erlbaum Associates, 1997.

Dunlap, Jack W., and Albert K. Kurtz. *Handbook of Statistical Nomographs, Tables, and Formulas.* Yonkers-on-Hudson, N.Y.: World Book Co., 1932.

Dunlap, Knight. "Antidotes for Superstitions Concerning Human Heredity." *Scientific Monthly* 51 (September 1940): 221.

Edgell, Beatrice, and W. Legge Symes. "The Wheatstone-Hipp Chronoscope. Its Adjustments, Accuracy, and Control." *British Journal of Psychology* 2 (1906): 58–88.

Educational Testing Service. *Nomograph for Computing Multiple Correlation Coefficients.* Princeton, N.J.: Educational Testing Service, 1955.

Fancher, Raymond. *The Intelligence Men: Makers of the IQ Controversy.* New York: Norton, 1985.

———. *Pioneers of Psychology.* New York: Norton, 1979.

———. *Psychoanalytic Psychology: The Development of Freud's Thought.* New York: Norton, 1973.

Faraday, Michael. "On A Peculiar Class of Acoustical Figures, and on Certain Forms Assumed by Groups of Particles Upon Vibrating Elastic Surfaces." *Philosophical Transactions* 1831 (1831b): 299–340.

————. "On A Peculiar Class of Optical Deceptions." *Journal of the Royal Institution* 1831 (1831a): 205–23.

Fechner, Gustav Theodor. *Elemente der Psychophysik*. Leipzig: Breitkopf und Haertel, 1860.

Fienberg, Stephen E. "Statistical Developments in World War II: An International Perspective." In *A Celebration of Statistics: The ISI Centenary Volume*. Edited by Anthony C. Atkinson and Stephen E. Fienberg. New York: Springer, 1985.

Fisher, Ronald A. *The Design of Experiments*. London: Oliver and Boyd, 1935.

————. *Statistical Methods for Research Workers*. London: Oliver and Boyd, 1925.

Fitts, Paul M. *Psychological Research on Equipment Design, Army Air Forces Aviation Psychology Program, Research Report No. 19*. Washington, D.C.: Government Printing Office, 1947.

Fitzgerald, F. Scott. "The Rich Boy." Reprinted in *All the Sad Young Men*. New York: Charles Scribner's Sons, 1926.

Flanagan, John C. *The Aviation Psychology Program in the Army Air Forces, Army Air Forces Aviation Psychology Program, Research Report No. 1*. Washington, D.C.: Government Printing Office, 1948.

Fleming, Allen Bruce. "Psychology, Medicine, and Religion: Early Twentieth-Century American Psychotherapy (1905–9)." Ph.D. diss., Fuller Theological Seminary, 1989. Abstract in *Dissertation Abstracts International* 50 (1990): 5313B.

Fowler, James W. *The Stages of Faith: The Psychology of Human Development and the Quest for Meaning*. New York: Harper & Row, 1981.

Friedlander, Saul. *Nazi Germany and the Jew, Vol. I: The Years of Persecution, 1933–1939*. New York: HarperCollins, 1997.

Fullerton, George Stuart, and James McKeen Cattell. *On the Perception of Small Differences, With Special Reference to the Extent, Force and Time of Movement*. Philadelphia, Pa.: University of Pennsylvania Press, 1892.

Furumoto, Laurel. "Shared Knowledge: The Experimentalists, 1904–1929." In *The Rise of Experimentation in American Psychology*. Edited by Jill G. Morawski. New Haven: Yale University Press, 1988.

Galison, Peter. *Image and Logic: A Material Culture of Microphysics*. Chicago: University of Chicago Press, 1997.

Garcia, John. "I. Krechevsky and I." In *Knowing, Thinking, and Believing: Festschrift for Professor David Krech*. Edited by Lewis Petrinovich and James L. McGaugh. New York: Plenum, 1976.

Geertz, Clifford. *A Life of Learning: Charles Homer Haskins Lecture for 1999*. New York: American Council of Learned Societies, 1999.

Gieson, Gerald L., ed. *Physiology in the American Context, 1850–1940*. Bethesda, MD: American Physiological Society, 1987.

Gigerenzer, Gerd, and David J. Murray. *Cognition as Intuitive Statistics*. Hillsdale, N.J.: Lawrence Erlbaum Associates, 1987.

Ginzburg, Carlo. "Morelli, Freud and Sherlock Holmes: Clues and Scientific Method." Translated by Anna Davin. *History Workshop Journal* 9 (1980): 5–36.

Gleason, John J., Jr. *Growing Up to God: Eight Steps in Religious Development*. Nashville: Abingdon Press, 1975.

Goddard, Henry H. "The Form Board as a Measure of Intellectual Development in Children." *The Training School* 9 (1912): 49–52.

———. "Psychological Work Among the Feeble-Minded." *Journal of Psycho-Asthenics* 12 (September 1907): 18.

Gooding, David, Trevor Pinch, and Simon Schaffer, eds. *The Uses of Experiment: Studies in the Natural Sciences.* Cambridge: Cambridge University Press, 1989.

Goodwin, C. James. "Maze Learning as Method: Origins and Early Development." Paper presented at the American Psychological Association, August 1991, San Francisco, California.

———. "On the Origins of Titchener's Experimentalists." *Journal of the History of the Behavioral Sciences* 21 (1985): 383–89.

Gosling, Francis G. "Neurasthenia in Pennsylvania: A Perspective on the Origins of American Psychotherapy." *Journal of the History of Medicine* 40 (1985): 188–206.

Gould, Daniel, and Sean Pick. "Sport Psychology: The Griffith Era, 1920–1940." *The Sport Psychologist* 9 (1995): 391–405.

Gould, Stephen Jay. *The Mismeasure of Man.* New York: Norton, 1981.

Groeschel, Benedict J. *Spiritual Passages: The Psychology of Spiritual Development.* New York: Crossroad, 1984.

Gruber, Carol Singer. "Academic Freedom at Columbia University, 1917–1918: The Case of James McKeen Cattell." *AAUP Bulletin* 58 (1972): 297–305.

Guilford, James P. *Printed Classification Tests, Army Air Forces Aviation Psychology Program, Research Report No. 5.* Washington, D.C.: Government Printing Office, 1947.

Guntrip, Harry. *Psychotherapy and Religion: The Constructive Use of Inner Conflict.* New York: Harper, 1957. Originally published as *Mental Pain and the Cure of Souls.* London: Independent Press, 1956.

Hacking, Ian. *Representing and Intervening: Introductory Topics in the Philosophy of Natural Science.* Cambridge: Cambridge University Press, 1983.

Hall, G. Stanley. *Jesus, the Christ, in the Light of Psychology.* Garden City, N.Y: Doubleday, Page, 1917.

Hankins, Thomas L. "Blood, Dirt, and Nomograms: A Particular History of Graphs." *Isis* 90 (1999): 50–80.

Harris, Benjamin. "Ceremonial Versus Critical History of Psychology." *American Psychologist* 35 (1980): 218–19.

Hastings, Donald W., David G. Wright, and Bernard C. Glueck. *Psychiatric Experiences of the Eighth Air Force: First Year of Combat (July 4, 1942-July 4, 1943).* Report prepared for The Air Surgeon, Army Air Forces. New York: Josiah Macy, Jr. Foundation, 1944.

Hebb, Donald O. "Alice in Wonderland or Psychology Among the Biological Sciences." In *Biological and Biochemical Bases of Behavior.* Edited by H. F. Harlow and C. N. Woolsey. Madison: University of Wisconsin Press, 1958.

———. "The American Revolution." *American Psychologist* 15 (1960): 735–45.

———. "Emotion in Man and Animal: An Analysis of the Intuitive Processes of Recognition." *Psychological Review* 53 (1954), 88–106.

———. "Heredity and Environment in Mammalian Behaviour." *British Journal of Animal Behaviour* 1 (1953): 243–54.

————. *Organization of Behavior.* New York: Wiley, 1949.

————. "The Role of Neurological Ideas in Psychology." *Journal of Personality* 20 (1951): 39–55.

Hebb, Donald O., and William R. Thompson. "The Social Significance of Animal Studies." In *Handbook of Social Psychology.* Vol. 1. Edited by Gardner Lindzey. Cambridge, Mass.: Addison-Wesley, 1954.

Herman, Ellen. *The Romance of American Psychology: Political Culture in the Age of Experts.* Berkeley: University of California Press, 1995.

Hester, Maureen P., and Martin D. Lampert. "Psychology of Religion in Academic Programs: Current Status." Poster presented at the annual meeting of the Western Psychological Association, Portland, Oreg., April 2000.

Hilgard, Ernest R. "Foreword." In *Wundt Studies: A Centennial Collection.* Edited by Wolfgang G. Bringmann and Ryan D. Tweney. Toronto: C. J. Hogrefe, 1980.

————. "Walter Richard Miles: 1885–1978." *American Journal of Psychology* 93 (1980): 565–68.

Hiltner, Seward. *Theological Dynamics.* Nashville: Abingdon, 1972.

Hirst, William, ed. *The Making of Cognitive Science: Essays in Honor of George A. Miller.* Cambridge: Cambridge University Press, 1988.

Hodos, William, and C. B. G. Campbell. *Scala Naturae*: Why There is No Theory in Comparative Psychology." *Psychological Review* 76 (1969): 337–50.

Hoffman, Louise E. "American Psychologists and Wartime Research on Germany, 1941–1945." *American Psychologist* 47 (1992): 264–73.

Holifield, E. Brooks. *A History of Pastoral Care in America: From Salvation to Self-Realization.* Nashville: Abingdon Press, 1983.

Hollingworth, Harry L. *Abnormal Psychology: Its Concepts and Theories.* New York: Ronald Press, 1930.

————. *Advertising and Selling: Principles of Appeal and Response.* New York: D. Appleton, 1913.

————. *Educational Psychology.* New York: D. Appleton, 1933.

————. "The Inaccuracy of Movement." *Archives of Psychology* 13 (1909) 1–80.

————. "The Influence of Caffein on Mental and Motor Efficiency." *Archives of Psychology* 22 (1912): 1–166.

————. *Judging Human Character.* New York: D. Appleton, 1922.

————. *Leta Stetter Hollingworth: A Biography.* 1943. Bolton, Mass.: Anker Publishing, 1990.

————. "Memories of the Early Development of the Psychology of Advertising suggested by Burtt's Psychology of Advertising." *Psychological Bulletin* 35 (1938): 307–11.

————. "Psycho-Dynamics of Chewing" *Archives of Psychology* No. 239 (1939): 1–90.

————. "Psychological Influence of Alcohol." *Journal of Abnormal and Social Psychology* 18 (1923): 204–37.

————. "Psychological Influence of Alcohol, Part 2." *Journal of Abnormal and Social Psychology* 18 (1924): 317–33.

————. *Psychology: Its Facts and Principles.* New York: D. Appleton, 1928.

————. *The Psychology of Functional Neuroses.* New York: D. Appleton, 1920.

————. *The Psychology of the Audience.* New York: American Book Company, 1935.

——. *Vocational Psychology: Its Problems and Methods*. New York: D. Appleton, 1916.

——. *Vocational Psychology and Character Analysis*. New York: D. Appleton, 1929.

——. "When is a Man Intoxicated?" *Journal of Applied Psychology* 9 (1925): 122–30.

Hollingworth, Harry L., and Albert T. Poffenberger. *Applied Psychology*. New York: D. Appleton, 1917.

Hubbard, Raymond, Rahul A. Parsa, and Michael R. Luthy. "The Spread of Statistical Significance Testing in Psychology: The Case of the *Journal of Applied Psychology*, 1917–1994." *Theory and Psychology* 7 (1997): 545–54.

Hull, Clark L. In *A History of Psychology in Autobiography, Volume IV*. Edited by Edwin G. Boring et al. Worcester, Mass.: Clark University Press, 1952.

Ippolito, Maria F., and Ryan D. Tweney. "The Inception of Insight." In *The Nature of Insight*. Edited by Robert J. Sternberg and Janet E. Davidson. Cambridge, Mass.: The MIT Press, 1995.

Jacoby, Russell, and Naomi Glauberman, eds. *The Bell Curve Debate: History, Documents, Opinions*. New York: Times Books, 1995.

James, Frank A.J.L., ed. *The Development of the Laboratory: Essays on the Place of Experiment in Industrial Civilization*. New York: American Institute of Physics, 1989.

James, William. *Psychology: The Briefer Course*. New York: Henry Holt, 1892.

——. *The Varieties of Religious Experience*. New York: Longmans, Green, 1902.

Johnson, David Paul. "The Contributions of Fritz Künkel to the Development of a Religious Psychology." Ph.D. diss., Fuller Theological Seminary, 1990. Abstract in *Dissertation Abstracts International* 51 (1990): 2624B.

Johnson, Paul E. *Personality and Religion*. New York: Abingdon, 1957.

Johnson, Thomas H. *The Oxford Companion to American History*. New York: Oxford University Press, 1966.

Judd, Charles H. *Laboratory Equipment for Psychological Experiments*. New York: Charles Scribner's Sons, 1907.

Kamin, Leon. *The Science and Politics of I.Q.* Potomac, Md.: Erlbaum, 1974.

Kearney, R. Timothy. "Psychology and the Soul: An Historical Investigation." Ph.D. diss., Fuller Theological Seminary, 1985. Abstract in *Dissertation Abstracts International* 47 (1985): 3526B.

Kevles, Daniel. "Testing the Army's Intelligence: Psychologists and the Military in World War I." *Journal of American History* 55 (1968): 565–81.

Knotts, Josephine R., and Walter R. Miles. "Notes on the History and Construction of the Stylus Maze." *Journal of General Psychology* 35 (1928): 415–25.

Kohlstedt, Sally Gregory, Michael M. Sokal, and Bruce V. Lewenstein. *The Establishment of Science in America: 150 Years of the American Association for the Advancement of Science*. New Brunswick: Rutgers University Press, 1999.

Kohs, Samuel C. "An Annotated Bibliography of Recent Literature on the Binet-Simon Scale (1913–1917)." *Journal of Educational Psychology*. Part I, 8, no. 7 (September 1917): 425–38.

——. "An Annotated Bibliography of Recent Literature on the Binet-Simon Scale (1913–1917)." *Journal of Educational Psychology*, Part II, 8, no. 8 (October 1917): 488–502.

——. "An Annotated Bibliography of Recent Literature on the Binet-Simon Scale

(1913–1917)." *Journal of Educational Psychology*, Part III, 8, no. 9 (November 1917): 559–65.

———. "An Annotated Bibliography of Recent Literature on the Binet-Simon Scale (1913–1917)." *Journal of Educational Psychology*, and Part IV, 8, no. 10 (December 1917): 609–18.

———. "The Binet-Simon Measuring Scale for Intelligence; An Annotated Bibliography." *Journal of Educational Psychology*, Part I, 5, no. 4 (April 1914): 215–24.

———. "The Binet-Simon Measuring Scale for Intelligence; An Annotated Bibliography." *Journal of Educational Psychology*, Part II, 5, no. 5 (May 1914): 279–90.

———. "The Binet-Simon Measuring Scale for Intelligence; An Annotated Bibliography." *Journal of Educational Psychology*, Part III, 5, no. 6 (June 1914): 335–46.

Kosslyn, Stephen M. *Elements of Graph Design.* New York: W. H. Freeman and Co., 1994.

Krech, David, . "David Krech." In *A History of Psychology in Autobiography* Vol. 6. Edited by G. Lindzey. Englewood Cliffs, NJ: Prentice Hall, 1974.

———. "Dynamic Systems, Psychological Fields, and Hypothetical Constructs." *Psychological Review* 57 (1950): 283–90.

———, ed. "Curriculum Vitae." In *The MacLeod Symposium.* Ithaca, N.Y.: Department of Psychology, Cornell University, 1973.

Krechevsky, Isadore. "Hereditary Nature of 'Hypotheses' in Rats." *Journal of Comparative Psychology* 16 (1933): 99–116.

Kulick, Henrika. "Assessing Research in the History of Sociology and Anthropology." *Journal of the History of the Behavioral Sciences* 35 (1999): 227–37.

Künkel, Fritz. "The Integration of Psychology and Religion." *Journal of Psychotherapy as a Religious Process* 1 (1954): 5–6.

Ladd, George Trumbull, and Robert Sessions Woodworth. *Elements of Physiological Psychology: A Treatise of the Activities and Nature of the Mind from the Physical and Experimental Points of View.* 2d ed. New York: Charles Scribner's Sons, 1911.

Lake, Frank. *Clinical Theology: A Theological and Psychological Basis to Clinical Pastoral Care.* London: Darton, Longman, & Todd, 1966.

Lapointe, François H. "Origin and Evolution of the Term 'Psychology.' " *American Psychologist* 25 (1970): 640–46.

———. "The Origin and Evolution of the Term 'Psychology.' " *Psychologia: An International Journal of Psychology in the Orient* 16 (1972): 1–16.

———. "Who Originated the Term 'Psychology'?" *Journal of the History of the Behavioral Sciences* 8 (1972): 328–35.

Lashley, Karl S. "Basic Neural Mechanisms in Behavior." *Psychological Review* 37 (1930): 1–24.

———. *Brain Mechanisms and Intelligence.* Chicago: University of Chicago Press, 1929.

———. "Cerebral Organization and Behavior." *Proceedings of the Association for Research on Nervous and Mental Diseases* 36(1958): 1–18.

———. "Experimental Analysis of Instinctive Behavior." *Psychological Review* 45 (1938): 445–71.

———. "Paul Harkai Schiller: 1908–1949." *Psychological Record* 44 (1994): 309–19.

———. "The Problem of Serial Order in Behavior." In *Cerebral Mechanisms in Behavior.* Edited by L. A. Jefress. New York: Wiley, 1951.

Latour, Bruno. *Science in Action: How to Follow Engineers and Scientists Through Society.* Cambridge, Mass.: Harvard University Press, 1987.

Lebeaux, Richard. *Thoreau's Seasons.* Amherst: University of Massachusetts Press, 1984.

Lehrman, Daniel S. "A Critique of Konrad Lorenz's Theory of Instinctive Behavior." *Quarterly Review of Biology* 28 (1953): 337–63.

Levinson, Daniel J., et al. *The Seasons of a Man's Life.* New York: Alfred A. Knopf, 1978.

Lockard, Robert B. "Reflections on the Fall of Comparative Psychology: Is There a Message for Us All?" *American Psychologist* 26 (1971): 168–79.

Loftus, Geoffrey R. "A Picture is Worth a Thousand p Values: On the Irrelevance of Hypothesis Testing in the Microcomputer Age." *Behavior Research Methods, Instruments, and Computers* 25 (1993): 250–56.

Lovie, A. D. "The Analysis of Variance in Experimental Psychology: 1934–1945." *British Journal of Mathematical and Statistical Psychology* 32 (1979): 151–78.

Lynch, Michael, and Steve Woolgar, eds. *Representation in Scientific Practice.* Cambridge, Mass.: MIT Press, 1990.

MacLeod, Robert Brodie. "An Experimental Investigation of Brightness Constancy." *Archives of Psychology* 135 (1932): 1, 102.

———. "Experimental Psychology." In *Religious Perspectives in College Teaching.* Edited by Roy Fairchild et al. New York: Ronald Press, 1952.

———. *Religious Perspectives of College Teaching in Experimental Psychology.* New Haven, Conn.: The Edward W. Hazen Foundation, n.d.

MacMurray, John. *The Form of the Personal in Two Volumes: The Self as Agent and Persons in Relation.* London: Faber & Faber, 1957–61.

Maier, Norman R. F. "Reasoning in White Rats." *Comparative Psychology Monographs* 6 (1929): 1–93.

Maier, Norman R. F., and Theodore C. Schneirla. *Principles of Animal Psychology.* New York: McGraw-Hill, 1935.

Malin, Patrick Murphy. "The National Council on Religion in Higher Education." In *Liberal Learning and Religion.* Edited by Amos Niven Wilder. New York: Harper & Brothers, 1951.

Marey, Étienne Jules. *La Méthode Graphique Dans Les Sciences Expérimentales, Et Principalement En Physiologie Et En Médecine.* 2d ed. Paris: G. Masson, 1885.

Marino, Andy. *A Quiet American: The Secret War of Varian Fry.* New York: St. Martin's Griffith, 1999.

Marr, David. *Vision: A Computational Investigation into the Human Representation and Processing of Visual Information.* San Francisco, Calif.: W.H. Freeman and Co., 1982.

Mateer, Florence. "The Vocabulary of a Four Year Old Boy." *Pedagogical Seminary* 15 (1908): 63–74.

Maudsley, Henry. *Natural Causes and Supernatural Seemings.* London: Kegan Paul, Trench, 1886.

McDargh, John. *Psychoanalytic Object Relations Theory and the Study of Religion.* Lanham, Md.: University Press of America, 1983.

Meehl, Paul Everett, et al. *What, Then, is Man? A Symposium of Theology, Psychology, and Psychiatry.* Saint Louis, Mo.: Concordia, 1958.

Melton, Arthur W. "Editorial." *Journal of Experimental Psychology* 64 (1962): 553–57.

———, ed. *Apparatus Tests, Army Air Forces Aviation Psychology Program, Research Report No. 4.* Washington, D.C.: Government Printing Office, 1947.

Miles, Walter R. "Accuracy of the Voice in Simple Pitch Singing." *Psychological Review Monographs* 16 (1914): 13–66.

———. "Age and Human Ability." *Psychological Review* 40 (1933): 99–123.

———. "Change of Dexterity with Age." *Proceedings for the Society of Experimental Biology and Medicine* 29 (1931): 136–38.

———. "The Effect of a Prolonged Reduced Diet on Twenty-five College Men." *Proceedings of the National Academy of Sciences* 4 (1918): 152–56.

———. "The High Relief Finger Maze for Human Learning." *Journal of General Psychology* 1 (1928): 3–14.

———. "Horizontal Eye Movements at the Onset of Sleep." *Psychological Review* 36 (1929): 122–41.

———. "The Narrow-Path Elevated Maze for Studying Rats." *Proceedings for the Society of Experimental Biology and Medicine* 24 (1927): 454–56.

———. "On the History of Research with Rats and Mazes: A Collection of Notes." *Journal of General Psychology* 3 (1930): 324–37.

———. "A Pursuit Pendulum." *Psychological Review* 27 (1920): 361–76.

———. "Pursuitmeter." *Journal of Experimental Psychology* 4 (1921): 77–105.

———. "Red Goggles for Producing Dark Adaptation." *Federal Proceedings of American Societies for Experimental Biology* 2 (1943): 109–15.

———. "Some Psycho-physiological Processes as Affected by Alcohol." *Proceedings of the National Academy of Sciences* 2 (1916): 703–9.

———. "Studies in Physical Exertion I: A Multiple Chronograph for Measuring Groups of Men." *American Physical Education Review* 33 (1928): 379–87.

———. "Studies in Physical Exertion II: Individual and Group Reaction Time in Football Charging." *Research Quarterly* 2, no. 3 (1931): 5–13.

———. "Studies in Physical Exertion III: Effect of Signal Variation in Football Charging." *Research Quarterly* 2, no. 3 (1931): 14–31.

———. "The Two-Story Duplicate Maze." *Journal of Experimental Psychology* 10 (1927): 365–77.

———. "Walter R. Miles." In *A History of Psychology in Autobiography, Volume 5.* Edited by E. G. Boring and Gardner Lindzey. New York: Appleton-Century-Crofts, 1967.

Miller, George A. "The Magical Number Seven, Plus or Minus Two; Some Limits on our Capacity for Processing Information." *Psychological Review* 63 (1956): 81–97.

Miller, George A., and Frederick C. Frick. "Statistical Behavioristics and Sequences of Responses." *Psychological Review* 56 (1949): 311–24.

Miller, George A., and Walter G. Taylor. "The Perception of Repeated Bursts of Noise." *Journal of the Acoustical Society of America* 20 (1949): 171–82.

Miller, Neal E., ed. *Psychological Research on Pilot Training. Army Air Forces Aviation Psychology Program, Research Report No. 8.* Washington, D.C.: Government Printing Office, 1947.

Minton, Henry. *Lewis M. Terman: Pioneer in Psychological Testing.* New York: New York University Press, 1988.

———. "Lewis Terman and Mental Testing: In Search of the Democratic Ideal." In *Psychological Testing and American Society, 1890–1930.* Edited by Michael Sokal. New Brunswick, N.J.: Rutgers University Press, 1987.

Mullan, E. H. *Mental Deficiency: Some of Its Public Health Aspects, With Special Reference to Diagnosis, Public Health Reports, Reprint 236.* 1914. Reprint, Washington, D.C.: Government Printing Office, 1919.

Münsterberg, Hugo. "The Place of Experimental Psychology" Dedication remarks at the opening of Emerson Hall, December, 1905. In *Harvard Psychological Studies Vol. 2.* Edited by Hugo Münsterberg, Boston: Houghton Mifflin, 1905.

Murdoch, Iris. *The Green Knight.* New York:Viking Press, 1993.

———. *The Message to the Planet.* New York: Penguin Books, 1989.

———. *Metaphysics as a Guide to Morals.* New York: Allen Lane, 1993.

Murphy, Gardner. "Robert Sessions Woodworth." *American Psychologist* 18 (1963): 131–33.

Myers, Charles S. *A Text-Book of Experimental Psychology.* London: Edward Arnold, 1909.

National Research Council. "Annual Meeting of the Division of Anthropology and Psychology, April 20 and 21, 1928." NRC Papers. Archives of the National Academy of Sciences, Washington, D.C.

National Research Council. "Annual Meeting of the Division of Anthropology and Psychology, April 12 and 13, 1929." NRC Papers. Archives of the National Academy of Sciences, Washington, D.C.

Nicholson, Ian. "Academic Professionalization and Protestant Reconstruction, 1890–1901: George Albert Coe's Psychology of Religion." *Journal of the History of the Behavioral Sciences* 30 (1994): 348–68.

———. "From the Kingdom of God to the Beloved Community, 1920–1930: Psychology and the Social Gospel in the Work of Goodwin Watson and Carl Rogers." *Journal of Psychology and Theology* 22 (1994): 196–206.

———. "Gordon Allport, Character, and the 'Culture of Personality'." *History of Psychology* 1 (1998): 52–68.

———. "Humanistic Psychology and Intellectual Identity: The 'Open' System of Gordon Allport." *Journal of Humanistic Psychology* 37 (1997): 60–78.

———. *Moral Projects and Disciplinary Practices: Gordon Allport and the Development of American Personality Psychology.* Ph.D. dissertation, York University, 1996.

———. "The Politics of Scientific Social Reform: Goodwin Watson and the Society for the Psychological Study of Social Issues." *Journal of the History of the Behavioral Sciences* 33 (1997): 39–60.

Noble, David F. *America by Design: Science, Technology, and the Rise of Corporate Capitalism.* Oxford: Oxford University Press, 1977.

Norman, Donald A. *Things That Make Us Smart: Defending Human Attributes in the Age of the Machine.* Reading, Mass.: Addison-Wesley, 1993.

Novick, Peter. *That Noble Dream: The "Objectivity Question" and the American Historical Profession.* New York: Cambridge University Press, 1988.

O'Donnell, John M. *The Origins of Behaviorism: American Psychology, 1870–1920.* New York: New York University Press, 1985.

Orbach, Jack. *The Neuropsychological Theories of Lashley and Hebb: Contemporary Perspectives Fifty Years After Hebb's The Organization of Behavior.* Lanham, Md.: University Press of America, 1998.

Parker, Robert P. "The Psychological Function of the Hymn Tune in a Service of Worship." *Religious Education* 38 (1943): 216–22.

Pastore, Nicholas. *The Nature-Nurture Controversy.* New York: King's Crown Press, 1949.

Pauly, Philip J. *Controlling Life: Jacques Loeb and the Engineering Ideal in Biology.* New York: Oxford University Press, 1987.

Peirce, Charles Saunders, and Joseph Jastrow. "On Small Differences of Sensation." *Memoirs of the National Academy of Sciences* 3, no. 1 (1884): 75–83.

Perry, William G. *Forms of Intellectual and Ethical Development in the College Years: A Scheme.* New York: Holt, Rinehart & Winston, 1970.

Pierce, Edgar. *The Philosophy of Character.* Cambridge: Harvard University Press, 1924.

Pillsbury, W. B. *Attention.* c. 1908 London: George Allen & Unwin, 1921.

Pillsbury, Walter B. "The Department of Psychology." In *The University of Michigan: An Encyclopedic Survey.* Edited by Wilfred B. Shaw. 4 Vols., Ann Arbor: University of Michigan Press, 1951.

———. "Walter B. Pillsbury." In *A History of Psychology in Autobiography, Volume II.* Edited by Carl Murchison. Worcester Mass.: Clark University Press, 1932.

Poffenberger, Albert T. "A History of the National Research Council, 1919–1933. VIII. Division of Anthropology and Psychology." *Science* 78 (25 August 1933): 158–61.

———. "Robert Sessions Woodworth: 1869–1962." *American Journal of Psychology* 75 (1962), 677–89.

Popplestone, John A., and Marion White McPherson. *An Illustrated History of American Psychology.* Akron, Ohio: The University of Akron Press, 1994.

———. "Pioneer Psychology Laboratories in Clinical Settings." In *Explorations in the History of Psychology in the United States.* Edited by Josef Brozek. Lewisburg, Pa.: Bucknell University Press, 1984.

———. "The Vitality of the Leipzig Model of 1880–1910 in the United States in 1950–1980." In *Wundt Studies: A Centennial Collection.* Edited by Wolfgang G. Bringmann and Ryan D. Tweney. Toronto: C.J. Hogrefe, 1980.

Popplestone, John A., and Ryan D. Tweney, eds. *The Great Catalog of the C.H. Stoelting Company, 1930–1937: A Facsimile Reproduction, With An Introduction.* Delmar, N.Y.: Scholars' Facsimiles and Reprints, 1997.

Pruyser, Paul W. *Between Belief and Unbelief.* New York: Harper & Row, 1974.

———. *A Dynamic Psychology of Religion.* New York: Harper & Row, 1968.

———. *The Play of the Imagination: Toward a Psychoanalysis of Culture.* New York: International Universities Press, 1983.

Reisman, John M. *A History of Clinical Psychology.* 2d ed. New York: Hemisphere Publishing Corporation, 1991.

"Review of The Kallikak Family." *Independent* 73 (October 3, 1912): 794.

Rheinberger, Hans-Jörg. *Toward A History of Epistemic Things: Synthesizing Proteins in the Test Tube.* Stanford, Calif.: Stanford University Press, 1997.

Roderick, Thomas H., Richard E. Wimer, and Cynthia C. Wimer. "Genetic Manipulation of Neuroanatomical Traits." In *Knowing, Thinking, and Believing: Festschrift for Professor David Krech*. Edited by Lewis Petrinovich and James L. McGaugh. New York: Plenum, 1976.

Rodgers, Daniel T. "In Search of Progressivism." *Reviews in American History* 10 (December 1982): 113–32.

Rokeach, Milton. "The Nature and Meaning of Dogmatism." *Psychological Review* 61 (1954): 194–204.

———. *The Open and Closed Mind*. New York: Basic Books, 1960.

———. "Political and Religious Dogmatism: An Alternative to the Authoritarian Personality." *Psychological Monographs 70* 18, no. 425 (1956).

Rokeach, Milton, Warren C. McGovney, and M. Ray Denny. "A Distinction between Dogmatic and Rigid Thinking." *Journal of Abnormal and Social Psychology* 51 (1955): 87–93.

Rosenthal, Robert, and Ralph H. Rosnow. *Essentials of Behavioral Research: Methods and Data Analysis*. 2d ed. New York: McGraw-Hill, 1991.

Rucci, Anthony J., and Ryan D. Tweney. "Analysis of Variance and the 'Second Discipline' of Scientific Psychology: A Historical Account." *Psychological Bulletin* 87 (1980): 166–84.

Samelson, Franz. "Assessing Research in the History of Psychology: Past, Present, and Future." *Journal of the History of the Behavioral Sciences* 35 (1999): 247–55.

———. "Organizing for the Kingdom of Behavior: Academic Battles and Organizing Policies in the Twenties." *Journal of the History of the Behavioral Science* 21 (1985): 33–47.

———. "Putting Psychology on the Map: Ideology and Intelligence Testing." In *Psychology in Social Context*. Edited by Allan R. Buss. New York: Irvington, 1979.

Sanford, Edmund C. *A Course in Experimental Psychology*. Boston: D. C. Heath and Co., 1898.

———. "A Laboratory Course in Physiological Psychology." *American Journal of Psychology* 4 (1891–92): 141–55.

Scarborough, Elizabeth, and Laurel Furumoto. *Untold Lives: The First Generation of American Women Psychologists*. New York: Columbia University Press, 1987.

Scott, Walter D. *The Psychology of Advertising*. Boston: Small, Maynard & Co., 1908.

———. *The Theory of Advertising*. Boston: Small, Maynard & Co., 1903.

Scull, Andrew. "A Quarter Century of the History of Psychiatry." *Journal of the History of the Behavioral Sciences* 35 (1999): 239–46.

Sears, Robert R. "Catherine Cox Miles: 1890–1984." *American Journal of Psychology* 99 (1986): 431–33.

Shaffer, Laurance F. "Frederic Lyman Wells: 1884–1964." *American Journal of Psychology* 77 (1964): 679–82.

Sharman, Henry Burton. *Jesus as Teacher: Student Edition*. New York: Harper & Brothers, 1935.

———. *Jesus in the Records*. New York: Association Press, 1918.

———. *The Records of the Life of Jesus*. New York: Association Press, 1917.

———. *Studies in the Records of the Life of Jesus*. New York: Harper & Brothers, 1938.

Sheehy, Gail. *Passages: Predictable Crises of Adult Life*. New York: Dutton, 1976.

Shideler, Mary McDermott. *Consciousness of Battle: An Interim Report on a Theological Journey.* Grand Rapids, Mich.: William B. Eerdmans, 1970.

———. *A Creed for a Christian Skeptic.* Grand Rapids, Mich.: William B. Eerdmans, 1968.

———. *In Search of the Spirit: A Primer.* New York: Ballantine/Epiphany, 1985.

———. *Starting Out. Stage 1 in the Series Visions and Nightmares, Ends and Beginnings. A Woman's Lifelong Journey.* Boulder, Colo.: Scribendi Press, 1996.

Shields, Stephanie A. "Ms. Pilgrim's Progress: The Contributions of Leta Stetter Hollingworth to the Psychology of Women." *American Psychologist* 30 (1975): 852–57.

Shrager Jeff. "High Throughout Discovery: Search and Interpretation on the Path to New Drugs." In *Designing for Science: Implications from Everyday, Classroom, and Professional Settings.* Edited by Kevin Crowley, Christian Schunn, and Takeshi Okada. Mahwah, N.J.: Lawrence Erlbaum Associates, 2001.

Simon, Herbert A. *The Sciences of the Artificial.* 3d ed.. Cambridge: MIT Press, 1996.

Smith, Laurence D., Lisa A. Best, D. Alan Stubbs, J. Johnston, and A. B. Archibald. "Scientific Graphs and the Hierarchy of the Sciences: A Latourian Survey of Inscription Practices." *Social Studies of Science* 30, (2000b): 73–94.

Smith, Laurence D., Lisa A. Best, Virginia A. Cylke, and D. Alan Stubbs. "Psychology Without Values: Data Analysis at the Turn of the 19th Century." *American Psychologist* 55 (2000a): 260–63.

Snow, C. P. *The Masters.* New York: Charles Scribner's Sons, 1951.

Sokal, Michael M. "Baldwin, Cattell, and the *Psychological Review*: A Collaboration and Its Discontents." *History of the Human Sciences* 10 (1997): 57–89.

———. "Companions in Zealous Research, 1886–1986." *American Scientist* 74 (1986): 486–508.

———. *An Education in Psychology: James McKeen Cattell's Journal and Letters from Germany and England, 1880–1888.* Cambridge, Mass.: MIT Press, 1981.

———. "Graduate Study with Wundt: Two Eyewitness Accounts." In *Wundt Studies: A Centennial Collection.* Edited by Wolfgang G. Bringmann and Ryan D. Tweney. Toronto: C. J. Hogrefe, 1980.

———. "History of Psychology and History of Science: Reflections on Two Subdisciplines, Their Relationship, and Their Convergence." In *Psychology in Its Historical Context: Essays in Honour of Prof. Josef Brozek.* Valencia: Monografias de la Revista de Historia de la Psicologia, 1985.

———. "James McKeen Cattell and American Psychology in the 1920s." In *Explorations in the History of Psychology in the United States.* Edited by Josef Brozek. Lewisburg, Pa.: Bucknell University Press, 1984.

———. "James McKeen Cattell and Mental Anthropometry: Nineteenth-Century Science and Reform and the Origins of Psychological Testing." In *Psychological Testing and American Psychology, 1890–1930.* Edited by Michael M. Sokal. New Brunswick, N.J.: Rutgers University Press, 1987.

———. "James McKeen Cattell and the Failure of Anthropometric Mental Testing." In *The Problematic Science: Psychology in Nineteenth-Century Thought.* Edited by William R. Woodward and Mitchell G. Ash. New York: Praeger, 1982.

———. "Life Span Developmental Psychology." In *Beyond History of Science: Essays in Honor of Robert E. Schofield*. Edited by Elizabeth Garber. Bethlehem, Pa.: Lehigh University Press, 1990.

———. "On *History of Psychology*'s Launch." *History of Psychology* 1 (1998): 3–7.

———. "Origins and Early Years of the American Psychological Association." *American Psychologist* 47 (1992): 111–22.

———. "Origins and Early Years of the American Psychological Association." In *The American Psychological Association: A Historical Perspective*. Edited by Rand B. Evans, Virginia S. Sexton, and Thomas C. Cadwallader. Washington, D.C.: American Psychological Association, 1992.

———. "The Origins of the Psychological Corporation." *Journal of the History of the Behavioral Sciences* 17 (1981): 54–67.

———. "Psychology at Victorian Cambridge—The Unofficial Laboratory of 1887–1888." *Proceedings of the American Philosophical Society* 116 (1972): 145–47.

———. "*Science* and James McKeen Cattell, 1894–1945." *Science* 209 (1980): 43–52.

———. "Stargazing: James McKeen Cattell, *American Men of Science*, and the Reward Structure of the American Scientific Community, 1906–1944." In *Psychology, Science, and Human Affairs: Essays in Honor of William Bevan*. Edited by Frank Kessel. Boulder, Colo.: Westview Press, 1995.

Sokal, Michael M., Audrey B. Davis, and Uta C. Merzbach. "Laboratory Instruments in the History of Psychology." *Journal of the History of the Behavioral Sciences* 12 (1976): 59–64.

Sommer, Robert. *Die Ausstellung von experimental-psychologischen Apparaten und Methoden, bei dem Kongress für experimentelle Psychologie, Giessen 18–21. April 1904*. Leipzig: Johann Ambrosius Barth, 1904. Reprinted with an introduction by Horst Gundlach. *Passauer Schriften zur Psychologiegeschichte, Nr. 2*. Passau: Passavia Universitätsverlag, 1984.

Stade, George. "A Romance for Highbrows." Review of *Nuns and Soldiers*, by Iris Murdoch. *New York Times*, January 4, 1981.

Staudt, Virginia. *Catholics in Psychology: A Historical Survey*. New York: McGraw–Hill, 1954.

Steigenga, J. John. "The Contribution of Henry Burton Sharman to the Development of a Christocentric Psychology." Ph.D. diss., Fuller Theological Seminary, 1990. Abstract in *Dissertation Abstracts International* 51 (1991): 5593B.

Stevens, S. Smith, ed. *Transmission and Reception of Sounds Under Combat Conditions*. Washington, D.C.: Office of Scientific Research and Development, 1946.

Stigler, Stephen M. "Statistical Concepts in Psychology." In *Statistics on the Table: The History of Statistical Concepts and Methods*. Edited by Stephen M. Stigler. Cambridge, Mass.: Harvard University Press, 1999.

Stoddard, George D. "Carl Emil Seashore." *American Journal of Psychology* 63 (1950): 456–62.

Stone, James. "War Music and War Psychology in the Civil War." *Journal of Abnormal and Social Psychology* 36 (1941): 543–60.

"Student [William Sealey Gosset]." "The Probable Error of A Mean." *Biometrika* 6 (1908): 1–25.

"SVHE Begins Year-Long 70th Anniversary Observance." *Society for Values in Higher Education Newsletter* 30, no. 1 (1993): 1.

Swijtink, Zeno G. "The Objectification of Observation: Measurement and Statistical Methods in the Nineteenth Century." In *The Probabilistic Revolution, Vol. 1: Ideas in History.* Edited by Lorenz Krüger, Lorraine J. Daston and Michael Heidelberger. Cambridge, Mass.: MIT Press, 1987.

Sylvester, Reuel Hull. "The Form Board Test." *Psychological Review Monographs* 15 (1913): 1–4.

———. "A Standardization of the Form Board Test." *Psychological Review Monographs* 15 (1913): 44–52.

Tart, Charles C., ed. *Altered States of Consciousness: A Book of Readings.* New York: John Wiley, 1969.

Terman, Lewis M., and Catherine Cox Miles. *Sex and Personality: Studies in Masculinity and Femininity.* New York: McGraw-Hill, 1936.

Thorndike, Edward L. *An Introduction to the Theory of Mental and Social Measurements.* New York: Science Press, 1904.

Tillich, Paul. *The Courage to Be.* New Haven, Conn.: Yale University Press, 1952.

Titchener, Edward Bradford. *Experimental Psychology: A Manual of Laboratory Practice. Vol. I: Qualitative Experiments; Vol. II: Quantitative Experiments.* New York: Macmillan, 1901–5.

Tobey, Ronald C. *The American Ideology of National Science, 1919–1930.* Pittsburgh, Pa.: University of Pittsburgh Press, 1971.

Toulmin, Stephen. "From Form to Function: Philosophy and History of Science in the 1950s and Now." *Daedalus* 106 (1977): 143–62.

Tufte, Edward R. *The Visual Display of Quantitative Information.* Cheshire, Conn.: The Graphics Press, 1983.

Turner, Gerard L. E. *The Great Age of the Microscope: The Collection of the Royal Microscopical Society Through 150 Years.* Bristol, U.K.: Adam Hilger, 1989.

Tweney, Ryan D. "Epistemic Artifacts: Michael Faraday's Search for the Optical Effects of Gold." In *Model-Based Reasoning: Science, Technology, Values.* Edited by Lorenzo Magnani and Nancy J. Nersessian. New York: Kluwer Academic/Plenum, 2002.

———. "Programmatic Research in Experimental Psychology: E. B. Titchener's Laboratory Investigations, 1887–1927." In *Psychology in Twentieth-Century Thought and Society.* Edited by Mitchell G. Ash and William R. Woodward. Cambridge: Cambridge University Press, 1987.

———. "Stopping Time: Faraday and the Scientific Creation of Perceptual Order." *Physis: Revista Internazionale di Storia Della Scienza* 29 (1992): 149–64.

Tweney, Ryan D., and Cheri A. Budzynski. "The Scientific Status of American Psychology in 1900." *American Psychologist* 55 (2000): 1014–17.

Ulrich, Laurel. *A Midwife's Tale: The Life of Martha Ballard, Based on Her Diary, 1785–1812.* New York: Vintage Books, 1990.

Vande Kemp, Hendrika. "Adler's Place in the Psychology and Religion Literature: An Empirical Investigation." Graduate School of Psychology, Fuller Theological Seminary, 2000.

———. "Christian Psychologies for the 21st Century: Lessons from History." *Journal of Psychology and Christianity* 17 (1998): 197–209.

———. "Dimensions of Religious Growth and Development in the College Years." Master's Thesis, the University of Massachusetts/Amherst, 1973.

———. "The Dream in Periodical Literature: 1860–1910." *The Journal of the History of the Behavioral Sciences* 17 (1981): 88–113.

———. "The Dream in Periodical Literature: 1860–1910. From Oneirocriticon to Die Traumdeutung via the Questionnaire." Ph.D. diss., University of Massachusetts/Amherst, 1976. Abstract in *Dissertation Abstracts International* 38 (1977): 342B.

———. "A Faculty Genealogy for the Travis Years." In *Psychology and the Cross: The Early History of Fuller Seminary's School of Psychology.* Edited by H. Newton Malony with Hendrika Vande Kemp. Pasadena, Calif.: Fuller Seminary Press, 1996.

———. "From Preacher's Kid to Phenomenologist: Robert B. MacLeod and the Religious 'Doctrine of Man.' " Invited address presented to The History of Psychology division at the meeting of the American Psychological Association, New Orleans, La., August 1989.

———. "Gordon Allport's Pre-1950 Writings on Religion: The Archival Record." In *Aspects and Contexts: Studies in the History of Psychology of Religion.* Edited by Jacob Belzen. Atlanta: Rodopi, 2000.

———. "Great Psychologists as 'Unknown' Psychologists of Religion." Paper presented at the annual meeting of the American Psychological Association, Los Angeles, Calif., August 1983.

———. "G. Stanley Hall and the Clark School of Religious Psychology." *American Psychologist* 47 (1992): 290–98.

———. "Historical Perspective: Religion and Clinical Psychology in America." In *Religion and the Clinical Practice of Psychology.* Edited by Edward Shafranske. Washington D.C.: American Psychological Association, 1996.

———. "In Memoriam: Virginia Staudt Sexton (1916–1997)." *The International Journal for the Psychology of Religion* 8 (1998): 27–32.

———. "Lectures in Psychology and Religion." Comprehensives paper, University of Massachusetts/Amherst, 1974.

———. "Lord Peter Wimsey in the Novel/Comedy of Manners: Courtesy, Intimacy, and the Courage to Be." *The Lamp-Post (of the Southern California C. S. Lewis Society) 23, no. 3 (1999): 11–23.*

———. *"Mate Selection and Marriage: A Psychodynamic Family Oriented Course." Teaching of Psychology* 12 (1985): 161–64.

———. "A Note on the Term Psychology in English Titles: Predecessors of Rauch." *Journal of the History of the Behavioral Sciences* 19 (1983): 185.

———. "On Seeing Yourself Through Another's Eyes: Response to Wagner and Struzynski." *Teaching of Psychology,* 6 (1979): 143–45.

———. "The Origin and Evolution of the Term 'Psychology': Addenda." *American Psychologist* 35 (1980): 774.

———. "Pastoral Counseling and Some Thoughts on the Psychology of Religion." Hope College, 1970.

———. "The Patient-Philosopher Evaluates the Scientist-Practitioner." In *Critical Issues in Psychotherapy: Translating New Ideas into Practice.* Edited by Brent D. Slife, Richard N. Williams, and Sally H. Barlow. Thousand Oaks, Calif.: Sage, 2001.

———. "Personal Reflections on Trauma and Head Injury." *American Family Therapy Academy Newsletter* 67 (1997): 38–42.

————. "Psyche and Soul." In *Encyclopedia of Psychology*. Edited by Allen E. Kazdin. Washington, D.C.: American Psychological Association, 2000.

————. "The Psychology of Paul Meehl." Hope College, 1969.

————. "Psycho-Spiritual Dreams in the Nineteenth Century. I. Dreams of Death." *Journal of Psychology and Theology* 22 (1994): 97–108.

————. "Psycho-Spiritual Dreams in the Nineteenth Century. II. Metaphysics and Immortality." *Journal of Psychology and Theology* 22 (1994): 109–19.

————. "Psychotheological Integration in the 1950s. The Journal of Psychotherapy as a Religious Process." Paper presented at the meeting of the American Psychological Association, Los Angeles, Calif., August 1985, and at the meeting of the American Academy of Religion, Anaheim, Calif., November 1985.

————. "Relational Ethics in the Novels of Charles Williams." *Family Process* 26 (1987): 283–94.

————. "Religion in College Textbooks: Allport's Historic 1948 Report." *The International Journal for the Psychology of Religion* 5 (1995): 197–209.

————. "The Rokeach Dogmatism Scale." Hope College, 1970.

————. "Spirit and Soul in No-Man's Land: Reflections on Haule's 'Care of Souls.' " *Journal of Psychology and Theology* 11 (1983): 117–22.

————. "Teaching Psychology of the Family: Bibliography and an Experiential Approach." *Teaching of Psychology* 8 (1981): 152–56.

————. "Teaching Psychology/Religion in the Seventies: Monopoly or Cooperation?" *Teaching of Psychology* 3, no. 1 (1976): 15.

————. "Teaching Psychology Through the Case Study Method." *Teaching of Psychology* 7 (1980): 38–41.

————. "The Tension between Psychology and Theology: I. The Etymological Roots." *Journal of Psychology and Theology* 10 (1982): 105–12.

————. "The Tension between Psychology and Theology: II. An Anthropological Solution." *Journal of Psychology and Theology* 10 (1982): 205–11.

————. "Wholeness, Holiness, and the Care of Souls: The Adler-Jahn Debate in Historical Perspective." *Journal of Individual Psychology* 56 (2000): 242–56.

Vande Kemp, Hendrika, and Beth Houskamp. "An Early Attempt at Integration: *The Journal of Psychotherapy as a Religious Process*," *Journal of Psychology and Theology* 14 (1986): 3–14.

Vande Kemp, Hendrika, with H. Newton Malony. *Psychology and Theology in Western Thought, 1672–1965: A Historical and Annotated Bibliography*. Millwood, N.Y.: Kraus International, 1984.

Wagner, Carl, and Anthony Struzynski. "On the Autonomy of Psychology in Psychology/Religion Courses: An Optimistic View." *Teaching of Psychology* 6 (1979): 140–43.

Ward, Steven. *Modernizing the Mind: Psychological Knowledge and the Remaking of Society*. Westport, Conn.: Greenwood Publishing Group, Praeger, 2002.

Warren, Roland L. "German *Parteilieder* and Christian Hymns as Instruments of Social Control." *Journal of Abnormal and Social Psychology* 38 (1943): 96–100.

Watson, John B. *Behavior: An Introduction to Comparative Psychology*. New York: Henry Holt and Co, 1914.

———. "Kinaesthetic and Organic Sensations: Their Role in the Reactions of the White Rat to the Maze." *Psychological Review, Monograph Supplements* 8, no. 2 (1907): whole no. 33.

———. "The Place of Kinaesthetic, Visceral, and Laryngeal Organization in Thinking." *Psychological Review* 31 (1924): 339–47

Wells, Frederic Lyman. "Critique of Impure Reason." *Journal of Abnormal Psychology* 7 (1912): 89–93.

Wertheimer, Michael. "Robert Brodie MacLeod (1907–1972)." *Journal of the History of the Behavioral Sciences* 9 (1973): 287–99.

Whipple, George Chandler. *Vital Statistics: An Introduction to the Science of Demography.* New York: John Wiley and Sons, 1919.

Whipple, Guy Montrose. *Manual of Mental and Physical Tests, A Book of Directions Compiled with Special Reference to the Experimental Study of School Children in the Laboratory or Classroom.* Baltimore, Md.: Warwick and York, 1910.

———. *Manual of Mental and Physical Tests, In Two Parts. Part II: Complex Processes.* Baltimore, Md.: Warwick and York, 1915.

Wissler, Clark. "The Correlation of Mental and Physical Tests." *Psychological Review Monograph Supplement* 3, no. 6 (1901).

Wundt, Wilhelm. *Handbuch der Medicinischen Physik.* Erlangen: Verlag von Ferdinand Enke, 1867.

———. *Lehrbuch der Physiologie des Menschen.* Erlangen: Verlag von Ferdinand Enke, 1865.

Wyczoikowska, Anna. "Theoretical and Experimental Studies in the Mechanism of Speech." *Psychological Review* 20 (1913): 448–59.

Wyss, Dieter. *Depth Psychology: A Critical History, Development, Problems, Crises.* Translated by Gerald Onn. 1961. Reprint, London: George Allen & Unwin, 1966. Also published as *Psychoanalytic Schools from the Beginning to the Present.* Translated by G. Onn. 1961. Reprint, New York: Jason Aronson, 1973.

Yerkes, Robert M. *Chimpanzees: A Laboratory Colony.* New Haven: Yale University Press, 1943.

———. "Raymond Dodge 1871–1942." *American Journal of Psychology* 55 (1942): 584–600.

———. "Report of the Psychology Committee of the National Research Council." *Psychological Review* 26 (1919): 83–149.

———. ed. *Psychological Examining in the United States Army.* Washington, D.C.: Government Printing Office, 1921.

Young, Kimball. "The Psychology of Hymns." *Journal of Abnormal and Social Psychology* 20 (1926): 391–406.

Zenderland, Leila. "Biblical Biology: American Protestant Social Reformers and the Early Eugenics Movement." *Science in Context,* 11: (3–4 Fall and Winter 1998): 511–25.

———. "Henry Herbert Goddard and the Medical Acceptance of Intelligence Testing." In *Psychological Testing and American Society.* Edited by Michael Sokal. New Brunswick: Rutgers University Press, 1987.

———. *Measuring Minds: Henry Herbert Goddard and the Origins of American Intelligence Testing.* New York: Cambridge University Press, 1998.

Zhang, Jiajie. "The Nature of External Representations in Problem Solving." *Cognitive Science* 21 (1997): 179–217.

———. "A Representational Analysis of Relational Information Displays." *International Journal of Human-Computer Studies* 45 (1996): 59–74.

Zhang, Jiajie, and Donald A. Norman. "A Representational Analysis of Numeration Systems." *Cognition* 57 (1995): 271–95.

———. "Representations in Distributed Cognitive Tasks." *Cognitive Science* 18 (1994): 87–122.

Zimmermann, E. *Preis-Liste über psycholgische und physiologische Apparate (XVIII).* 1903. Reprint, Passau: Institut für Geschichte der Neueren Psychologie, Universität Passau, 1983.

Archive Collections

Archives of the History of American Psychology, The University of Akron, Akron, Ohio
> Beach, Frank A., Papers
> Dodge, Raymond, Papers
> Fischer, Robert, Papers
> Goddard, Henry H., Papers
> Hollingworth, Harry L., Papers
> Maier, Norman R.F., Papers
> Miles, Walter R., Papers
> Verplanck, William S., Papers

California Institute of Technology Archives, Pasadena, Calif.
> Hale, George Ellery Papers

Clark University Archives

Columbia University, New York, N.Y.
> Cattell, James McKeen, Files

Harvard University Archives, Boston, Mass.
> Boring, E. G., Papers

Library of Congress, Washington, D.C.
> Cattell, James McKeen, Papers
> Manuscript Division

McGill University Archives, Montreal, Quebec, Canada
> Hebb, Donald O., Papers

National Archives, Washington, D.C.
> Lathrop, Julia C., Records of the Children's Bureau. Department of Labor

Skillman Library, Lafayette College, Easton, Pa.

Stanford University Archives, Stanford, Calif.
> Terman, Lewis M., Papers

University of Rochester Library, Rochester, N.Y.
> Fairchild, Herman L., Papers

Yale University Library, New Haven, Conn.
> Yerkes, Robert M., Papers

Index

ability testing, 167
abnormal psychology, 28, 50, 87
abstract thinking, 101
academic freedom, 12
Adler, A., 31, 122
Advertising Men's League of New York
    City, 44
aging, 64
Agnew, N., 163
aircrib, 39
Allport, G., 112–13, 119–21, 165, 171–72
Alpha Psi Zeta Foundation, 117
American Association for Applied Psychol-
    ogy (AAAP), 38
American Association for the Advance-
    ment of Science (AAAS), 4–5, 12, 18,
    158
American Council on Education, 119
American Journal of Psychology, 26, 30, 157
American Medical Association, 114
American Men of Science, 4
American Orthopsychiatric Association,
    35
American Psychiatric Association, 16
American Psychoanalytic Association, 114
American Psychological Association
    (APA), 26–27, 35, 39, 59, 62, 66–67,
    70, 73, 108, 118, 159, 161, 163, 172–
    73
Amherst College, 113
Angell, J. R., 25, 147, 149
animal psychology, 39
animal research, 167
anthropology, 34, 62, 67
anthropometric laboratory, 77
anthropometric tests, 3, 12

apparatus, 58–64, 68, 71, 123, 128–32,
    158
applied psychology, 38–56, 67
applied social psychology, 151
archival methods, 83, 87, 110, 112–13,
    150, 160–61,165, 168, 171
Archives of the American Philosophical
    Society, 146
Archives of the History of American Psy-
    chology 6, 13, 19, 38, 57, 64, 78,
    107–8, 122, 125, 141, 145, 162, 165–
    66, 173
Arkell, B., 51
Army Air Forces Aviation Psychology Pro-
    gram, 136
Army Alpha and Beta Tests, 133
Association of Consulting Psychologists
    (ACP), 38
auditory perception, 60
automatic correlating machine, 68
automatisms, 51

Bakan, D., 163–64
Baker, D. B., 39, 108
Baldwin, J. M., 4
Ballantyne, P., 165–68
Ballard, M., 74–75
Baritz, L., 168
Barnard College, 39–40, 43, 46–47, 55
Barr, M., 100
Barrett, A., 28
Beach, F. A., 151, 154–57, 159, 161
Beecher, H. W., 113
behaviorism, 22,26, 28, 73, 132, 152
Bell, A. G., 4
Bell Labs, 140